NEW COLLECTED POEMS

NEW COLLECTED POEMS

MARIANNE MOORE

EDITED BY

HEATHER CASS WHITE

FARRAR, STRAUS AND GIROUX • NEW YORK

Farrar, Straus and Giroux
18 West 18th Street, New York 10011

Printed in the United States of America
Originally published in 2017 by Faber and Faber Ltd., Great Britain
Published in the United States by Farrar, Straus and Giroux
First American edition, 2017

Library of Congress Cataloging-in-Publication Data
Names: Moore, Marianne, 1887–1972, author. | White, Heather Cass,
    editor.
Title: New collected poems / Marianne Moore ; edited by Heather
    Cass White.
Description: First American edition. | New York : Farrar, Straus and
    Giroux, 2017.
Identifiers: LCCN 2017003857 | ISBN 9780374221041 (hardback) |
    ISBN 9780374716059 (ebook)
Subjects: BISAC: POETRY / American / General.
Classification: LCC PS3525.O5616 A6 2017 | DDC 811/.54—dc23
LC record available at https://lccn.loc.gov/2017003857

Our books may be purchased in bulk for promotional,
educational, or business use. Please contact your local bookseller
or the Macmillan Corporate and Premium Sales Department
at 1-800-221-7945, extension 5442, or by e-mail at
MacmillanSpecialMarkets@macmillan.com.

www.fsgbooks.com
www.twitter.com/fsgbooks • www.facebook.com/fsgbooks

10 9 8 7 6 5 4 3 2 1

CONTENTS

POEMS 1932–1936

EDITOR'S NOTES

ACKNOWLEDGMENTS

I am grateful to David Moore, Administrator of the Literary Estate of Marianne C. Moore, for entrusting me with this project. I thank Paul Keegan and Matthew Hollis at Faber for commissioning it. Jonathan Galassi, at Farrar, Straus and Giroux, published the American edition, for which Viking Books generously gave its permission. My gratitude to them all. The Department of English at the University of Alabama supported research for this book in the spring of 2016.

The painting by Isaac Oliver, *Young Man Seated under a Tree*, is reproduced by permission of the Royal Collection Trust / © Her Majesty Queen Elizabeth II 2017.

For their valuable feedback on the editorial apparatus I thank Robert Baker, Luke Carson, Randy Fowler, Fiona Green, Ellen Levy, Anouk Markovitz, Albert Pionke, Steve Tedeschi, Liza White, Stuart White, Fred Whiting, Patricia Willis, and Emily Wittman. Elizabeth Gregory, Cristanne Miller, and Robin Schulze provided Moore-ish sustenance and zeal. Linda Leavell consulted, condoled, and graciously shared her vast accumulation. My family, Fowler, Otts, White, and especially Fowler-White, is with me in everything I do.

My special thanks go to Patricia Willis for her wise and warm support. Without the early enthusiasm of Luke Carson and ELS Editions, this book would not have come to be.

*

Moore's work is not mine to dedicate, but my work on Moore is dedicated, with deep affection and gratitude, to Ellen Sue Levy.

CONVENTIONS FOLLOWED

Throughout the main text I have silently corrected misspellings and printer's errors. I have occasionally modernized a spelling. Punctuation has been standardized to American usage throughout. Ellipses in brackets indicate my omissions, not Moore's.

Abbreviations

AO	*The Arctic Ox*. London: Faber, 1964
ColP	*Collected Poems*. New York: Macmillan, 1951
ComP	*Complete Poems*. New York: Macmillan/Viking, 1967
ComP (1981)	*Complete Poems*. Eds. Clive Driver and Patricia Willis. New York: Penguin, 1981
LB	*Like a Bulwark*. New York: Viking, 1956
N	*Nevertheless*. New York: Macmillan, 1944
O	*Observations*. New York: The Dial Press, 1924
OD	*O to Be a Dragon*. New York: Viking, 1959
P	*Poems*. London: The Egoist Press, 1921
POV	*The Pangolin and Other Verse*. London: The Brendin Publishing Company, 1936
SP	*Selected Poems*. New York: Macmillan/London: Faber, 1935
TM	*Tell Me, Tell Me*. New York: Viking, 1966
WAY	*What Are Years*. New York: Macmillan, 1941

Symbols

/	Indicates a line break in quotations from verse
//	Indicates a stanza break in quotations from verse

INTRODUCTION

What should one call a new edition of Marianne Moore's poetry? What *can* one call it, given the titles of her books that have been or are currently in use? During her life there were books of her poems called *Poems* (1921), *Selected Poems* (1935), *Collected Poems* (1951), and *Complete Poems* (1967). After her death came a revised version of *Complete Poems* (1981), and the *Poems of Marianne Moore* (2003). Looking over this list a reader might wonder what is left to do with a body of work already selected, collected, and presented complete several times over. The answer is that "selected" is the only adjective that accurately describes any book of Moore's work thus far produced, or any that can be produced. Moore's art has no straight path from beginning to end; there is no vantage point from which one can see it whole. She created new poems throughout her life, but she also created new arrangements of the old. At her direction major poems disappeared from print, early poems appeared in late collections, carefully planned series of poems were broken up and dispersed, and intricate stanzaic forms were truncated and left ragged as she revised her poems, sometimes out of all recognition.

Even in an age known for poets who reshaped their own work, Moore's revisions are unique in their sheer number and in the length of time over which she persisted in making them. For Moore, the publication of a poem in a periodical, or the ordering of poems in a book, marked resting-places in her poetry's development, not its final form. There is good reason to think that her own death is, in effect, only a particularly protracted pause in a process of revision that would otherwise have had no end. The complex, involuted textual history Moore left behind means that forty years after her death we have just begun to explore the ways her poems may be presented, and little about our view of her work as a poet is complete.

The outlines of her career, by contrast, are well known. She was born in 1887, in Kirkwood, Missouri. She and her brother, John Warner Moore (called Warner), were raised by their mother, Mary

Warner Moore, in Carlisle, Pennsylvania.[1] Mrs. Moore, an educated and devout woman, was the daughter of a Presbyterian minister; Moore's brother Warner became a Navy chaplain. The tightly knit Moore household was unified by devotion to family, spiritual values, and academic study. Moore herself never married, and lived with her mother from 1910, when Moore was twenty-three, until Mrs Moore's death in 1947.[2] She began publishing her poems in student magazines during her undergraduate years at Bryn Mawr (1905–1909) and continued to publish them until her death in 1972.

Moore's poetic maturity coincided with that of American Modernism, a movement in which she was a defining figure. Her poems appeared in its journals, both radical and established, and for four years, between 1925 and 1929, she edited the *Dial,* the most prestigious literary journal of its day. Her decisions in that role, about what to publish and from whom to solicit work, along with the hundreds of commentary pieces and book reviews she wrote, meant that her ideas directly shaped the literary landscape in which she and her peers worked. Among her friends, correspondents, and colleagues were Robert Frost, T. S. Eliot, W. H. Auden, Ezra Pound, Wallace Stevens, H.D., Mina Loy, William Carlos Williams, and Langston Hughes. The next generation consciously challenged and enriched by her work includes John Ashbery, Elizabeth Bishop, Louise Bogan, Robert Duncan, James Merrill, Lorine Niedecker, May Swenson, and countless others.

In the later decades of her life she had a career as a more popular public figure as well. In 1955 the Ford Motor Company invited her to suggest names for their new model (she gave them more than forty suggestions, including "Utopian Turtletop" and "Mongoose Civique"; they declined all of them and named it the "Edsel" instead). In 1963 she contributed to the liner notes for Muhammad Ali's (then Cassius Clay's) spoken-word album *I am the Greatest!,* and in 1968 she threw the first pitch of the season at Yankee Stadium, a privilege

---

1   Moore's father, John Milton Moore (1858–1925), was institutionalized before her birth after a series of psychotic episodes and a prolonged period of religious mania. He died in institutional care. Moore never met him, never even saw a picture of him until she was an adult, and his name was never mentioned in the Mary–Warner–Marianne household.

2   Warner Moore (1886–1974) married and had children of his own, but the lifelong primacy of the Moores' bonds with each other has prompted Moore's biographer to characterize it this way: "so intense was the mutual devotion of Mary Warner Moore and her two adult children that it bewildered and incensed outsiders" (Leavell, 12).

usually reserved for presidents and Hollywood celebrities. That late fame is now largely forgotten, founded as it was on a protective persona Moore developed and then inhabited until the end of her life: America's beloved, eccentric maiden aunt, costumed in tri-corn hat and cape. There are many arresting and engaging photographs of Moore from that time, but they depict an artist far removed from the young, ambitious, driven, and voraciously intellectual poet who mattered to her Modernist peers and matters to poets today.

Moore's private life was mismatched with the popular image of sexually free-wheeling and politically radical bohemian living in Greenwich Village of the 1920s. Nevertheless, she was drawn early to New York as a center of experimental and progressive art. She first visited the city in 1909, documenting her sense of being "*bewitched, with pleasure*" (*Letters*, 55) and "*flourishing like a bay tree*" (*Letters*, 57) in a series of letters to her mother and brother. When Moore visited New York City again, in December 1915, she was an informed cultural explorer, visiting Alfred Stieglitz's gallery at 291 Fifth Avenue to see the latest in avant-garde art, and meeting the writers and editors who would become her friends and peers when she (and her mother) moved there for good in 1918. By 1925, having published several of her longest and best poems, and having assumed the editorship of the *Dial*, she was herself a writer and editor younger artists came to New York to meet.

Ten years later, in 1935, T. S. Eliot, an admirer of Moore's work since he first published it in the London-based *Egoist*, edited and wrote an introductory essay for Moore's *Selected Poems*. In this essay he articulates her value for him in definite terms:

> Miss Moore's poems form part of the small body of durable poetry written in our time; of that small body of writings, among what passes for poetry, in which an original sensibility and alert intelligence and deep feeling have been engaged in maintaining the life of the English language.   (xiv)

Moore's best readers have often been fellow poets, who, like Eliot, celebrate her artistry in uninflated, even technical terms. The precision of Moore's poems taught her readers precision in their praise, as when William Carlos Williams writes "Miss Moore's [work] holds its bloom today . . . by the aesthetic pleasure engendered when pure crafts-manship joins hard surfaces skillfully" (Williams, 315). Williams calls her craftsmanship "pure" for some of the same reasons Eliot calls her sensibility "original." "Using the same materials as all others before her," Williams writes, "[Moore] comes at it so effectively at a new angle as to throw out of fashion the classical conventional poetry to which one is used and puts her own and that about her in its place . . . [T]here is a multiplication, a quickening, a burrowing through, a blasting aside, a dynamization, a flight over" (Williams, 311). In his review of *Selected Poems* Wallace Stevens, like Eliot and Williams, suggests that the newness of Moore's "angle" on poetry arises from the singular quality of her mind. "Instead of being intentionally one of the most original of contemporary or modern poets," he writes, "she is merely one of the most truthful. People with a passion for the truth are always original" (Stevens, 780). Elizabeth Bishop, recalling her first reading of *Observations*, put in a succinct question her sense of Moore's unlikeness to anyone preceding her: "Why had no one ever written about things in this clear and dazzling way before?" (Bishop, 123).

Readers' sense of Moore's uniqueness has not diminished over time. Her poems are as startling today as they were when they first appeared; Moore's work sounds like no one else's. At its best it appears to have no precedents, to disclose no influences, to move in a self-created field of metrical, syntactical, and referential energy. One of her work's persistent themes is the fight to value singular things in the face of the world's propensity to dismiss what it cannot easily categorize. Moore's work, especially of the 1920s, defends against many names people give to that which they don't wish to take seriously: "idiosyncrasy," "peculiarity," "curio," "delightful happenstance," and so on. She understood all of these as potential synonyms for her poetry, and some of them have actually been used to describe it. Moore was working in no previously discovered vein of poetics when she wrote her poems, and in the decades following their publication they have gained new generations of admirers but almost no imitators.

The tension latent between Bishop's terms of praise, "clear" and "dazzling," suggests why this has been so. Moore's poems are "clear" in the sense that they present for inspection real objects, immediately recognizable as parts of the everyday world, that are nevertheless transformed by the poet's minute attention to them. Moore is her century's greatest poet of visual analogy, as when she describes a cat's whiskers as "shadbones regularly set about his mouth, to droop or rise//in unison like the porcupine's quills" (45), or notes that the ostrich's "comic duckling head on its/great neck, revolves with compass-/needle nervousness"(151), or describes how "a sea the purple of the peacock's neck is/paled to greenish azure as Dürer changed/the pine green of the Tyrol to peacock blue and guinea grey" (93). Moore's poems value *looking* at the world as a form of experience in itself, reporting in exact terms on what is to be found by paying attention.

Careful descriptive discriminations are also one of Moore's keenest ironic tools when she has a point to make about human behavior. Are Americans "students" or merely "undergraduates"? What is the difference between living with "too much" and with "abundance"? Is marriage an "institution" or an "enterprise"? Moore structures some of her best poems around shades of meaning as finely differentiated as any of the visual detail she observes.

Yet another part of Moore's poems' "clarity" lies in the consistent presence of her authorial voice as she describes and thinks about the world. Her poems are often in first-person singular ("I too, dislike it," [27] her poem on poetry notoriously begins). Even when they are not in the first person, the effect of a unified, particular, personal perspective pervades her poems first to last. Moore's "I" is rarely a persona, and her poems in the third person are not written by a detached observer. "A/black savage or such/as was subject to the/deer-fur Crown is not all brawn/and animality" (135) we are firmly informed in "Virginia Britannia," by the same poet who notes in "The Jerboa" that

> Africanus meant
> the conqueror sent
>   from Rome. It should mean the
>   untouched: the sand-brown jumping-rat—free-born; and
>   the blacks, that choice race with an elegance
>   ignored by one's ignorance.   (102)

While such clarities of the eye and voice are touchstones throughout Moore's work, they are also part of its simultaneous "dazzlement," the poems' sometimes overwhelming complexities of statement, form, and metaphor. If clarity allows us to see better, dazzlement, however exciting, may mean we can hardly see at all. It is seldom easy to say what a Moore poem as a whole is about, even when it comes with a seemingly straightforward title. Moore was serious, but also witty, and not above liking to shock her readers. Her titles range from the brisk ("Bowls," "Novices") to the comically gigantic: she titled an early poem "So far as the future is concerned, 'Shall not one say, with the Russian philosopher, "How is one to know what one doesn't know?"' So far as the present is concerned."

Her poem "Poetry" (27) is pointedly catholic about the range of things appropriate to be subjects of poetry, including "the baseball/ fan, the statistician [. . .] business documents and//school-books," and she lived that precept, writing with equal ease about steamrollers, snails, New York, racehorses, unicorns, the Brooklyn Dodgers, and Yul Brynner (to choose examples at random). Her own best commentary on the wild heterogeneity of her poetic materials is the impish "Index" she prepared for *Observations*. A sample (chosen, again, at random) from the "S" section lists:

> snobbishness, 54
> snowshoes, 76
> SOJOURN IN THE WHALE, 35, 298
> Southey, R., 302
> Spanish, 13
> spectrum, a fish, 16; as food, 7
> Spenser, E., 307
> spider fashion, 72, 305; returning, 60
> STATECRAFT EMBALMED, TO, 25
> Statue of Liberty, 13[3]

Moore's poems are often studded with quotations, pieces of found language from the books, newspapers, and magazines Moore read in quantity. John Ashbery, in writing about "An Octopus," calls it the greatest of her poems and describes its author "tacking imperturbably among excerpts from Ruskin, the *Illustrated London News*, the London *Graphic*, *The National Parks Portfolio* and a remark overheard at the circus" (111).

Moore's poems compass floods of detailed images, only occasionally making connections between them explicit for the reader. Understanding a Moore poem means keeping pace with her own exactingly nimble mind. For example, the unwary reader of "Marriage" might be surprised to encounter this description of Adam:

> "something feline,
> something colubrine"—how true!
> a crouching mythological monster
> in that Persian miniature of emerald mines,
> raw silk—ivory white, snow white,

---

3 The page numbers included in "Index" on pp. 81–9 below, and in the extract here, have been changed to match the layout of the present edition.

oyster white and six others—
that paddock full of leopards and giraffes—
long lemon-yellow bodies
sown with trapezoids of blue.   (64)

Moore's notes on the poem will not help; they report only that
the quoted lines about "something feline, something colubrine" come
from a book review in the *New Republic*. The first three lines suggest
that Adam is alluring and dangerous, catlike and snakelike, poised
to spring and so rare and unfamiliar as to seem "mythological." The
lines that follow, however, veer sharply into an aesthetic reverie in
which the literal referent is private (what Persian miniature? does it
contain raw silk in nine shades of white and a paddock of leopards
and giraffes as well as an emerald mine, or is the poet recalling a series
of artworks?). In the absence of answers to these questions all that is
present to the reader is the poet's pleasure in detail, in workmanship,
and in the sensuous possibilities of color. To the extent that the lines
are unified by anything it is by the intensity of that pleasure, expressed
most strongly by the last two lines' resolution into a regular trochaic
pulse enriched with alliterative "l"s and assonant "o"s.

The reader who, like F. R. Leavis in 1935, finds herself "defeated
and exasperated" (Gregory, 110) by the quick motions of Moore's
sidelong, associative method, will not be consoled by many of
the usual pleasures of poetic form. With respect to meter Moore's
poems usually follow strict and strange rules of her own invention.
Her characteristic unit of poetic measurement is the syllable rather
than the foot; her stanzas are syllabic grids, shaped to please the eye
rather than reward the ear. Through those grids her long, hypotactic
sentences flow with a syntactical music distinct from their metrical
scansion. The poems nearly always rhyme, but Moore's parenthetical
qualification on the subject must be taken seriously: "after 1929—
perhaps earlier—[I] wrote no verse that did not (in my opinion)
rhyme" (*Reader*, xvi). The last three stanzas of "The Fish" (39–40)
neatly exemplify her characteristic form, and suggest why her use of
rhyme might seem like a matter of opinion:

All
external
    marks of abuse are present on
        this
            defiant edifice—
    all the physical features of

ac-
cident—lack
   of cornice, dynamite grooves, burns
     and
     hatchet strokes, these things stand
   out on it; the chasm side is

dead.
Repeated
   evidence has proved that it can
     live
     on what cannot revive
   its youth. The sea grows old in it.

Each stanza of "The Fish" follows the same pattern of syllable count, indentation, and rhyme. A schematic representation of these elements might look like this:

1		a
3		a
	8	b
	1	c
	6	c
	8	d

Such patterning of language calls attention to itself, and in particular to its arbitrariness. It does not call back to a history of other poems written in the same form. It does not arrange its words into recognizable units of meaning (as, say, do the quatrains and couplet of a Shakespearian sonnet). Its rhyme scheme is difficult to hear out loud, hard to see unless one is looking for it, and based purely on phonemes: "ac" rhymes with "lack," a fact of the ear that in itself means little to the mind. Partly on the basis of Moore's choice to rhyme words on conjunctions like "and" (and/stand), and participial suffixes like "-ed" (dead/repeated), T. S. Eliot called Moore "the greatest living master" of light rhyme. Opinion differed on that point; even an early admirer of Moore's "invariably interesting" poems like Edith Sitwell was driven to wonder "why end a line—and sometimes a stanza—in the middle of a word? Miss Moore is too good of a poet to do that kind of thing" (Gregory, 35). Moore herself, in thanking Eliot for his introduction, wrote:

I might tell you with regard to my froward rhymes that my
mother acknowledges being converted from what for years
has been an aggrieved sense of the family gone astray. When a
friend recently noted my "using no rhymes," she said, "don't
enlighten him." (*Letters*, 329)

Moore was not "froward," however. Her nearly inaudible rhymes,
along with her lack of interest in both end-stopped and conventionally
enjambed lines, remained integral parts of her work's topography, in
which the sentence and the image, rather than the stanza and the
word, function as magnetic poles. Moore's form was not the trick of a
young attention-seeker, but the preternaturally accomplished artistry
of a poet for whom the sound and sense of words were always to have
equal, though sometimes competing and seemingly inharmonious
claims. Moore's early poems are unapologetic about form that looks
ungainly to the uninitiated. In "Diligence is to Magic as Progress is
to Flight" (18), for example, she praises laborious travel by elephants
rather than the "semblance of speed" attaching to magic carpets. She
calls the latter "scarecrows/of aesthetic procedure":

> With an elephant to ride upon—"with rings on her fingers
> and bells on her toes,"
> she shall outdistance calamity anywhere she goes.
> Speed is not in her mind inseparable from carpets.
> Locomotion arose
> in the shape of an elephant; she clambered up and chose
> to travel laboriously. So far as magic carpets are concerned,
> she knows
> that although the semblance of speed may attach to
> scarecrows
> of aesthetic procedure, the substance of it is embodied in such
> of those
> tough-grained animals as have outstripped man's whim to
> suppose
> them ephemera, and have earned that fruit of their ability to
> endure blows,
> which dubs them prosaic necessities—not curios.

Moore's identification of "the substance of aesthetic procedure"
with whatever is able to "endure blows" and earn the title "prosaic
necessities—not curios" is a mission statement of sorts for her work
up through the 1930s. These poems often thematize her commitment
to formal innovation, however unconventional, and her belief in it as

the only way to create what will last. In her eye beauty and resilience are one: "Black Earth" admires the elephant's thick skin for being "cut/into checkers by rut/upon rut of unpreventable experience" (41). "Roses Only" tells a rose approvingly that its thorns, "Guarding the/infinitesimal pieces of your mind [. . .] are the best part of you" (37). The creation of an original, densely worked, highly controlled formal structure was at the heart of Moore's poetry and the reason she is lastingly important. Her poems through the 1930s derive their power from the tension they create between the poet's exquisite attunement to the pleasures of sound and the strictness of the form she employs to concentrate and refine that pleasure. The poems are also closely concerned with questions of morality, but those questions function as Robert Frost says subject matter, in a real poem, must: as the "dramatic tones of meaning struck across the rigidity of a limited meter" out of which arise "endless possibilities for tune" (Frost, 776).

By the early 1940s, however, her poetic priorities had changed, as had a number of circumstances in her life. 1940 was a hard year for Moore. She suffered significant professional disappointments, including primarily Macmillan's rejection of a novel on which she had worked in secret for at least a decade.[4] Right after that rejection *Selected Poems,* the book in which T. S. Eliot made his case for her work's membership in "the small body of durable poetry written in our time," was remaindered. She was also, for the first time in at least a decade, having trouble finding an audience for her new work: her most recent poems were being rejected by the *Atlantic* and the *New Yorker,* magazines with the wider reading audience she now sought. Her letters from this time frequently mention her own and her mother's ill-health, and show how much of Moore's time was devoted to caring for her mother. The war, and the United States's potential involvement in it, troubled Moore deeply. Throughout the late thirties she corresponded about the rise of Fascism with her European-based friend and patron Bryher (an artist, philanthropist, and the companion of the poet H.D.), and was an early and impassioned partisan of European Jews.

These pressures, and most especially her commitment to the Allied cause, are evident in her next book, 1941's *What Are Years.* The title poem meditates on the nature of individual courage against the implicit backdrop of war, beginning with a stark assessment: "What

---

4   The novel is called *The Way We Live Now.* A typescript of it is in the archive
    of her papers at the Rosenbach Museum and Library in Philadelphia. A
    specific instruction in her will prevents it ever being published, suggesting
    that Moore came to agree with Macmillan's decision.

is our innocence,/what is our guilt? All are/naked, none is safe" (147). The book's final poem, "The Paper Nautilus," ends with an ode to maternal love, calling it "the only fortress/strong enough to trust to" (158). Moore had always been an epigram-maker, but in the 1940s the epigrams began to drive the poems' attention to sensuous detail and expressive form, rather than the other way around.

Moore's poems through the 1930s have urgent things to say about the world, but they understand the complexity of their forms as part of what they need to say. After the 1940s, by contrast, Moore increasingly prioritized saying what she thought her readers ought to hear in the simplest terms she could manage. Readers' responses to that change varied widely when it happened, as they still do today. Peers equally as ardent about her work as W. H. Auden and Randall Jarrell, for example, split sharply. Writing about Moore's 1944 war poem "In Distrust of Merits" Auden called it "the best" of all recent war poems, and "a surprise to those who think of Miss Moore as a poet incapable of, or too reticent to employ, the organ note" (Gregory, 138). Jarrell, while asserting his ongoing admiration of Moore, calls the same poem a collection of "abstractions she is unfamiliar with and finds it hard not to be heroic about" and "a mistake we sympathize with thoroughly" (Gregory, 141).

Whatever one thinks of it, the shift in her poems' emphasis has had enormous repercussions for her reputation. Nearly 60 percent of the poems she chose to reprint in her *Complete Poems,* which has been the text of record since its first publication in 1967, were written after 1940 (the figure for the present edition is closer to 45 percent). Moreover, the poems from the twenties and thirties that she did reprint in 1967 are often extensively revised versions of their originals. In other words, Moore frequently did what she could to turn her poems written before the 1940s into poems she would have written later. The end result is that Moore has been widely misperceived as primarily a (witty, but nonetheless insistent) moralist, and this has happened because she took pains to ensure it would.

By the 1950s Moore was publicly disavowing her earlier work, in person and in print. In 1950 she introduced a talk at New York's Museum of Modern Art with what would become a standard joke, saying she would read some "verse," but would "scruple to call it poetry" (Leavell, 341).[5] Such charming self-deprecation made her

---

5 This aperçu became a refrain for Moore in her later years. In her remarks on accepting the National Book Award in 1952 she wrote, "I can see no reason for calling my work poetry except that there is no other category in which to put it" (*Prose*, 648). She repeated the joke in her 1958 essay "Subject,

audiences laugh and augmented her growing popularity, but she was serious about it, ominously so for those readers who valued the complexities of which she made light. In a 1951 letter to a family member she referred disparagingly to her poems of the teens, twenties, and thirties, the poems that made her name and on which her achievement still rests, as "my 'cats and dogs' of former days," calling them "hard reading" (Leavell, 344). In editing her 1951 *Collected Poems* she pared away many brilliant early poems, and printed revised (which nearly always meant shortened) versions of many more. She repeated the process in editing her 1967 *Complete Poems,* further pruning and shaping (or truncating and deforming, depending on one's perspective) her oeuvre.

*

The complex history of Moore's revisions requires a separate essay, which can be found within the "Editor's Notes" to this volume. That essay also lays out in detail the work I have done in selecting and arranging the contents of this book. In essence, however, my aim is simple: I have here presented Moore's poems as they were when she first wrote and published them, not as she later revised them. In her own collections Moore treated her early work as ephemeral forms of what it later became. I have reversed her procedure, treating later revisions as footnotes to the original poems.

My underlying belief (which I share with Moore herself) is that there are at least two major Moores: pre- and post-war. Where Moore sought to bring the former into line with the latter, however, I have worked to keep them distinct. The reader who values Moore's late achievements, including the way she refashioned her earlier work, can find them here. The reader in search of the poet Moore was before she changed her mind about many important things will find her here as well. That poet whom Eliot, Stevens, Williams, and Bishop loved has been substantially, increasingly lost with each passing decade since 1951, when Moore herself began her long erasure. An accurate assessment not only of Moore's work, but of the Modernist culture she helped create, requires that we come to terms with the poet she was in the beginning. It is not too late to bring her back.

Predicate, Object" (*Prose,* 504), and again in her 1961 interview with the poet Donald Hall.

THE POEMS

OBSERVATIONS (1924)

To an Intra-Mural Rat

You make me think of many men
Once met to be forgot again
   Or merely resurrected
In a parenthesis of wit
That found them hastening through it
   Too brisk to be inspected.

Reticence and Volubility

"When I am dead,"
The wizard said,
　"I'll look upon the narrow way
　And this Dante,
　　And know that he was right
　　And he'll delight
　　　In my remorse,
　　　Of course."
"When I am dead,"
The student said,
　"I shall have grown so tolerant,
　I'll find I can't
　　Laugh at your sorry plight
　　Or take delight
　　　In your chagrin,
　　　Merlin."

To a Chameleon

Hid by the august foliage and fruit of the grape vine,
Twine,
   Your anatomy
     Round the pruned and polished stem,
      Chameleon.
      Fire laid upon
    An emerald as long as
   The Dark King's massy
One,
Could not snap the spectrum up for food as you have done.

A Talisman

Under a splintered mast,
Torn from the ship and cast
  Near her hull,

A stumbling shepherd found
Embedded in the ground,
  A seagull

Of lapis lazuli,
A scarab of the sea,
  With wings spread—

Curling its coral feet,
Parting its beak to greet
  Men long dead.

To a Prize Bird

You suit me well, for you can make me laugh,
Nor are you blinded by the chaff
   That every wind sends spinning from the rick.

You know to think, and what you think you speak
With much of Samson's pride and bleak
   Finality; and none dare bid you stop.

Pride sits you well, so strut, colossal bird.
No barnyard makes you look absurd;
   Your brazen claws are staunch against defeat.

Injudicious Gardening

If yellow betokens infidelity,
   I am an infidel.
      I could not bear a yellow rose ill will
      Because books said that yellow boded ill,
   White promised well;

However, your particular possession—
   The sense of privacy
      In what you did—deflects from your estate
      Offending eyes, and will not tolerate
   Effrontery.

Fear is Hope

"No man may him hyde
From Deth holow eyed."
  For us two spirits this shall not suffice,
    To whom you are symbolic of a plan
    Concealed within the heart of man.
      Splendid with splendor hid you come, from your Arab abode,
      An incandescence smothered in the hand of an astrologer
                who rode
    Before you, Sun—whom you outran,
    Piercing his caravan.

Sun, you shall stay
With us. Holiday
  And day of wrath shall be as one, wound in a device
    Of Moorish gorgeousness, round glasses spun
    To flame as hemispheres of one
      Great hourglass dwindling to a stem. Consume hostility;
      Employ your weapons in this meeting place of surging enmity.
    Insurgent feet shall not outrun
    Multiplied flames, O Sun.

To a Strategist

You brilliant Jew,
You bright particular chameleon, you
  Regild a shabby fence.

They understood
Your stripes and particolored mind, who could
  Begrudge you prominence

And call you cold!
But when has prejudice been glad to hold
  A lizard in its hand—

A subtle thing?
To sense fed on a fine imagining,
  Sound sense is contraband.

Is Your Town Nineveh?

Why so desolate?
   in phantasmagoria about fishes,
      what disgusts you? Could
         not all personal upheaval in
            the name of freedom, be tabooed?

Is it Nineveh
   and are you Jonah
      in the sweltering east wind of your wishes?
         I myself, have stood
            there by the aquarium, looking
               at the Statue of Liberty.

A Fool, a Foul Thing, a Distressful Lunatic

With webs of cool
  Chain mail and his stout heart, is not the gander
  Mocked, and ignorantly designated yet,
To play the fool?
    "Egyptian vultures clean as cherubim,
    All ivory and jet," are they most foul?
And nature's child,
  That most precocious water bird, the loon—why
  Is he foremost in the madman's alphabet;
Why is he styled
  In folly's catalogue, distressful lunatic?

To Military Progress

You use your mind
Like a millstone to grind
   Chaff.
You polish it
And with your warped wit
   Laugh

At your torso,
Prostrate where the crow
   Falls
On such faint hearts
As its god imparts,
   Calls

And claps its wings
Till the tumult brings
   More
Black minute-men
To revive again,
   War

At little cost.
They cry for the lost
   Head
And seek their prize
Till the evening sky's
   Red.

An Egyptian Pulled Glass Bottle in the Shape of a Fish

Here we have thirst
And patience from the first,
   And art, as in a wave held up for us to see
   In its essential perpendicularity;

Not brittle but
Intense—the spectrum, that
   Spectacular and nimble animal the fish,
   Whose scales turn aside the sun's sword with their polish.

To a Steam Roller

The illustration
is nothing to you without the application.
   You lack half wit. You crush all the particles down
      into close conformity, and then walk back and forth on them.

Sparkling chips of rock
are crushed down to the level of the parent block.
   Were not "impersonal judgment in aesthetic
      matters, a metaphysical impossibility," you

might fairly achieve
it. As for butterflies, I can hardly conceive
   of one's attending upon you, but to question
      the congruence of the complement is vain, if it exists.

Diligence is to Magic as Progress is to Flight

With an elephant to ride upon—"with rings on her fingers and bells
      on her toes,"
   she shall outdistance calamity anywhere she goes.
Speed is not in her mind inseparable from carpets. Locomotion arose
   in the shape of an elephant; she clambered up and chose
to travel laboriously. So far as magic carpets are concerned, she
      knows
   that although the semblance of speed may attach to scarecrows
of aesthetic procedure, the substance of it is embodied in such of
      those
   tough-grained animals as have outstripped man's whim to suppose
them ephemera, and have earned that fruit of their ability to endure
      blows,
   which dubs them prosaic necessities—not curios.

To a Snail

If "compression is the first grace of style,"
you have it. Contractility is a virtue
as modesty is a virtue.
It is not the acquisition of any one thing
that is able to adorn,
or the incidental quality that occurs
as a concomitant of something well said,
that we value in style,
but the principle that is hid:
in the absence of feet, "a method of conclusions";
"a knowledge of principles,"
in the curious phenomenon of your occipital horn.

"The Bricks are Fallen Down, We Will Build with
Hewn Stones. The Sycamores are Cut Down, We Will
Change to Cedars."

In what sense shall we be able to
    secure to ourselves peace and do as they did—
who, when they were not able to rid
        themselves of war, cast out fear?
            They did not say: "We shall not be brought
                into subjection by the naughtiness of the sea;
though we have 'defeated ourselves with
    false balances' and laid weapons in the scale,
glory shall spring from in-glory; hail,
        flood, earthquake, and famine shall
            not intimidate us nor shake the
                foundations of our inalienable energy."

George Moore

In speaking of "aspiration,"
 From the recesses of a pen more dolorous than blackness itself,
  Were you presenting us with one more form of imperturbable
   French drollery,
  Or was it self directed banter?
  Habitual ennui
   Took from you, your invisible hot helmet of anemia
  While you were filling your little glass from the decanter
  Of a transparent-murky, would-be-truthful
   "hobohemia"—
  And then facetiously
  Went off with it? Your soul's supplanter,
 The spirit of good narrative, flatters you, convinced that in
   reporting briefly
One choice incident, you have known beauty other than that
   of stys, on
Which to fix your admiration.

"Nothing will Cure the Sick Lion but to Eat an Ape"

Perceiving that in the masked ball
attitude, there is a hollowness
that beauty's light momentum can't redeem,
   since disproportionate satisfaction anywhere
   lacks a proportionate air,

he let us know without offense
by his hands' denunciatory
upheaval, that he despised the fashion
   of curing us with an ape—making it his care
   to smother us with fresh air.

To the Peacock of France

In "taking charge of your possessions when you saw them,"
        you became a golden jay.
Scaramouche said you charmed his charm away,
    But not his color? Yes, his color when you liked.
    Of chiseled setting and black-opalescent dye,
        You were the jewelry of sense;
            Of sense, not license; you but trod the pace
            Of liberty in market-place
                And court. Molière,
                The huggermugger repertory of your first adventure, is
                    your own affair.

"Anchorites do not dwell in theatres," and peacocks do not flourish
        in a cell.
Why make distinctions? The results were well
    When you were on the boards; nor were your triumphs bought
    At horrifying sacrifice of stringency.
        You hated sham; you ranted up
            And down through the conventions of excess;
            Nor did the King love you the less
                Nor did the world,
                In whose chief interest and for whose spontaneous delight,
                    your broad tail was unfurled.

In this Age of Hard Trying, Nonchalance is Good and

"really, it is not the
   business of the gods to bake clay pots." They did not
     do it in this instance. A few
       revolved upon the axes of their worth
   as if excessive popularity might be a pot;

they did not venture the
   profession of humility. The polished wedge
     that might have split the firmament
       was dumb. At last it threw itself away
   and falling down, conferred on some poor fool, a privilege.

"Taller by the length of
   a conversation of five hundred years than all
     the others," there was one, whose tales
       of what could never have been actual—
   were better than the haggish, uncompanionable drawl

of certitude; his by-
   play was more terrible in its effectiveness
     than the fiercest frontal attack.
       The staff, the bag, the feigned inconsequence
   of manner, best bespeak that weapon, self protectiveness.

To Statecraft Embalmed

There is nothing to be said for you. Guard
Your secret. Conceal it under your hard
  Plumage, necromancer.
    O
Bird, whose tents were "awnings of Egyptian
Yarn," shall Justice' faint, zigzag inscription—
  Leaning like a dancer—
    Show
The pulse of its once vivid sovereignty?
You say not, and transmigrating from the
  Sarcophagus, you wind
    Snow
Silence round us and with moribund talk,
Half limping and half ladified, you stalk
  About. Ibis, we find
    No
Virtue in you—alive and yet so dumb.
Discreet behavior is not now the sum
  Of statesmanlike good sense.
    Though
It were the incarnation of dead grace?
As if a death mask ever could replace
  Life's faulty excellence!
    Slow
To remark the steep, too strict proportion
Of your throne, you'll see the wrenched distortion
  Of suicidal dreams
    Go
Staggering toward itself and with its bill,
Attack its own identity, until
  Foe seems friend and friend seems
    Foe.

The Monkey Puzzler

A kind of monkey or pine-lemur
not of interest to the monkey,
but to the animal higher up which resembles it,
in a kind of Flaubert's Carthage, it defies one—
this "Paduan cat with lizard," this "tiger in a bamboo thicket."
"An interwoven somewhat," it will not come out.
Ignore the Foo dog and it is forthwith more than a dog,
its tail superimposed upon itself in a complacent half spiral,
incidentally so witty;
but this pine-tree—this pine-tiger, is a tiger, not a dog.
It knows that if a nomad may have dignity,
Gibraltar has had more—
that "it is better to be lonely than unhappy."
A conifer contrived in imitation of the glyptic work of jade and
                    hard stone cutters,
a true curio in this bypath of curio collecting,
it is worth its weight in gold but no one takes it
from these woods in which society's not knowing is colossal,
the lion's ferocious chrysanthemum head seeming kind in
                    comparison.
This porcupine-quilled, infinitely complicated starkness—
this is beauty—"a certain proportion in the skeleton which gives
                    the best results."
One is at a loss, however, to know why it should be here,
in this morose part of the earth—
to account for its origin at all;
but we prove, we do not explain our birth.

Poetry

I too, dislike it: there are things that are important beyond all this
               fiddle.
  Reading it, however, with a perfect contempt for it, one discovers
               that there is in
  it after all, a place for the genuine.
     Hands that can grasp, eyes
       that can dilate, hair that can rise
         if it must, these things are important not because a

high sounding interpretation can be put upon them but because
               they are
  useful; when they become so derivative as to become unintelligible,
  the same thing may be said for all of us, that we
     do not admire what
     we cannot understand: the bat,
       holding on upside down or in quest of something to

eat, elephants pushing, a wild horse taking a roll, a tireless wolf
               under
  a tree, the immovable critic twitching his skin like a horse that feels
               a flea, the base-
  ball fan, the statistician—
     nor is it valid
       to discriminate against "business documents and

school-books"; all these phenomena are important. One must make
               a distinction
  however: when dragged into prominence by half poets, the result
               is not poetry,
  nor till the poets among us can be
     "literalists of
     the imagination"—above
       insolence and triviality and can present

for inspection, imaginary gardens with real toads in them, shall
               we have
  it. In the meantime, if you demand on one hand,
  the raw material of poetry in
     all its rawness and

that which is on the other hand
   genuine, then you are interested in poetry.

The Past is the Present

If external action is effete
   and rhyme is outmoded,
     I shall revert to you,
    Habakkuk, as on a recent occasion I was goaded
       into doing, by XY, who was speaking of unrhymed verse.
This man said—I think that I repeat
   his identical words:
     "Hebrew poetry is
prose with a sort of heightened consciousness. 'Ecstasy affords
    the occasion and expediency determines the form.'"

Pedantic Literalist

Prince Rupert's drop, paper muslin ghost,
    White torch—"with power to say unkind
Things with kindness, and the most
        Irritating things in the midst of love and
            Tears," you invite destruction.

You are like the meditative man
    With the perfunctory heart; its
Carved cordiality ran
        To and fro at first like an inlaid and royal
            Immutable production;

Then afterward "neglected to be
    Painful, deluding him with
Loitering formality,"
        "Doing its duty as if it did it not,"
            Presenting an obstruction

To the motive that it served. What stood
    Erect in you has withered. A
Little "palm tree of turned wood"
        Informs your once spontaneous core in its
            Immutable production.

"He Wrote The History Book"

There! You shed a ray
    of whimsicality on a mask of profundity so
        terrific, that I have been dumbfounded by
it oftener than I care to say.
            The book? Titles are chaff.

Authentically
    brief and full of energy, you contribute to your father's
        legibility and are sufficiently
synthetic. Thank you for showing me
        your father's autograph.

Critics and Connoisseurs

There is a great amount of poetry in unconscious
    fastidiousness. Certain Ming
        products, imperial floor coverings of coach
wheel yellow, are well enough in their way but I have seen
                something
      that I like better—a
         mere childish attempt to make an imperfectly ballasted
            animal stand up,
        similar determination to make a pup
          eat his meat on the plate.

I remember a swan under the willows in Oxford
    with flamingo colored, maple-
      leaflike feet. It reconnoitered like a battle
ship. Disbelief and conscious fastidiousness were the staple
      ingredients in its
         disinclination to move. Finally its hardihood was not
            proof against its
        proclivity to more fully appraise such bits
         of food as the stream

bore counter to it; it made away with what I gave it
    to eat. I have seen this swan and
      I have seen you; I have seen ambition without
understanding in a variety of forms. Happening to stand
      by an ant hill, I have
         seen a fastidious ant carrying a stick, north, south, east,
            west, till it turned on
        itself, struck out from the flower bed into the lawn,
        and returned to the point

from which it had started. Then abandoning the stick as
    useless and overtaxing its
      jaws with a particle of whitewash pill-like but
heavy, it again went through the same course of procedure. What is
      there in being able
         to say that one has dominated the stream in an attitude of
            self defense,
        in proving that one has had the experience
         of carrying a stick?

To be Liked by You Would be a Calamity

"Attack is more piquant than concord," but when
  You tell me frankly that you would like to feel
    My flesh beneath your feet,
      I'm all abroad; I can but put my weapon up, and
        Bow you out.
Gesticulation—it is half the language.
  Let unsheathed gesticulation be the steel
    Your courtesy must meet,
      Since in your hearing words are mute, which to my senses
        Are a shout.

Like a Bulrush

or the spike
of a channel marker or the
moon, he superintended the demolition of his image in
the water by the wind; he did not strike

them at the
time as being different from
any other inhabitant of the water; it was as if he
were a seal in the combined livery

of bird plus
snake; it was as if he knew that
the penguins were not fish and as if in their bat blindness,
                    they did not
realize that he was amphibious.

Sojourn in the Whale

Trying to open locked doors with a sword, threading
   the points of needles, planting shade trees
     upside down; swallowed by the opaqueness of one whom the seas
love better than they love you, Ireland—

you have lived and lived on every kind of shortage.
   You have been compelled by hags to spin
     gold thread from straw and have heard men say: "There is
              a feminine
temperament in direct contrast to

ours which makes her do these things. Circumscribed by a
   heritage of blindness and native
     incompetence, she will become wise and will be forced to give
in. Compelled by experience, she

will turn back; water seeks its own level": and you
   have smiled. "Water in motion is far
     from level." You have seen it when obstacles happened to bar
the path—rise automatically.

My Apish Cousins

winked too much and were afraid of snakes. The zebras, supreme in
their abnormality; the elephants with their fog-colored skin
   and strictly practical appendages
      were there, the small cats; and the parakeet—
         trivial and humdrum on examination, destroying
      bark and portions of the food it could not eat.

I recall their magnificence, now not more magnificent
than it is dim. It is difficult to recall the ornament,
   speech, and precise manner of what one might
      call the minor acquaintances twenty
         years back; but I shall not forget him—that Gilgamesh among
      the hairy carnivora—that cat with the

wedge-shaped, slate-gray marks on its forelegs and the resolute tail,
astringently remarking: "They have imposed on us with their pale
   half fledged protestations, trembling about
      in inarticulate frenzy, saying
         it is not for us to understand art; finding it
      all so difficult, examining the thing

as if it were inconceivably arcanic, as symmet-
rically frigid as if it had been carved out of chrysoprase
   or marble—strict with tension, malignant
      in its power over us and deeper
         than the sea when it proffers flattery in exchange for hemp,
      rye, flax, horses, platinum, timber, and fur."

Roses Only

You do not seem to realise that beauty is a liability rather than
   an asset—that in view of the fact that spirit creates form we are
          justified in supposing
     that you must have brains. For you, a symbol of the unit, stiff
          and sharp,
   conscious of surpassing by dint of native superiority and liking
          for everything
self-dependent, anything an

ambitious civilization might produce: for you, unaided to attempt
          through sheer
   reserve, to confute presumptions resulting from observation,
          is idle. You cannot make us
     think you a delightful happen-so. But rose, if you are brilliant, it
   is not because your petals are the without-which-nothing of
          pre-eminence. You would, minus thorns,
look like a what-is-this, a mere

peculiarity. They are not proof against a worm, the elements, or
          mildew
   but what about the predatory hand? What is brilliance without
          co-ordination? Guarding the
     infinitesimal pieces of your mind, compelling audience to
   the remark that it is better to be forgotten than to be remembered
          too violently,
your thorns are the best part of you.

Reinforcements

The vestibule to experience is not to
  be exalted into epic grandeur. These men are going
to their work with this idea, advancing like a school of fish through

still water—waiting to change the course or dismiss
  the idea of movement, till forced to. The words of the Greeks
ring in our ears, but they are vain in comparison with a sight
            like this.

The pulse of intention does not move so that one
  can see it, and moral machinery is not labeled, but
the future of time is determined by the power of volition.

The Fish

wade
through black jade.
   Of the crow-blue mussel shells, one
     keeps
     adjusting the ash heaps;
   opening and shutting itself like

an
injured fan.
   The barnacles which encrust the
     side
     of the wave, cannot hide
   there for the submerged shafts of the

sun,
split like spun
   glass, move themselves with spotlight swift-
     ness
     into the crevices—
   in and out, illuminating

the
turquoise sea
   of bodies. The water drives a
     wedge
     of iron through the iron edge
   of the cliff, whereupon the stars,

pink
rice grains, ink
   bespattered jelly-fish, crabs like
     green
     lilies and submarine
   toadstools, slide each on the other.

All
external
   marks of abuse are present on

this
    defiant edifice—
  all the physical features of

ac-
cident—lack
    of cornice, dynamite grooves, burns
        and
            hatchet strokes, these things stand
    out on it; the chasm side is

dead.
Repeated
    evidence has proved that it can
        live
            on what cannot revive
    its youth. The sea grows old in it.

Black Earth

Openly, yes,
with the naturalness
   of the hippopotamus or the alligator
   when it climbs out on the bank to experience the

sun, I do these
things which I do, which please
   no one but myself. Now I breathe and now I am submerged;
   the blemishes stand up and shout when the object

in view was a
renaissance; shall I say
   the contrary? The sediment of the river which
   encrusts my joints, makes me very gray but I am used

to it, it may
remain there; do away
   with it and I am myself done away with, for the
   patina of circumstance can but enrich what was

there to begin
with. This elephant skin
   which I inhabit, fibered over like the shell of
   the coconut, this piece of black glass through which no light

can filter—cut
into checkers by rut
   upon rut of unpreventable experience—
   it is a manual for the peanut-tongued and the

hairy toed. Black
but beautiful, my back
   is full of the history of power. Of power? What
   is powerful and what is not? My soul shall never

be cut into
by a wooden spear; through-
   out childhood to the present time, the unity of
   life and death has been expressed by the circumference

described by my
trunk; nevertheless, I
   perceive feats of strength to be inexplicable after
   all; and I am on my guard; external poise, it

has its center
well nurtured—we know
   where—in pride, but spiritual poise, it has its center where?
   My ears are sensitized to more than the sound of

the wind. I see
and I hear, unlike the
   wandlike body of which one hears so much, which was made
   to see and not to see; to hear and not to hear;

that tree trunk without
roots, accustomed to shout
   its own thoughts to itself like a shell, maintained intact
   by one who knows what strange pressure of the atmosphere; that

spiritual
brother to the coral
   plant, absorbed into which, the equable sapphire light
   becomes a nebulous green. The I of each is to

the I of each,
a kind of fretful speech
   which sets a limit on itself; the elephant is?
   Black earth preceded by a tendril? It is to that

phenomenon
the above formation,
   translucent like the atmosphere—a cortex merely—
   that on which darts cannot strike decisively the first

time, a substance
needful as an instance
   of the indestructibility of matter; it
   has looked at the electricity and at the earth-

quake and is still
here; the name means thick. Will
   depth be depth, thick skin be thick, to one who can see no
   beautiful element of unreason under it?

Radical

Tapering
to a point, conserving everything,
   this carrot is predestined to be thick.
     The world is
      but a circumstance, a mis-
         erable corn-patch for its feet. With ambition, imagination,
              outgrowth,

nutriment,
with everything crammed belligerent-
  ly inside itself, its fibers breed mon-
     opoly—
     a tail-like, wedge-shaped engine with the
        secret of expansion, fused with intensive heat to color
            of the set-

ting sun and
stiff. For the man in the straw hat, stand-
  ing still and turning to look back at it,
     as much as
     to say my happiest moment has
        been funereal in comparison with this, the conditions
            of life pre-

determined
slavery to be easy and freedom hard. For
  it? Dismiss
     agrarian lore; it tells him this:
     that which it is impossible to force, it is impossible
        to hinder.

In the Days of Prismatic Color

not in the days of Adam and Eve but when Adam
   was alone; when there was no smoke and color was
fine, not with the fineness of
   early civilization art but by virtue
of its originality; with nothing to modify it but the

mist that went up, obliqueness was a varia-
   tion of the perpendicular, plain to see and
to account for: it is no
   longer that; nor did the blue red yellow band
of incandescence that was color keep its stripe: it also is one of

those things into which much that is peculiar can be
   read; complexity is not a crime but carry
it to the point of murki-
   ness and nothing is plain. Complexity
moreover, that has been committed to darkness, instead of
                    granting it-

self to be the pestilence that it is, moves all a-
   bout as if to bewilder us with the dismal
fallacy that insistence
   is the measure of achievement and that all
truth must be dark. Principally throat, sophistication is as it al-

ways has been—at the antipodes from the init-
   ial great truths. "Part of it was crawling, part of it
was about to crawl, the rest
   was torpid in its lair." In the short legged, fit-
ful advance, the gurgling and all the minutiae—we have the classic

multitude of feet. To what purpose! Truth is no Apollo
   Belvedere, no formal thing. The wave may go over it if it likes.
Know that it will be there when it says:
   "I shall be there when the wave has gone by."

Peter

Strong and slippery, built for the midnight grass-party confronted by
　　　　　　four cats,
　　he sleeps his time away—the detached first claw on his foreleg
　　　　　　which corresponds
to the thumb, retracted to its tip; the small tuft of fronds
　　or katydid legs above each eye, still numbering the units in
　　　　　　each group;
　　　　the shadbones regularly set about his mouth, to droop or rise

in unison like the porcupine's quills—motionless. He lets himself
　　　　　　be flat-
　　tened out by gravity, as it were a piece of seaweed tamed and
　　　　　　weakened by
exposure to the sun; compelled when extended, to lie
　　stationary. Sleep is the result of his delusion that one must do as
　　　　well as one can for oneself; sleep—epitome of what is to

him as to the average person, the end of life. Demonstrate on
　　　　　　him how
the lady caught the dangerous southern snake, placing a forked
　　　　　　stick on either
side of its innocuous neck; one need not try to stir
　　him up; his prune shaped head and alligator eyes are not a
　　　　　　party to the
　　　　joke. Lifted and handled, he may be dangled like an eel or set

up on the forearm like a mouse; his eyes bisected by pupils of a pin's
　　width, are flickeringly exhibited, then covered up. May be?
　　　　　　I should say,
　　might have been; when he has been got the better of in a
　　　　dream—as in a fight with nature or with cats—we all know it.
　　　　　　Profound sleep is
　　　　not with him, a fixed illusion. Springing about with
　　　　　　froglike ac-

curacy, emitting jerky cries when taken in the hand, he is himself
　　again; to sit caged by the rungs of a domestic chair would be
　　　　　　unprofit-
able—human. What is the good of hypocrisy? It

is permissible to choose one's employment, to abandon the wire
            nail, the
    roly-poly, when it shows signs of being no longer a pleas-

ure, to score the adjacent magazine with a double line of strokes.
            He can
    talk, but insolently says nothing. What of it? When one is frank,
            one's very
  presence is a compliment. It is clear that he can see
    the virtue of naturalness, that he is one of those who do
            not regard
    the published fact as a surrender. As for the disposition

invariably to affront, an animal with claws wants to have to use
  them; that eel-like extension of trunk into tail is not an accident.
            To
  leap, to lengthen out, divide the air—to purloin, to pursue,
    to tell the hen: fly over the fence, go in the wrong way—in
            your perturba-
    tion—this is life; to do less would be nothing but dishonesty.

Dock Rats

There are human beings who seem to regard the place as craftily
    as we do—who seem to feel that it is a good place to come
    home to. On what a river; wide—twinkling like a chopped sea
                under some
    of the finest shipping in the

world: the square-rigged Flemish four-master, the liner, the battleship
              like the two-
    thirds submerged section of an iceberg; the tug
    dipping and pushing, the bell striking as it comes; the steam yacht,
             lying
    like a new made arrow on the

stream; the ferry-boat—a head assigned, one to each compartment,
             making
    a row of chessmen set for play. When the wind is from the east,
    the smell is of apples, of hay; the aroma increased and decreased
        as the wind changes;

of rope, of mountain leaves for florists; as from the west,
    it is aromatic of salt. Occasionally a parakeet
    from Brazil, arrives clasping and clawing; or a monkey—tail and
             feet
    in readiness for an over-

ture; all arms and tail; how delightful! There is the sea, moving the
             bulk-
    head with its horse strength; and the multiplicity of rudders
    and propellers; the signals, shrill, questioning, peremptory, diverse;
    the wharf cats and the barge dogs; it

is easy to overestimate the value of such things. One does
    not live in such a place from motives of expediency
    but because to one who has been accustomed to it, shipping is the
    most interesting thing in the world.

Picking And Choosing

Literature is a phase of life: if
  one is afraid of it, the situation is irremediable; if
one approaches it familiarly,
    what one says of it is worthless. Words are constructive
when they are true; the opaque allusion—the simulated flight

upward—accomplishes nothing. Why cloud the fact
  that Shaw is self-conscious in the field of sentiment but is
           otherwise re-
warding? that James is all that has been
  said of him, if *feeling* is profound? It is not Hardy
the distinguished novelist and Hardy the poet, but one man

"interpreting life through the medium of the
  emotions." If he must give an opinion, it is permissible that the
critic should know what he likes. Gordon
  Craig with his "this is I" and "this is mine," with his three
wise men, his "sad French greens" and his Chinese cherries—Gordon
           Craig, so

inclinational and unashamed—has carried
  the precept of being a good critic, to the last extreme; and
           Burke is a
psychologist—of acute, raccoon-
  like curiosity. *Summa diligentia*;
to the humbug, whose name is so amusing—very young and ve-

ry rushed, Caesar crossed the Alps on the "top of a
  diligence." We are not daft about the meaning but this familiarity
with wrong meanings puzzles one. Humming-
  bug, the candles are not wired for electricity.
Small dog, going over the lawn, nipping the linen and saying

that you have a badger—remember Xenophon;
  only the most rudimentary sort of behavior necessary
to put us on the scent; "a right good
  salvo of barks," a few "strong wrinkles" puckering the
skin between the ears, are all we ask.

England

with its baby rivers and little towns, each with its abbey or its
        cathedral,
    with voices—one voice perhaps, echoing through the transept—the
criterion of suitability and convenience: and Italy with its equal
        shores—contriving an epicureanism from which the grossness
            has been

extracted: and Greece with its goats and its gourds, the nest of
        modified illusions:
    and France, the "chrysalis of the nocturnal butterfly" in
whose products, mystery of construction diverts one from what
            was originally one's
        object—substance at the core: and the East with its snails,
            its emotional

shorthand and jade cockroaches, its rock crystal and its
        imperturbability,
    all of museum quality: and America where there
is the little old ramshackle victoria in the south, where cigars are
            smoked on the
        street in the north; where there are no proofreaders, no
            silkworms, no digressions;

the wild man's land; grass-less, links-less, language-less country in
            which letters are written
    not in Spanish, not in Greek, not in Latin, not in shorthand
but in plain American which cats and dogs can read! The letter "a"
            in psalm and calm when
        pronounced with the sound of "a" in candle, is very noticeable
            but

why should continents of misapprehension have to be accounted for
            by the
    fact? Does it follow that because there are poisonous toadstools
which resemble mushrooms, both are dangerous? In the case of
            mettlesomeness which may be
        mistaken for appetite, of heat which may appear to be haste,
            no con-

clusions may be drawn. To have misapprehended the matter, is to
    have confessed
that one has not looked far enough. The sublimated wisdom
of China, Egyptian discernment, the cataclysmic torrent of emotion
    compressed
    in the verbs of the Hebrew language, the books of the man
        who is able

to say, "I envy nobody but him and him only, who catches more
        fish than
    I do,"—the flower and fruit of all that noted superi-
ority—should one not have stumbled upon it in America, must
        one imagine
    that it is not there? It has never been confined to one locality.

When I Buy Pictures

or what is closer to the truth,
when I look at that of which I may regard myself as the imaginary
                possessor,
I fix upon what would give me pleasure in my average moments:
the satire upon curiosity in which no more is discernible than the
                intensity of the mood;
or quite the opposite—the old thing, the medieval decorated
                hat-box,
in which there are hounds with waists diminishing like the waist of
                the hourglass
and deer and birds and seated people;
it may be no more than a square of parquetry; the literal biography
                perhaps,
in letters standing well apart upon a parchment-like expanse;
an artichoke in six varieties of blue; the snipe-legged hieroglyphic in
                three parts;
the silver fence protecting Adam's grave, or Michael taking Adam by
                the wrist.
Too stern an intellectual emphasis upon this quality or that, detracts
                from one's enjoyment;
it must not wish to disarm anything; nor may the approved triumph
                easily be honored—
that which is great because something else is small.
It comes to this: of whatever sort it is,
it must be "lit with piercing glances into the life of things";
it must acknowledge the spiritual forces which have made it.

A Grave

Man looking into the sea,
taking the view from those who have as much right to it as you have
        to it yourself,
it is human nature to stand in the middle of a thing
but you cannot stand in the middle of this:
the sea has nothing to give but a well excavated grave.
The firs stand in a procession, each with an emerald turkey-foot
        at the top,
reserved as their contours, saying nothing;
repression, however, is not the most obvious characteristic of the sea;
the sea is a collector, quick to return a rapacious look.
There are others besides you who have worn that look—
whose expression is no longer a protest; the fish no longer investigate
        them
for their bones have not lasted:
men lower nets, unconscious of the fact that they are desecrating
        a grave,
and row quickly away—the blades of the oars
moving together like the feet of water-spiders as if there were no
        such thing as death.
The wrinkles progress upon themselves in a phalanx—beautiful
        under networks of foam,
and fade breathlessly while the sea rustles in and out of the seaweed;
the birds swim through the air at top speed, emitting catcalls as
        heretofore—
the tortoise-shell scourges about the feet of the cliffs, in motion
        beneath them
and the ocean, under the pulsation of lighthouse and noise of
        bell-buoys,
advances as usual, looking as if it were not that ocean in which
        dropped things are bound to sink—
in which if they turn and twist, it is neither with volition nor
        consciousness.

Those Various Scalpels

Those
various sounds consistently indistinct, like intermingled echoes
    struck from thin glasses successively at random—the
    inflection disguised: your hair, the tails of two fighting-cocks head
            to head in stone—like sculptured scimitars re-
        peating the curve of your ears in reverse order: your eyes,
            flowers of ice

and
snow sown by tearing winds on the cordage of disabled ships: your
            raised hand
    an ambiguous signature: your cheeks, those rosettes
    of blood on the stone floors of French châteaux, with regard to
            which the guides are so affirmative:
        your other hand

a
bundle of lances all alike, partly hid by emeralds from Persia
    and the fractional magnificence of Florentine
    goldwork—a collection of half a dozen little objects made fine
        with enamel in gray, yellow, and dragon fly blue; a lemon, a

pear
and three bunches of grapes, tied with silver: your dress, a
            magnificent square
        cathedral of uniform
    and at the same time, diverse appearance—a species of vertical
            vineyard rustling in the storm
        of conventional opinion. Are they weapons or scalpels?
            Whetted

to
brilliance by the hard majesty of that sophistication which is su-
    perior to opportunity, these things are rich
    instruments with which to experiment but surgery is not tentative.
        Why dissect destiny with instruments which
    are more highly specialized than the tissues of destiny itself?

The Labors of Hercules

To popularize the mule, its neat exterior
expressing the principle of accommodation reduced to a minimum:
to persuade one of austere taste, proud in the possession of home,
        and a musician—
that the piano is a free field for etching; that his "charming
        tadpole notes"
belong to the past when one had time to play them:
to persuade those self-wrought Midases of brains
whose fourteen-karat ignorance aspires to rise in value
"till the sky is the limit,"
that excessive conduct augurs disappointment,
that one must not borrow a long white beard and tie it on
and threaten with the scythe of time, the casually curious:
to teach the bard with too elastic a selectiveness
that one detects creative power by its capacity to conquer
        one's detachment;
that while it may have more elasticity than logic,
it knows where it is going;
it flies along in a straight line like electricity
depopulating areas that boast of their remoteness:
to prove to the high priests of caste
that snobbishness is a stupidity,
the best side out, of age-old toadyism,
kissing the feet of the man above,
kicking the face of the man below:
to teach the patron-saints-to-atheists, the Coliseum
meet-me-alone-by-moonlight maudlin troubadour
that kickups for catstrings are not life
nor yet appropriate to death—that we are sick of the earth,
sick of the pig-sty, wild geese and wild men:
to convince snake-charming controversialists
that it is one thing to change one's mind,
another to eradicate it—that one keeps on knowing
"that the Negro is not brutal,
that the Jew is not greedy,
that the Oriental is not immoral,
that the German is not a Hun."

New York

the savage's romance,
accreted where we need the space for commerce—
the center of the wholesale fur trade,
starred with tepees of ermine and peopled with foxes,
the long guard-hairs waving two inches beyond the body of the pelt;
the ground dotted with deer-skins—white with white spots
"as satin needlework in a single color may carry a varied pattern,"
and wilting eagles' down compacted by the wind;
and picardels of beaver skin; white ones alert with snow.
It is a far cry from the "queen full of jewels"
and the beau with the muff,
from the gilt coach shaped like a perfume bottle,
to the conjunction of the Monongahela and the Allegheny,
and the scholastic philosophy of the wilderness
to combat which one must stand outside and laugh
since to go in is to be lost.
It is not the dime-novel exterior,
Niagara Falls, the calico horses and the war canoe;
it is not that "if the fur is not finer than such as one sees others wear,
one would rather be without it—"
that estimated in raw meat and berries, we could feed the universe;
it is not the atmosphere of ingenuity,
the otter, the beaver, the puma skins
without shooting-irons or dogs;
it is not the plunder,
it is the "accessibility to experience."

People's Surroundings

they answer one's questions:
a deal table compact with the wall;
in this dried bone of arrangement,
one's "natural promptness" is compressed, not crowded out;
one's style is not lost in such simplicity:

the palace furniture, so old fashioned, so old fashionable;
Sèvres china and the fireplace dogs—
bronze dromios with pointed ears, as obsolete as pugs;
one has one's preference in the matter of bad furniture
and this is not one's choice:

the vast indestructible necropolis
of composite Yawman-Erbe separable units;
the steel, the oak, the glass, the Poor Richard publications
containing the public secrets of efficiency
on "paper so thin that one thousand four hundred and twenty pages
            make one inch,"
exclaiming so to speak, When you take my time, you take something
            I had meant to use:

the highway hid by fir trees in rhododendron twenty feet deep,
the peacocks, hand-forged gates, old Persian velvet—
roses outlined in pale black on an ivory ground—
the pierced iron shadows of the cedars,
Chinese carved glass, old Waterford,
lettered ladies; landscape gardening twisted into permanence:

straight lines over such great distances as one finds in Utah or in
            Texas
where people do not have to be told
that "a good brake is as important as a good motor,"
where by means of extra sense cells in the skin,
they can like trout, smell what is coming—
those cool sirs with the explicit sensory apparatus of common sense,
who know the exact distance between two points as the crow flies;
there is something attractive about a mind that moves in a straight
            line—
the municipal bat-roost of mosquito warfare, concrete statuary,

medicaments for "instant beauty" in the hands of all,
and that live wire, the American string quartet:

and Bluebeard's tower above the coral reefs,
the magic mousetrap closing on all points of the compass,
capping like petrified surf, the furious azure of the bay
where there is no dust and life is like a lemon-leaf,
a green piece of tough translucent parchment,
where the crimson, the copper, and the Chinese vermilion of
                the poincianas
set fire to the masonry and turquoise blues refute the clock;
this dungeon with odd notions of hospitality,
with its "chessmen carved out of moonstones,"
its mocking-birds, fringed lilies, and hibiscus,
its black butterflies with blue half circles on their wings,
tan goats with onyx ears, its lizards glittering and without thickness
like splashes of fire and silver on the pierced turquoise of the lattices
and the acacia-like lady shivering at the touch of a hand,
lost in a small collision of the orchids—
dyed quicksilver let fall
to disappear like an obedient chameleon in fifty shades of mauve
                and amethyst:
here where the mind of this establishment has come to the conclusion
that it would be impossible to revolve about one's self too much,
sophistication has like "an escalator, cut the nerve of progress."

In these noncommittal, personal-impersonal expressions of
                appearance,
the eye knows what to skip;
the physiognomy of conduct must not reveal the skeleton;
"a setting must not have the air of being one"
yet with x-raylike inquisitive intensity upon it, the surfaces go back;
the interfering fringes of expression are but a stain on what
                stands out,
there is neither up nor down to it;
we see the exterior and the fundamental structure—
captains of armies, cooks, carpenters,
cutlers, gamesters, surgeons and armorers,
lapidaries, silkmen, glovers, fiddlers and ballad-singers,
sextons of churches, dyers of black cloth, hostlers and chimney-
                sweeps,
queens, countesses, ladies, emperors, travelers and mariners,

dukes, princes and gentlemen
in their respective places—
camps, forges and battlefields,
conventions, oratories and wardrobes,
dens, deserts, railway stations, asylums and places where engines
        are made,
shops, prisons, brickyards and altars of churches—
in magnificent places clean and decent,
castles, palaces, dining-halls, theatres and imperial audience-
        chambers.

Snakes, Mongooses, Snake-Charmers, and the Like

I have a friend who would give a price for those long fingers all of
        one length—
those hideous bird's claws, for that exotic asp and the mongoose—
products of the country in which everything is hard work, the
        country of the grass-getter,
the torch-bearer, the dog-servant, the message-bearer, the holy-man.
Engrossed in this distinguished worm nearly as wild and as fierce as
        the day it was captured,
he gazes as if incapable of looking at anything with a view to
        analysis.
"The slight snake rippling quickly through the grass,
the leisurely tortoise with its pied back,
the chameleon passing from twig to stone, from stone to straw,"
lit his imagination at one time; his admiration now converges
        upon this:
thick, not heavy, it stands up from its traveling-basket,
the essentially Greek, the plastic animal, all of a piece from nose
        to tail;
one is compelled to look at it as at the shadows of the alps
imprisoning in their folds like flies in amber, the rhythms of the
        skating-rink.
This animal to which from the earliest times, importance has
        attached,
fine as its worshippers have said—for what was it invented?
To show that when intelligence in its pure form
has embarked on a train of thought which is unproductive, it will
        come back?
We do not know; the only positive thing about it is its shape, but
        why protest?
The passion for setting people right is in itself an afflictive disease.
Distaste which takes no credit to itself is best.

Bowls

on the green
with lignum vitae balls and ivory markers,
the pins planted in wild duck formation,
and quickly dispersed:
by this survival of ancient punctilio
in the manner of Chinese lacquer carving,
layer after layer exposed by certainty of touch and unhurried incision
so that only so much color shall be revealed as is necessary to the
picture
I learn that we are precisians—
not citizens of Pompeii arrested in action
as a cross section of one's correspondence would seem to imply.
Renouncing a policy of boorish indifference
to everything that has been said since the days of Matilda,
I shall purchase an Etymological Dictionary of Modern English
that I may understand what is written
and like the ant and the spider
returning from time to time to headquarters,
shall answer the question
as to "why I like winter better than I like summer"
and acknowledge that it does not make me sick
to look modern playwrights and poets and novelists straight in the
face—
that I feel just the same;
and I shall write to the publisher of the magazine
which will "appear the first day of the month
and disappear before one has had time to buy it
unless one takes proper precaution,"
and make an effort to please—
since he who gives quickly gives twice
in nothing so much as in a letter.

Novices

anatomize their work
in the sense in which Will Honeycomb was jilted by a duchess,
the little assumptions of the scared ego confusing the issue
so that they do not know "whether it is the buyer or the seller
        who gives the money"—
an abstruse idea plain to none but the artist,
the only seller who buys, and holds on to the money.
Because one expresses oneself and entitles it wisdom, one is not
        a fool. What an idea!
"Dracontine cockatrices, perfect and poisonous from the beginning,"
they present themselves as a contrast to sea-serpented regions "unlit
        by the half-lights of more conscious art."
Acquiring at thirty what at sixty they will be trying to forget,
blind to the right word, deaf to satire
which like "the smell of the cypress strengthens the nerves of
        the brain,"
averse from the antique
with "that tinge of sadness about it which a reflective mind always
        feels,
it is so little and so much"—
they write the sort of thing that would in their judgment interest
        a lady;
curious to know if we do not adore each letter of the alphabet that
        goes to make a word of it—
according to the Act of Congress, the sworn statement of the
        treasurer and all the rest of it—
the counterpart to what we are:
stupid man; men are strong and no one pays any attention:
stupid woman; women have charm and how annoying they can be.
Yes, "the authors are wonderful people, particularly those that write
        the most,"
the masters of all languages, the supertadpoles of expression.
Accustomed to the recurring phosphorescence of antiquity,
the "much noble vagueness and indefinite jargon" of Plato,
the lucid movements of the royal yacht upon the learned scenery
        of Egypt—
king, steward, and harper seated amidships while the jade and the
        rock crystal course about in solution,
their suavity surmounts the surf—

the willowy wit, the transparent equation of Isaiah, Jeremiah,
Ezekiel, Daniel.
Bored by "the detailless perspective of the sea," reiterative and naive,
and its chaos of rocks—the stuffy remarks of the Hebrews—
the good and alive young men demonstrate the assertion
that it is not necessary to be associated with that which has
bored one;
they have never made a statement which they found so easy
to prove—
"split like a glass against a wall"
in this "precipitate of dazzling impressions,
the spontaneous unforced passion of the Hebrew language—
an abyss of verbs full of reverberations and tempestuous energy,"
in which action perpetuates action and angle is at variance with angle
till submerged by the general action;
obscured by "fathomless suggestions of color,"
by incessantly panting lines of green, white with concussion,
in this drama of water against rocks—this "ocean of hurrying
consonants"
with its "great livid stains like long slabs of green marble,"
its "flashing lances of perpendicular lightning" and "molten fires
swallowed up,"
"with foam on its barriers,"
"crashing itself out in one long hiss of spray."

Marriage

This institution,
perhaps one should say enterprise
out of respect for which
one says one need not change one's mind
about a thing one has believed in,
requiring public promises
of one's intention
to fulfill a private obligation:
I wonder what Adam and Eve
think of it by this time,
this firegilt steel
alive with goldenness;
how bright it shows—
"of circular traditions and impostures,
committing many spoils,"
requiring all one's criminal ingenuity
to avoid!
Psychology which explains everything
explains nothing
and we are still in doubt.
Eve: beautiful woman—
I have seen her
when she was so handsome
she gave me a start,
able to write simultaneously
in three languages—
English, German and French
and talk in the meantime;
equally positive in demanding a commotion
and in stipulating quiet:
"I should like to be alone";
to which the visitor replies,
"I should like to be alone;
why not be alone together?"
Below the incandescent stars
below the incandescent fruit,
the strange experience of beauty;
its existence is too much;
it tears one to pieces

and each fresh wave of consciousness
is poison.
"See her, see her in this common world,"
the central flaw
in that first crystal-fine experiment,
this amalgamation which can never be more
than an interesting impossibility,
describing it
as "that strange paradise
unlike flesh, gold, or stately buildings,
the choicest piece of my life:
the heart rising
in its estate of peace
as a boat rises
with the rising of the water";
constrained in speaking of the serpent—
that shed snakeskin in the history of politeness
not to be returned to again—
that invaluable accident
exonerating Adam.
And he has beauty also;
it's distressing—the O thou
to whom, from whom,
without whom nothing—Adam;
"something feline,
something colubrine"—how true!
a crouching mythological monster
in that Persian miniature of emerald mines,
raw silk—ivory white, snow white,
oyster white and six others—
that paddock full of leopards and giraffes—
long lemon-yellow bodies
sown with trapezoids of blue.
Alive with words,
vibrating like a cymbal
touched before it has been struck,
he has prophesied correctly—
the industrious waterfall,
"the speedy stream
which violently bears all before it,
at one time silent as the air
and now as powerful as the wind."

"Treading chasms
on the uncertain footing of a spear,"
forgetting that there is in woman
a quality of mind
which as an instinctive manifestation
is unsafe,
he goes on speaking
in a formal, customary strain
of "past states, the present state,
seals, promises,
the evil one suffered,
the good one enjoys,
hell, heaven,
everything convenient
to promote one's joy."
There is in him a state of mind
by force of which,
perceiving what it was not
intended that he should,
"he experiences a solemn joy
in seeing that he has become an idol."
Plagued by the nightingale
in the new leaves,
with its silence—
not its silence but its silences,
he says of it:
"It clothes me with a shirt of fire."
"He dares not clap his hands
to make it go on
lest it should fly off;
if he does nothing, it will sleep;
if he cries out, it will not understand."
Unnerved by the nightingale
and dazzled by the apple,
impelled by "the illusion of a fire
effectual to extinguish fire,"
compared with which
the shining of the earth
is but deformity—a fire
"as high as deep as bright as broad
as long as life itself,"
he stumbles over marriage,

"a very trivial object indeed"
to have destroyed the attitude
in which he stood—
the ease of the philosopher
unfathered by a woman.
Unhelpful Hymen!
"a kind of overgrown cupid"
reduced to insignificance
by the mechanical advertising
parading as involuntary comment,
by that experiment of Adam's
with ways out but no way in—
the ritual of marriage,
augmenting all its lavishness;
its fiddle-head ferns,
lotus flowers, opuntias, white dromedaries,
its hippopotamus—
nose and mouth combined
in one magnificent hopper,
"the crested screamer—
that huge bird almost a lizard,"
its snake and the potent apple.
He tells us
that "for love
that will gaze an eagle blind,
that is like a Hercules
climbing the trees
in the garden of the Hesperides,
from forty-five to seventy
is the best age,"
commending it
as a fine art, as an experiment,
a duty or as merely recreation.
One must not call him ruffian
nor friction a calamity—
the fight to be affectionate:
"no truth can be fully known
until it has been tried
by the tooth of disputation."
The blue panther with black eyes,
the basalt panther with blue eyes,
entirely graceful—

one must give them the path—
the black obsidian Diana
who "darkeneth her countenance
as a bear doth,
causing her husband to sigh,"
the spiked hand
that has an affection for one
and proves it to the bone,
impatient to assure you
that impatience is the mark of independence
not of bondage.
"Married people often look that way"—
"seldom and cold, up and down,
mixed and malarial
with a good day and bad."
"When do we feed?"
We occidentals are so unemotional,
we quarrel as we feed;
one's self quite lost,
the irony preserved
in "the Ahasuerus tête à tête banquet"
with its "good monster, lead the way,"
with little laughter
and munificence of humor
in that quixotic atmosphere of frankness
in which "Four o'clock does not exist
but at five o'clock
the ladies in their imperious humility
are ready to receive you";
in which experience attests
that men have power
and sometimes one is made to feel it.
He says, "What monarch would not blush
to have a wife
with hair like a shaving-brush?
The fact of woman
is not 'the sound of the flute
but very poison.'"
She says, "'Men are monopolists
of stars, garters, buttons
and other shining baubles'—
unfit to be the guardians

of another person's happiness."
He says, "These mummies
must be handled carefully—
'the crumbs from a lion's meal,
a couple of shins and the bit of an ear';
turn to the letter M
and you will find
that 'a wife is a coffin,'
that severe object
with the pleasing geometry
stipulating space and not people,
refusing to be buried
and uniquely disappointing,
revengefully wrought in the attitude
of an adoring child
to a distinguished parent."
She says, "This butterfly,
this waterfly, this nomad
that has 'proposed
to settle on my hand for life.'—
What can one do with it?
There must have been more time
in Shakespeare's day
to sit and watch a play.
You know so many artists who are fools."
He says, "You know so many fools
who are not artists."
The fact forgot
that "some have merely rights
while some have obligations,"
he loves himself so much,
he can permit himself
no rival in that love.
She loves herself so much,
she cannot see herself enough—
a statuette of ivory on ivory,
the logical last touch
to an expansive splendor
earned as wages for work done:
one is not rich but poor
when one can always seem so right.
What can one do for them—

these savages
condemned to disaffect
all those who are not visionaries
alert to undertake the silly task
of making people noble?
This model of petrine fidelity
who "leaves her peaceful husband
only because she has seen enough of him"–
that orator reminding you,
"I am yours to command."
"Everything to do with love is mystery;
it is more than a day's work
to investigate this science."
One sees that it is rare—
that striking grasp of opposites
opposed each to the other, not to unity,
which in cycloid inclusiveness
has dwarfed the demonstration
of Columbus with the egg—
a triumph of simplicity—
that charitive Euroclydon
of frightening disinterestedness
which the world hates,
admitting:

> "I am such a cow,
> if I had a sorrow,
> I should feel it a long time;
> I am not one of those
> who have a great sorrow
> in the morning
> and a great joy at noon";

which says: "I have encountered it
among those unpretentious
protegés of wisdom,
where seeming to parade
as the debater and the Roman,
the statesmanship
of an archaic Daniel Webster
persists to their simplicity of temper
as the essence of the matter:

'Liberty and union
now and forever';

the book on the writing-table;
the hand in the breast-pocket."

Silence

My father used to say,
"Superior people never make long visits,
have to be shown Longfellow's grave
nor the glass flowers at Harvard.
Self reliant like the cat—
that takes its prey to privacy,
the mouse's limp tail hanging like a shoelace from its mouth—
they sometimes enjoy solitude,
and can be robbed of speech
by speech which has delighted them.
The deepest feeling always shows itself in silence;
not in silence, but restraint."
Nor was he insincere in saying, "'Make my house your inn.'"
Inns are not residences.

An Octopus

of ice. Deceptively reserved and flat,
it lies "in grandeur and in mass"
beneath a sea of shifting snow dunes;
dots of cyclamen red and maroon on its clearly defined pseudopodia
made of glass that will bend—a much needed invention—
comprising twenty-eight ice fields from fifty to five hundred feet
                    thick,
of unimagined delicacy.
"Picking periwinkles from the cracks"
or killing prey with the concentric crushing rigor of the python,
it hovers forward "spider fashion
on its arms" misleadingly like lace;
its "ghostly pallor changing
to the green metallic tinge of an anemone starred pool."
The fir trees in "the magnitude of their root systems,"
rise aloof from these maneuvers "creepy to behold,"
austere specimens of our American royal families,
"each like the shadow of the one beside it.
The rock seems frail compared with their dark energy of life,"
its vermilion and onyx and manganese blue interior expensiveness
left at the mercy of the weather;
"stained transversely by iron where the water drips down,"
recognized by its plants and its animals.
Completing a circle,
you have been deceived into thinking that you have progressed,
under the polite needles of the larches
"hung to filter not to intercept the sunlight"—
met by tightly wattled spruce twigs
"conformed to an edge like clipped cypress
as if no branch could penetrate the cold beyond its company";
and dumps of gold and silver ore enclosing The Goat's Mirror—
that lady-fingerlike depression in the shape of the left human foot,
which prejudices you in favor of itself
before you have had time to see the others;
its indigo, pea-green, blue-green, and turquoise,
from a hundred to two hundred feet deep,
"merging in irregular patches in the middle lake
where like gusts of a storm

obliterating the shadows of the fir trees, the wind makes lanes of
              ripples."
What spot could have merits of equal importance
for bears, elk, deer, wolves, goats, and ducks?
Preempted by their ancestors,
this is the property of the exacting porcupine,
and of the rat "slipping along to its burrow in the swamp
or pausing on high ground to smell the heather";
of "thoughtful beavers
making drains which seem the work of careful men with shovels,"
and of the bears inspecting unexpectedly
ant hills and berry bushes.
Composed of calcium gems and alabaster pillars,
topaz, tourmaline crystals and amethyst quartz,
their den is somewhere else, concealed in the confusion
of "blue forests thrown together with marble and jasper and agate
as if whole quarries had been dynamited."
And farther up, in stag-at-bay position
as a scintillating fragment of these terrible stalagmites,
stands the goat,
its eye fixed on the waterfall which never seems to fall—
an endless skein swayed by the wind,
immune to force of gravity in the perspective of the peaks.
A special antelope
acclimated to "grottoes from which issue penetrating draughts
which make you wonder why you came,"
it stands its ground
on cliffs the color of the clouds, of petrified white vapor—
black feet, eyes, nose, and horns engraved on dazzling ice-fields,
the ermine body on the crystal peak;
the sun kindling its shoulders to maximum heat like acetylene,
              dyeing them white—
upon this antique pedestal—
"a mountain with those graceful lines which prove it a volcano,"
its top a complete cone like Fujiyama's
till an explosion blew it off.
Maintaining many minds, distinguished by a beauty
of which "the visitor dare never fully speak at home
for fear of being stoned as an imposter,"
Big Snow Mountain is the home of a diversity of creatures:
those who "have lived in hotels
but who now live in camps—who prefer to";

the mountain guide evolving from the trapper,
"in two pairs of trousers, the outer one older,
wearing slowly away from the feet to the knees";
"the nine-striped chipmunk
running with unmammallike agility along a log";
the water ouzel
with "its passion for rapids and high pressured falls,"
building under the arch of some tiny Niagara;
the white-tailed ptarmigan "in winter solid white,
feeding on heather bells and alpine buckwheat";
and the eleven eagles of the west,
"fond of the spring fragrance and the winter colors,"
used to the unegoistic action of the glaciers
and "several hours of frost every midsummer night."
"They make a nice appearance, don't they,"
happy seeing nothing?
Perched on treacherous lava and pumice—
those unadjusted chimney-pots and cleavers
which stipulate "the names and addresses of persons to notify
in case of disaster—"
they hear the roar of ice and supervise the water
winding slowly through the cliffs,
the road "climbing like the thread
which forms the groove around a snail-shell,
doubling back and forth until where snow begins, it ends."
No "deliberate wide-eyed wistfulness" is here
among the boulders sunk in ripples and white water
where "when you hear the best wild music of the mountains it is sure
                    to be a marmot,"
the victim on some slight observatory,
of "a struggle between curiosity and caution,"
inquiring what has scared it:
a stone from the moraine descending in leaps,
another marmot, or the spotted ponies with "glass eyes,"
brought up on frosty grass and flowers
and rapid draughts of ice water.
Instructed none knows how, to climb the mountain,
by "business men who as totemic scenery of Canada,
require for recreation,
three hundred and sixty-five holidays in the year,"
these conspicuously spotted little horses are peculiar;
hard to discern among the birch trees, ferns, and lily pads,

avalanche lilies, Indian paintbrushes,
bears' ears and kittentails,
and miniature cavalcades of chlorophylless fungi
magnified in profile on the moss beds like moonstones in the water;
the cavalcade of calico competing
with the original American "menagerie of styles"
among the white flowers of the rhododendron surmounting rigid
                            leaves
upon which moisture works its alchemy,
transmuting verdure into onyx.
Larkspur, blue pincushions, blue peas, and lupin;
white flowers with white, and red with red;
the blue ones "growing close together
so that patches of them look like blue water in the distance":
this arrangement of colors
as in Persian designs of hard stones with enamel,
forms a pleasing equation—
a diamond outside and inside, a white dot;
on the outside, a ruby; inside, a red dot;
black spots balanced with black
in the woodlands where fires have run over the ground—
separated by aspens, cat's paws, and woolly sunflowers,
fireweed, asters, and Goliath thistles
"flowering at all altitudes as multiplicitous as barley,"
like pink sapphires in the pavement of the glistening plateau.
Inimical to "bristling, puny, swearing men
equipped with saws and axes,"
this treacherous glass mountain
admires gentians, lady's slippers, harebells, mountain dryads,
and "Calypso, the goat flower—
that greenish orchid fond of snow"—
anomalously nourished upon shelving glacial ledges
where climbers have not gone or have gone timidly,
"the one resting his nerves while the other advanced,"
on this volcano with the blue jay, her principal companion.
"Hopping stiffly on sharp feet" like miniature icehacks—
"secretive, with a look of wisdom and distinction, but a villain,
fond of human society or the crumbs that go with it,"
he knows no Greek,
"that pride producing language,"
in which "rashness is rendered innocuous, and error exposed
by the collision of knowledge with knowledge."

"Like happy souls in Hell," enjoying mental difficulties,
the grasshoppers of Greece
amused themselves with delicate behavior
because it was "so noble and so fair";
not practiced in adapting their intelligence
to eagle traps and snowshoes,
to alpenstocks and other toys contrived by those
"alive to the advantage of invigorating pleasures."
Bows, arrows, oars, and paddles for which trees provide the wood,
in new countries are more eloquent than elsewhere—
augmenting evidence for the assertion
that essentially humane,
"the forest affords wood for dwellings and by its beauty stimulates
the moral vigor of its citizens."
The Greeks liked smoothness, distrusting what was back
of what could not be clearly seen,
resolving with benevolent conclusiveness,
"complexities which still will be complexities
as long as the world lasts";
ascribing what we clumsily call happiness,
to "an accident or a quality,
a spiritual substance or the soul itself,
an act, a disposition, or a habit,
or a habit infused to which the soul has been persuaded,
or something distinct from a habit, a power—"
such power as Adam had and we are still devoid of.
"Emotionally sensitive, their hearts were hard";
their wisdom was remote
from that of these odd oracles of cool official sarcasm,
upon this game preserve
where "guns, nets, seines, traps and explosives,
hired vehicles, gambling and intoxicants are prohibited,
disobedient persons being summarily removed
and not allowed to return without permission in writing."
It is self evident
that it is frightful to have everything afraid of one;
that one must do as one is told
and eat "rice, prunes, dates, raisins, hardtack, and tomatoes"
if one would "conquer the main peak" of Mount Tacoma
this fossil flower concise without a shiver,
intact when it is cut,
damned for its sacrosanct remoteness—

like Henry James "damned by the public for decorum";
not decorum, but restraint;
it was the love of doing hard things
that rebuffed and wore them out—a public out of sympathy
                    with neatness.
Neatness of finish! Neatness of finish!
Relentless accuracy is the nature of this octopus
with its capacity for fact.
"Creeping slowly as with meditated stealth,
its arms seeming to approach from all directions,"
it receives one under winds that "tear the snow to bits
and hurl it like a sandblast,
shearing off twigs and loose bark from the trees."
Is tree the word for these strange things
"flat on the ground like vines";
some "bent in a half circle with branches on one side
suggesting dustbrushes, not trees;
some finding strength in union, forming little stunted groves,
their flattened mats of branches shrunk in trying to escape"
from the hard mountain "planed by ice and polished by the wind"—
the white volcano with no weather side;
the lightning flashing at its base,
rain falling in the valleys, and snow falling on the peak—
the glassy octopus symmetrically pointed,
its claw cut by the avalanche
"with a sound like the crack of a rifle,
in a curtain of powdered snow launched like a waterfall."

Sea Unicorns and Land Unicorns

with their respective lions—
"mighty monoceroses with immeasured tayles"—
these are those very animals
described by the cartographers of 1539,
defiantly revolving
in such a way that the hard steel
in the long keel of white exhibited in tumbling,
disperses giant weeds
and those sea snakes whose forms looped in the foam, "disquiet
        shippers."
Not ignorant of how a voyager obtained the horn of a sea unicorn
to give Queen Elizabeth
who thought it worth a hundred thousand pounds,
they persevere in swimming where they like,
finding the place where lions live in herds,
strewn on the beach like stones with lesser stones—
and bears are white;
discovering Antarctica, its penguin kings and icy spires,
and Sir John Hawkins' Florida
"abounding in land unicorns and lions,
since where the one is,
its arch enemy cannot be missing."
Thus personalities by nature much opposed,
can be combined in such a way
that when they do agree, their unanimity is great,
"in politics, in trade, law, sport, religion,
china collecting, tennis, and church going."
You have remarked this fourfold combination of strange animals,
upon embroideries,
enwrought with "polished garlands" of agreeing indifference—
thorns, "myrtle rods, and shafts of bay,"
"cobwebs, and knotts, and mulberries"
of lapis lazuli and pomegranate and malachite—
Britannia's sea unicorn with its rebellious child
now ostentatiously indigenous of the new English coast
and its land lion oddly tolerant of those pacific counterparts to it,
the water lions of the west.
This is a strange fraternity—these sea lions and land lions,

land unicorns and sea unicorns:
the lion civilly rampant,
tame and concessive like the long-tailed bear of Ecuador—
the lion standing up against this screen of woven air
which is the forest:
the unicorn also, on its hind legs in reciprocity.
A puzzle to the hunters, is this haughtiest of beasts,
to be distinguished from those born without a horn,
in use like Saint Jerome's tame lion, as domestics,
rebelling proudly at the dogs
which are dismayed by the chain lightning
playing at them from its horn—
the dogs persistent in pursuit of it as if it could be caught,
"deriving agreeable terror" from its "moonbeam throat"
on fire like its white coat and unconsumed as if of salamander's skin.
So wary as to disappear for centuries and reappear,
yet never to be caught,
the unicorn has been preserved
by an unmatched device
wrought like the work of expert blacksmiths,
with which nothing can compare—
this animal of that one horn
throwing itself upon which head foremost from a cliff,
it walks away unharmed,
proficient in this feat, which like Herodotus,
I have not seen except in pictures.
Thus this strange animal with its miraculous elusiveness,
has come to be unique,
"impossible to take alive,"
tamed only by a lady inoffensive like itself—
as curiously wild and gentle;
"as straight and slender as the crest,
or antlet of the one-beam'd beast."
Upon the printed page,
also by word of mouth,
we have a record of it all
and how, unfearful of deceit,
etched like an equine monster on an old celestial map,
beside a cloud or dress of Virgin-Mary blue,
improved "all over slightly with snakes of Venice gold,
and silver, and some O's,"

the unicorn "with pavon high," approaches eagerly;
until engrossed by what appears of this strange enemy,
upon the map, "upon her lap,"
its "mild wild head doth lie."

INDEX

giraffes, 64
glass, "eyes," 74, 306; pulled,
    16; that will bend, 72, 305;
    Waterford, 56, 301
goat, 73
Godwin, 304
Goliath thistles, 75
Gordon, A. R., conscious art, 61,
    302; piercing glances, 51, 299;
    precipitate, 62, 302
grasshoppers of Greece, 76
GRAVE, A, 52
grave, Adam's, 51, 299
Greece, grasshoppers of, 76;
    goats, gourds, 49
Greek, essentially, 59; language,
    75, 306; letters in, 49
Greeks, smoothness, 76; words
    of, 38

H

Habakkuk, 29
Hardy, Thomas, 48, 298
Hartman, C. B., 304
Harvard, glass flowers at, 71
Hawkins, Sir John, 78, 307
Hazlitt, 303
Hebrew language, verbs of, 62;
    spontaneous passion of, 62
Hebrew poetry, 29, 297
Hebrews, remarks of, 62
Hegel, 302
Hell, in, 75, 307; heaven, 65
HERCULES, LABORS OF, 54,
    299
Hercules climbing trees, a, 66
Herodotus, 79, 308
Hesperides, 66, 303
HE WROTE THE HISTORY
    BOOK, 31, 298
hippopotamus, 41
HISTORY BOOK, see HE

hollowness, 22
holow eyed, 11
Homans, Miss A. M., 305
Honeycomb, Will, 61
HOPE, FEAR IS, 11
Hueber, M., 298
humility, ladies', 67, 304
Hunt, Leigh, agreeable terror, 79,
    308; authors, 61, 302; flashing
    lances, 62, 303
Hyde, W. D., 307
Hymen, 66, 304

I

ibis, 25
icehacks, 75
Ideas of Good and Evil, 297
imagination, 43; literalists of, 27
impersonal judgment, 17
incandescence, of color, 44; the
    sun's, 11
incandescent, fruit, 63; stars, 63
India paper, 56, 301
INJUDICIOUS GARDENING,
    10, 296
In Memory, 298
inn, 71, 305
IN THE DAYS OF PRISMATIC
    COLOR, 44, 298
IN THIS AGE OF HARD
    TRYING, 24
INTRA-MURAL RAT, TO AN,
    5
Ireland, 35
IS YOUR TOWN NINEVEH?,
    13
ivory, and jet, 14; markers, 60;
    statuette, 68

J

jade, black, 39; cockroaches, 49;
    water, 61

water lions, 78; seeks its own
level, 35, 298
waterfall, industrious, 64;
swayed by the wind, 73
Waterford glass, 56, 301
wave, may go over me, 44;
perpendicular, 16
Webbe, 301
Webster, Daniel, 305
Weniger, M., 298
Wescott, G., 304
WHALE, SOJOURN IN THE,
35, 298
WHEN I BUY PICTURES, 51,
299
white, nine kinds, 75; tailed deer,
55, 300
wife, a coffin, 68, 304
Wilcox, W. D., clipped cypress,
72, 306; crack of a rifle, 77,
307; "glass eyes," 74, 306;

grottoes, 73, 306; two pairs
of trousers, 74, 306
Will Honeycomb, 61
willows at Oxford, 32
Wilson, V. A., Cavendish, 307;
cobwebs, 78, 307; Queen
Elizabeth's Maids of Honour,
307

X
Xenophon, 48, 299
x-ray, 57

Y
Yawman-Erbe, 56
Yeats, W. B., 297
yellow, 10, 296

Z
zebras, 36

POEMS 1932–1936

Part of a Novel, Part of a Poem, Part of a Play

The Steeple-Jack

Dürer would have seen a reason for living
    in a town like this, with eight stranded whales
to look at; with the sweet sea air coming into your house
on a fine day, from water etched
    with waves as formal as the scales
on a fish.

One by one, in two's, in three's, the seagulls keep
    flying back and forth over the town clock,
or sailing around the lighthouse without moving the wings—
rising steadily with a slight
    quiver of the body—or flock
mewing where

a sea the purple of the peacock's neck is
    paled to greenish azure as Dürer changed
the pine green of the Tyrol to peacock blue and guinea
grey. You can see a twenty-five
    pound lobster; and fishnets arranged
to dry. The

whirlwind fifeanddrum of the storm bends the salt
    marsh grass, disturbs stars in the sky and the
star on the steeple; it is a privilege to see so
much confusion. Disguised by what
    might seem austerity, the sea-
side flowers and

trees are favored by the fog so that you have
    the tropics at first hand: the trumpet-vine,
fox-glove, giant snap-dragon, a salpiglossis that has
spots and stripes; morning-glories, gourds,
    or moon-vines trained on fishing-twine
at the back

door; cat-tails, flags, blueberries and spiderwort,
    striped grass, lichens, sunflowers, asters, daisies—

the yellow and the crab-claw blue ones with green bracts—
        toad-plant,
petunias, ferns; pink lilies, blue
    ones, tigers; poppies; black sweet-peas.
The climate

is not right for the banyan, frangipani, the
    jack-fruit tree; nor for exotic serpent
life. Ring lizard and snake-skin for the foot if you see fit,
but here they've cats not cobras to
    keep down the rats. The diffident
little newt

with white pin-dots on black horizontal spaced
    out bands lives here; yet there is nothing that
ambition can buy or take away. The college student
named Ambrose sits on the hill-side
    with his not-native books and hat
and sees boats

at sea progress white and rigid as if in
    a groove. Liking an elegance of which
the source is not bravado, he knows by heart the antique
sugar-bowl shaped summer-house of
    interlacing slats, and the pitch
of the church

spire, not true, from which a man in scarlet lets
    down a rope as a spider spins a thread;
he might be part of a novel, but on the sidewalk a
sign says C. J. Poole, Steeple-jack,
    in black and white; and one in red
and white says

Danger. The church portico has four fluted
    columns, each a single piece of stone, made
modester by white-wash. This would be a fit haven for
waifs, children, animals, prisoners,
    and presidents who have repaid
sin-driven

senators by not thinking about them. There
    are a school-house, a post-office in a

store, fish-houses, hen-houses, a three-masted schooner on
the stocks. The hero, the student,
    the steeple-jack, each in his way,
is at home.

It could not be dangerous to be living
    in a town like this, of simple people,
who have a steeple-jack placing danger signs by the church
while he is gilding the solid-
    pointed star, which on a steeple
stands for hope.

The Student

"In America everybody must have a degree," the French man
says, "but the French do not think that all can have it; they don't
    say everyone must go to college." We
    may feel as he says we do; five kinds of superiority

might be unattainable by all, but one degree is not too much.
In each school there is a pair of fruit-trees like that twin tree
    in every other school: tree-of-knowledge—
    tree-of-life—each with a label like that of the other college:

lux, or *lux et veritas, Christo et ecclesiae, sapiet
felici*, and if science confers immortality,
    these apple-trees should be for everyone.
    Oriental arbor vitae we say lightly. Yet you pardon

it as when one thinking of the navy does not know not to infer
dishonorable discharge from a D. D. It is a
    thoughtful pupil has two thoughts for the word
    valet; or for bachelor, child, damsel; though no one having heard

them used as terms of chivalry would make the medieval use of
them. Secluded from domestic strife, Jack Bookworm led a
    college life says Goldsmith. He might not say
    it of the student who shows interest in the stranger's resumé

by asking "when will your experiment be finished, Doctor Einstein?"
and is pleased when Doctor Einstein smiles and says politely
    "science is never finished." But we're not
    hypocrites, we're rustics. The football huddle in the vacant lot

is impersonating calculus and physics and military
books; and is gathering the data for genetics. If
   scholarship would profit by it, sixteen-
    foot men should be grown; it's for the football men to say.
             We must lean

on their experience. There is vitality in the world of sport.
If it is not the tree of knowledge, it's the tree of life.
   When Audubon adopted us he taught
    us how to dance. It was the great crab-flounder of Montana caught

and changed from that which creeps to that which is angelic.
             He taught us how
to turn as the airport wind-sock turns without an error;
   like Alligator, Downpour, Dynamite,
    and Wotan, gliding round the course in a fast neat school,
             with the white

of the eye showing; or as sea-lions keep going round and round the
pool. But there is more to learn—the difference between cow
   and zebu; lion, tiger; barred and brown
    owls; horned owls have one ear that opens up and one that opens
             down.

The golden eagle is the one with feathered legs. The penguin wing is
ancient, not degenerate. Swordfish are different from
   gars, if one may speak of gars when the big
    gamehunters are using the fastidious singular—say pig,

and that they have seen camelsparrow, tigerhorse, rat, mouse,
             butterfly,
snake, elephant, fruit-bat, et cet'ra. No fact of science—
   theology or biology—might
    not as well be known; one does not care to hold opinions that
             fright

could dislocate. Education augments our natural forces and
prompts us to extend the machinery of advantage
   to those who are without it. One fitted
    to be a scholar must have the heroic mind, Emerson said.

The student concentrates and does not like to fight;
          "gives his opinion
firmly and rests on it"—in the manner of the poet;

is reclusive, and reserved; and has such
ways, not because he has no feeling but because he has so much.

Boasting provokes jibes, and in this country we've no cause to boast;
       we are
as a nation perhaps, undergraduates not students.
    But anyone who studies will advance.
    Are we to grow up or not? They are not all college boys in France.

The Hero

Where there is personal liking we go.
    Where the ground is sour; where there are
    weeds of beanstalk height,
    snakes' hypodermic teeth, or
    the wind brings the "scarebabe voice"
    from the neglected yew set with
    the semi-precious cat's eyes of the owl—
awake, asleep, "raised ears extended to fine points," and so
on—love won't grow.

We do not like some things and the hero
    doesn't; deviating head-stones
    and uncertainty;
    going where one does not wish
    to go; suffering and not
    saying so; standing and listening where something
    is hiding. The hero shrinks
as what it is flies out on muffled wings, with twin yellow
eyes—to and fro—

with quavering water-whistle note, low,
    high, in basso-falsetto chirps
    until the skin creeps.
    Jacob when a-dying, asked
    Joseph: Who are these? and blessed
    both sons, the younger most, vexing Joseph. And
    Joseph was vexing to some.
Cincinnatus was; Regulus; and some of our fellow
men have been, though

devout, like Pilgrim having to go slow
    to find his roll; tired but hopeful—

hope not being hope
until all ground for hope has
vanished; and lenient, looking
upon a fellow creature's error with the
feelings of a mother—a
woman or a cat. The decorous frock-coated Negro
by the grotto

answers the fearless sightseeing hobo
    who asks the man she's with, what's this,
    what's that, where's Martha
    buried, "Gen-ral Washington
    there; his lady, here"; speaking
    as if in a play—not seeing her; with a
    sense of human dignity
and reverence for mystery, standing like the shadow
of the willow.

Moses would not be grandson to Pharaoh.
    It is not what I eat that is
    my natural meat,
    the hero says. He's not out
    seeing a sight but the rock
    crystal thing to see—the startling El Greco
    brimming with inner light—that
covets nothing that it has let go. This then you may know
as the hero.

No Swan So Fine

"No water so still as the
   dead fountains of Versailles." No swan,
with swart blind look askance
and gondoliering legs, so fine
   as the chintz china one with fawn-
brown eyes and toothed gold
collar on to show whose bird it was.

Lodged in the Louis Fifteenth
   candelabrum-tree of cockscomb-
tinted buttons, dahlias,
sea-urchins, and everlastings,
   it perches on the branching foam
of polished sculptured
flowers—at ease and tall. The king is dead.

The Jerboa

Too Much

A Roman hired an
artist, a freedman,
   to make a cone—pine-cone
   or fir-cone—with holes for a fountain. Placed on
      the Prison of St. Angelo, this cone
      of the Pompeys which is known

now as the Popes', passed
for art. A huge cast
   bronze, dwarfing the peacock
   statue in the garden of the Vatican,
      it looks like a work of art made to give
      to a Pompey, or native

of Thebes. Others could
build, and understood
   making colossi and
   how to use slaves, and kept crocodiles and put
      baboons on the necks of giraffes to pick
      fruit, and used serpent magic.

They had their men tie
hippopotami
   and bring out dapple dog-
   cats to course antelopes, dikdik, and ibex;
      or used small eagles. They looked on as theirs,
      impalas and onagers,

the wild ostrich herd
with hard feet and bird
   necks rearing back in the
   dust like a serpent preparing to strike, cranes,
      storks, anoas, mongooses, and Nile geese.
      And there were gardens for these—

combining planes, dates,
limes, and pomegranates,
   in avenues—with square
   pools of pink flowers, tame fish, and small frogs. Besides

yarns dyed with indigo, and red cotton,
they had a flax which they spun

into fine linen
cordage for yachtsmen.
   These people liked small things;
   they gave to boys little paired playthings such as
      nests of eggs, ichneumon and snake, paddle
      and raft, badger and camel;

and made toys for them-
selves: the royal totem;
   and toilet-boxes marked
   with the contents. Lords and ladies put goose-grease
      paint in round bone boxes with pivoting
      lid incised with the duck-wing

or reverted duck-
head; kept in a buck
   or rhinoceros horn,
   the ground horn; and locust oil in stone locusts.
      It was a picture with a fine distance;
      of drought, and of assistance

in time, from the Nile
rising slowly, while
   the pig-tailed monkey on
   slab-hands, with arched-up slack-slung gait, and the brown
      dandy, looked at the jasmine two-leafed twig
      and bud, cactus-pads, and fig.

Dwarfs here and there, lent
to an evident
   poetry of frog grays,
   duck-egg greens, and egg-plant blues, a fantasy
      and a verisimilitude that were
      right to those with, everywhere,

power over the poor.
The bees' food is your
   food. Those who tended flower-
   beds and stables were like the king's cane in the
      form of a hand, or the folding bedroom
      made for his mother of whom

he was fond. Princes
clad in queens' dresses
    calla or petunia
    white that trembled at the edge, and queens in a
        king's underskirt of fine-twilled thread like silk-
        worm gut, as bee-man and milk-

maid, kept divine cows
and bees; limestone brows,
    and gold-foil wings. They made
    basalt serpents and portraits of beetles; the
        king gave his name to them and he was named
        for them. He feared snakes and tamed

Pharaoh's rat, the rust-
backed mongoose. No bust
    of it was made, but there
    was pleasure for the rat. Its restlessness was
        its excellence; it was praised for its wit;
        and the jerboa, like it,

a small desert rat,
and not famous, that
    lives without water, has
    happiness. Abroad seeking food, or at home
        in its burrow, the Sahara field-mouse
        has a shining silver house

of sand. O rest and
joy, the boundless sand,
    the stupendous sand-spout,
    no water, no palm-trees, no ivory bed,
        tiny cactus; but one would not be he
        who has nothing but plenty.

Abundance

Africanus meant
the conqueror sent
    from Rome. It should mean the
    untouched: the sand-brown jumping-rat—free-born; and
        the blacks, that choice race with an elegance
        ignored by one's ignorance.

Part terrestrial,
and part celestial,
   Jacob saw, cudgel staff
   in claw-hand—steps of air and air angels; his
      friends were the stones. The translucent mistake
      of the desert, does not make

hardship for one who
can rest and then do
   the opposite—launching
   as if on wings, from its match-thin hind legs, in
      daytime or at night; that departs with great
      speed, followed by, as a weight,

a double length, thin
tail furred like the skin;
   that curls round it when it
   sleeps "round"—the nose nested in fur, a hind leg
      at each side of the head—or lies lengthwise,
      in view, when the body lies

flat. Seen by daylight,
the body is white
   in front; and on the back,
   buffy-brown like the breast of the fawn-breasted
      bower-bird. It hops like the fawn-breast, but has
      chipmunk contours—perceived as

it turns its bird head—
the nap directed
   neatly back and blending
   with the ear which reiterates the slimness
      of the body. The fine hairs on the tail,
      repeating the other pale

markings, lengthen till
at the tip they fill
   out in a tuft—black and
   white; strange detail of the simplified creature,
      fish-shaped and silvered to steel by the force
      of the large desert moon. Course

the jerboa, or
plunder its food store,
  and you will be cursed. It
  honors the sand by assuming its color;
    closed upper paws seeming one with the fur
    in its flight from a danger.

By fifths and sevenths,
in leaps of two lengths,
  like the uneven notes
  of the Bedouin flute, it stops its gleaning
    on little wheel casters, and makes fern-seed
    foot-prints with kangaroo speed.

Its leaps should be set
to the flageolet;
  pillar body erect
  on a three-cornered smooth-working Chippendale
    claw—propped on hind legs, and tail as third toe,
    between leaps to its burrow.

Camellia Sabina

and the Bordeaux plum
from Marmande (France in parentheses) with
A. G. on the base of the jar—Alexis Godillot—
unevenly blown beside a bubble that
is green when held up to the light; they
are a fine duet; the screw-top for this graft-grown
    briar-black bloom on black-thorn pigeon's-blood
    is, like Certosa, sealed with foil. Appropriate custom.

And they keep under
glass also, camellias catalogued by
lines across the leaf. The French are a cruel race—willing
to squeeze the diner's cucumber or broil a
meal on vine-shoots. Gloria mundi
with a leaf two inches, nine lines broad, they have; and
    the smaller, Camellia Sabina
    with amanita-white petals; there are several of her

    pale pinwheels, and pale
    stripe that looks as if on a mushroom the
    sliver from a beet-root carved into a rose were laid. "Dry
    the windows with a cloth fastened to a staff.
    In the camellia-house there must be
    no smoke from the stove, nor dew on the windows, lest
        the plants ail," the amateur is told;
        "mistakes are irreparable and nothing will avail."

The scentless nosegay
is thus formed in the midst of the bouquet
from bottles casks and corks for: sixty-four million red wines
and twenty million white, which Bordeaux merchants
and lawyers "have spent a great deal of
trouble" to select, from what was and what was not
    Bordeaux. A food-grape, however—"born
    of nature and of art"—is true ground for the grape-holiday.

    The food of a wild
    mouse in some countries is wild parsnip- or sunflower- or
    morning-glory-seed, with an occasional
    grape. Underneath the vines of the Bolzano

grape of Italy, the Prince of Tails
might stroll. Does yonder mouse with a grape in its hand
  and its child in its mouth, not portray
  the Spanish fleece suspended by the neck? In that well-piled

  larder above your
head, the picture of what you will eat is
looked at from the end of the avenue. The wire cage is
locked, but by bending down and studying the
roof, it is possible to see the
pantomime of Persian thought: the gilded, too tight,
  undemure coat of gems unruined
  by the rain—each small pebble of jade that refused to mature,

    plucked delicately
  off. Off jewelry not meant to keep Tom
  Thumb, the cavalry cadet, on his Italian upland
  meadow-mouse, from looking at the grapes beneath
  the interrupted light from them, and
  dashing round the *concours hippique* of the tent, in
    a flurry of eels, scallops, serpents,
    and other shadows from the blue of the green canopy.

  The wine-cellar? No.
It accomplishes nothing and makes the
soul heavy. The gleaning is more than the vintage, though the
history *de la vigne et du vin* place a
mirabelle in the *bibliothèque*
unique depuis seventeen-ninety-seven. (Close
  the window, says the Abbé Berlèse,
  for Sabina born under glass.) O generous Bolzano!

The Plumet Basilisk

In Costa Rica

In blazing driftwood
    the green keeps showing at the same place;
as, intermittently, the fire-opal shows blue and green.
    In Costa Rica the true Chinese lizard face
is found, of the amphibious falling dragon, the living firework.

He leaps and meets his
    likeness in the stream and, king with king,
helped by his three-part plume along the back, runs on two legs,
    tail dragging; faints upon the air; then with a spring
dives to the stream-bed, hiding as the chieftain with gold body hid in

Guatavita Lake.
    He runs, he flies, he swims, to get to
his basilica—"the ruler of Rivers, Lakes, and Seas,
    invisible or visible," with clouds to do
as bid—and can be "long or short, and also coarse or fine at
                    pleasure." With a

modest quiver, he
    ascends the bank on clinging tree-frog
hands, and waits; the water draining, forms a lizard there, from
    skin now looking a little newer than the log
it rested on & the thick mass of verdure all about. This is the

feather basilisk
    of travelers' tales, of which a pair stood
bodyguard beside Confucius' crib: aquatic flying
    lizard-fairy detested by such dragonhood
as Michael fought. One has seen animals like his, though smaller,
                    collide

and fight, brother matched
    with brother, as if immune to pain;
push, struggle and breathe hard; swell out and muster strength,
                    withdraw,
    advance; and swerving, almost fall—hoping to gain
the mortal hold and that some fang should pierce the marrow.
            But when plumet

territories touch,
   the masters of them are dramatic
without shedding blood, exerting charm as Chinese dragon-
   whiskers in a crystal handle charm; or as thick-
flowering orchids gather dragons, in the east, by forming clouds
               for them.

The Malay Dragon

We have ours; and they
   have theirs. Ours has a skin feather crest;
theirs has wings out from the waist which is snuff-brown or sallow.
   Ours falls from trees on water; theirs is the smallest
dragon that knows how to dive head-first from a tree-top to
               something dry.

Floating on spread ribs,
   the boat-like body settles on the
clamshell-tinted spray sprung from the nutmeg-tree—minute legs
   trailing half akimbo—the true divinity
of Malay. Among unfragrant orchids, on the unnutritious nut

tree, *myristica*
   fragrans, the harmless god spreads ribs that
do not raise a hood. This is the serpent-dove peculiar
   to the East; that lives as the butterfly or bat
can, in a brood, conferring wings on what it grasps, as the
               air-plant does.

The Tuatera

Elsewhere, sea lizards—
   congregated so there is not room
to step, with tails laid criss-cross, alligator-style, among
   birds toddling in and out—are innocent of whom
they neighbor. Bird-reptile social life is pleasing. The tuatera

will tolerate a
   petrel in its den, and lays ten eggs
or nine—the number laid by dragons since "a true dragon
   has nine sons." The frilled lizard, the kind with no legs,

and the three-horned chameleon, are non-serious ones that take to
            flight

if you do not. In
    Copenhagen the principal door
of the bourse is roofed by two pairs of dragons standing on
    their heads—twirled by the architect—so that the four
green tails conspiring upright, symbolize four-fold security. Now,

In Costa Rica

where sapotans drop
    their nuts out on the stream, there is, as
I have said, one of the quickest lizards in the world—the
    basilisk—that feeds on leaves and berries and has
shade from palm-vines, ferns, and peperomias; or lies basking on a

horizontal branch
    from which sour-grass and orchids sprout. If
best, he lets go, smites the water, and runs on it—a thing
    difficult for fingered feet. But when captured—stiff
and somewhat heavy, like fresh putty on the hand—he is no longer

the slight lizard that
    can stand in a receding flattened
S—small, long and vertically serpentine or, sagging,
    span the bushes in a fox's bridge. Vines suspend
the weight of something's shadow fixed on silk. By the Chinese
                brush, eight green

bands are painted on
    the tail—as piano keys are barred
by five black stripes across the white. This octave of faulty
    decorum hides the extraordinary lizard
till night-fall, which is for man the basilisk whose look will kill; but is

for lizards men can
    kill, the welcome dark—with the galloped
ground-bass of the military drum, the squeak of bag-pipes
    and of bats. Hollow whistled monkey-notes disrupt
the castanets. Taps from the back of the bow sound odd on last year's
                gourd,

or when they touch the
   kettledrums—at which, for there's no light,
a scared frog screaming like a bird, leaps out from weeds in which
   it could have hid, with curves of the meteorite,
the curve of whose diving no diver refutes. Upon spider-hands, with

            wide water-bug strokes,
         in jerks which express
         a regal and excellent awkwardness,

            the plumet portrays
         mythology's wish
         to be interchangeably man and fish—

         traveling rapidly upward, as
         spider-clawed fingers can twang the
         bass strings of the harp, and with steps
         as articulate, make their way
         back to retirement on strings that
         vibrate till the claws are spread flat.

            Among tightened wires,
         minute noises swell
         and change as in the woods' acoustic shell

            they will, with trees as
         avenues of steel
         to veil invisibleness ears must feel—

         black opal emerald opal
         emerald—the prompt-delayed loud-
         low chromatic listened-for down-
         scale which Swinburne called in prose, the
         noiseless music that hangs about
         the serpent when it stirs or springs.

No anonymous
   nightingale sings in a swamp, fed on
sound from porcupine-quilled palm-trees blurring at the edge, that
   rattle like the rain. This is our Tower-of-London
jewel that the Spaniards failed to see, among the feather capes and
            hawk's-

head moths and black-chinned
   humming-birds; the innocent, rare, gold-
defending dragon that as you look begins to be a
   nervous naked sword on little feet, with three-fold
separate flame above the hilt, inhabiting fringe equidistant

from itself, of white
   fire eating into air. Thus nested
in the phosphorescent alligator that copies each
   digression of the shape, he pants and settles—head
up and eyes black as the molested bird's, with look of whetted
                     fierceness,

in what is merely
   breathing and recoiling from the hand.
Thinking himself hid among the yet unfound jade axeheads,
   silver jaguars and bats, and amethysts and
polished iron, gold in a ten-ton chain, and pearls the size of
                     pigeon-eggs,

he is alive there
   in his basilisk cocoon beneath
the one of living green; his quicksilver ferocity
   quenched in the rustle of his fall into the sheath
which is the shattering sudden splash that marks his temporary loss.

The Frigate Pelican

Rapidly cruising or lying on the air there is a bird
   that realizes Rasselas's friend's project
   of wings uniting levity with strength. This
      hell-diver, frigate-bird, hurricane-
bird; unless swift is the proper word
   for him, the storm omen when
he flies close to the waves, should be seen
      fishing, although oftener
      he appears to prefer

to take, on the wing, from industrious cruder-winged species
   the fish they have caught, and is seldom successless.
   A marvel of grace, no matter how fast his
      victim may fly or how often may
turn, the dishonest pelican's ease
   in pursuit, bears him away
with the fish that the badgered bird drops.
      A kind of superlative
      swallow, that likes to live

on food caught while flying, he is not a pelican. The toe
   with slight web, air-boned body, and very long wings
   with the spread of a swan's—duplicating a
      bow-string as he floats overhead—feel
the changing V-shaped scissor swallow-
   tail direct the rigid keel.
And steering beak to windward always,
      the fleetest foremost fairy
      among birds, outflies the

aeroplane which cannot flap its wings nor alter any quill-
   tip. For him, the feeling in a hand, in fins, is
   in his unbent downbent crafty oar. With him
      other pelicans aimlessly soar
as he does; separating, until
   not flapping they rise once more,
closing in without looking and move
      outward again to the top
      of the circle and stop

and blow back, allowing the wind to reverse their direction.
   This is not the stalwart swan that can ferry the
   woodcutter's two children home; no. Make hay; keep
      the shop; I have one sheep; were a less
limber animal's mottoes. This one
      finds sticks for the swan's-down dress
   of his child to rest upon and would
      not know Gretel from Hänsel.
      As impassioned Handel—

meant for a lawyer and a masculine German domestic
   career—clandestinely studied the harpsichord
   and never was known to have fallen in love,
      the unconfiding frigate-bird hides
in the height and in the majestic
      display of his art. He glides
   a hundred feet or quivers about
      as charred paper behaves—full
      of feints; and an eagle

of vigilance, earns the term aquiline; keeping at a height
   so great the feathers look black and the beak does not
   show. It is not retreat but exclusion from
      which he looks down and observes what went
secretly, as it thought, out of sight
      among dense jungle plants. Sent
   ahead of the rest, there goes the true
      knight in his jointed coat that
      covers all but his bat

ears; a-trot, with stiff pig gait—our tame armadillo, loosed by
   his master and as pleased as a dog. Beside the
   spattered blood—that orchid which the native fears—
      the fer-de-lance lies sleeping; centaur-
like, this harmful couple's amity
      is apropos. A jaguar
   and crocodile are fighting. Sharp-shinned
      hawks and peacock-freckled small
      cats, like the literal

merry-go-round, come wandering within the circular view
   of the high bird for whom from the air they are ants
   keeping house all their lives in the crack of a

crag with no view from the top. And here,
unlikely animals learning to
    dance, crouch on two steeds that rear
    behind a leopard with a frantic
        face, tamed by an Artemis
        who wears a dress like his,

and hampering haymaker's hat. *Festina lente.* Be gay
    civilly. How so? "If I do well I am blessed
    whether any bless me or not, and if I do
    ill I am cursed." We watch the moon rise
on the Susquehanna. In his way
        this most romantic bird, flies
    to a more mundane place, the mangrove
        swamp, to sleep. He wastes the moon.
        But he, and others, soon

rise from the bough, and though flying are able to foil the tired
    moment of danger, that lays on heart and lungs the
    weight of the python that crushes to powder.
        The tune's illiterate footsteps fail;
the steam hacks are not to be admired.
        These, unturbulent, avail
    themselves of turbulence to fly—pleased
        with the faint wind's varyings,
        on which to spread fixed wings.

The reticent lugubrious ragged immense minuet
    descending to leeward, ascending to windward
    again without flapping, in what seems to be
    a way of resting, are now nearer,
but as seemingly bodiless yet
        as they were. Theirs are somber
    quills for so wide and lightboned a bird
        as the frigate pelican
        of the Caribbean.

The Buffalo

Black in blazonry means
prudence; and niger, unpropitious. Might
hematite-
black incurved compact horns on a bison
have significance? The
soot brown tail-tuft on
a kind of lion-

tail; what would that express?
And John Steuart Curry's Ajax pulling
grass—no ring
in his nose—two birds standing on his back?
though prints like this cannot
show if they were black
birds, nor the color

of the back. The modern
ox does not look like the Augsburg ox's
portrait. Yes,
the great extinct wild Aurochs was a beast
to paint, with stripe and six-
foot horn-spread—decreased
to Siamese-cat-

Brown Swiss size, or zebu
shape with white plush dewlap and warm-blooded
hump; to red-
skinned Hereford or to piebald Holstein. Yet
some would say the sparse-haired
buffalo has met
human notions best—

unlike the elephant,
both jewel and jeweler in the hairs
that he wears—
no white-nosed Vermont ox yoked with its twin
to haul the maple sap,
up to their knees in
snow; no freakishly

Over-Drove Ox drawn by
Rowlandson, but the Indian buffalo,
albino-
    footed, standing in the mud-lake, with a
    day's work to do. No white
    Christian heathen, way-
        laid by the Buddha,

    serves him so well as the
buffalo—as mettlesome as if check-
reined—free neck
    stretching out, and snake-tail in a half twist
    on the flank; nor will so
    cheerfully assist
        the Sage sitting with

    feet at the same side, to
dismount at the shrine; nor are there any
ivory
    tusks like those two horns which when a tiger
    coughs, are lowered fiercely
    and convert the fur
        to harmless rubbish.

    The Indian buffalo,
led by bare-leggèd herd-boys to a hay
hut where they
    stable it, need not fear comparison
    with bison, with the twins,
    nor with anyone
        of ox ancestry.

Nine Nectarines and Other Porcelain

Arranged by two's as peaches are,
at intervals that all may live—
    eight and a single one, on twigs that
    grew the year before—they look like
a derivative;
    although not uncommonly
    the opposite is seen—
nine peaches on a nectarine.
        Fuzzless through slender crescent leaves
            of green or blue—or both,
            in the Chinese style—the four

    pairs' half-moon leaf-mosaic turns
out to the sun the sprinkled blush
    of puce-American-Beauty pink
    applied to beeswax gray by the
unenquiring brush
    of mercantile bookbinding.
Like the peach *Yu*, the red-
cheeked peach which cannot aid the dead,
        but eaten in time prevents death,
            the Italian peach-
            nut, Persian plum, Ispahan

    secluded wall-grown nectarine,
as wild spontaneous fruit was
    found in China first. But was it wild?
    Prudent de Candolle would not say.
We cannot find flaws
    in this emblematic group
    of nine, with leaf window
unquilted by curculio—
        which someone once depicted on
            this much-mended plate; or
            in the also accurate

    unantlered moose, or Iceland horse,
or ass, asleep against the old
    thick, low-leaning nectarine that is the
    color of the shrub-tree's brownish

flower. From manifold
   small boughs, productive as the
magic willow that grew
above the mother's grave and threw
   on Cinderella what she wished,
      a bat is winging. It
      is a moonlight scene, bringing

   the animal so near, its eyes
are separate from the face—mere
   delicately drawn gray discs, out from
   itself in space. Imperial
happiness lives here
   on the peaches of long life
that make it permanent.
A fungus could have meant
   long life; a crane, a stork, a dove.
      China, with flowers and birds
      and half-beasts, became the land

   of the best china-making first.
Hunts and domestic scenes occur
   in France on dinner-plates, signed on the
   back with a two-finned fish; England
has an officer
   in jack-boots seated in a
bosquet, the cow, the flock
of sheep, the pheasant, the peacock
   sweeping near with lifted claw; the
      skilled peonian rose
      and the rosebud that began

   with William Billingsley (once poor,
like a monkey on a dolphin, tossed
   by Ocean, mighty monster) until
   Josiah Spode adopted him.
Yet with the gold-glossed
   serpent handles, are there green
cocks with "brown beaks and cheeks
and dark blue combs" and mammal freaks
   that, like the Chinese Certainties
      and sets of Precious Things,
      dare to be conspicuous?

Theirs is a race that "understands
the spirit of the wilderness"
    and the nectarine-loving kylin
    of pony appearance—the long-
tailed or the tailless
    small cinnamon-brown common
camel-haired unicorn
with antelope feet and no horn,
    here enamelled on porcelain.
        It was a Chinese who
        imagined this masterpiece.

Pigeons

Older than the ancient Greeks, than
  Solomon, the pigeon family is a
  ramifying one, a
  banyan of banyans; to begin
with, bluish slate,
    but with ability. Modesty cannot dull
    the lustre of the pigeon
    swift and sure, coming quickest and
straightest just after a storm. The great
    lame war hero Cher Ami, the
    Lost Battalion's gallant bird; and
    Mocker with one eye
      destroyed, delivering his dispatch
    to his superiors; and Sergeant Dunn,
    civilian pigeon who flew eight
    hundred sixty-eight miles
    in four days and six hours;
      and destined to hatch
    in France, Spike, veteran of
    the division in which Mocker
      served—exceptional messenger.
    "Rarely was confidence misplaced" a newspaper
    says. Dastardly comment
      inexactly phrased, as used of Her-
    mes, Ariel, or Leander—
    pigeons of the past. Neither was confidence
    misplaced in the Javan-
    Sumatran birds the Dutch had had
brought from Baghdad.
    Mysterious animal with a magnetic
    feel by which he traces back-
    ward his transportation outward,
even in a fog at sea, though glad
    to be tossed near enough the loft
    or coop to get back the same day.
    "Home on time without
      his message." What matter since he has
    got back. Migrating always in the same
    direction, bringing all letters

to the same address, see-
ing better homes than his,
   he is not Theudas
boasting himself to be some-
body, this anonymous post-
     man who, as soon as he could fly,
was carrying valentines and messages of
state; or soberer news—
     "So please write me and believe that I
am yours very truly"; fine words
those. An instrument not just an instinctive
individual, this
dove, that lifts his right foot over
the alighting-
   board to rejoin his ungainly pin-clad dark-skinned
brood as domestic turtle-
doves might; two. Invariably
two. The turtle, a not exciting
   bird—in Britain shy, detected
by its constantly heard coo, with-
out a song but not
     without a voice—does well to stay far
out of sight; but the Pelew pigeon with
black head, metallic wasp-lustred
grass-green breast and purple
legs and feet, need not; nor
    need the Nicobar,
novel, narrow-feathered dove.
And one should see the Papuan
    fancrests with six-sided scale which
coats the foot; "not much is known about these splendid
birds" hid in unimag-
     inably weak lead-colored ostrich-
plumes a third of an inch long, and
needle-fine cat-whisker-fibered battleship-
gray lace. The Samoan
tooth-billed pigeon fortunately
survives also—
   saved from destruction by no longer feeding on
the ground, a bird with short legs
and heavy bill, remarkable
because related to the dodo.

Didus ineptus; man's remorse
enshrines it now, abundant still
in sixteen-one. "A
   little bigger than our swans, these birds
want wings and lay but one egg" the traveler
said—"defenceless unsuspicious
things, with a cry like the
cry of a Gosling." *Il*
   dóudo (the words
mean simple one)—extinct as
the Solitaires which having "raised
   their young one do not disunite."
A new pigeon cannot compensate, but we have
it. With neat-cered eye, long
   face, trim form and posture, this delight-
ful bird outdoes the dashingly
black and white Dalmatian dog and map-freckled
pony that Indians dress
with feathers seriatim down
the mane and tail;—
   a slender Cinderella deliberately
pied, so she on each side is
   the same, an all-feather piebald,
cuckoo-marked on a titanic scale
   taking perhaps sixteen birds to
show the whole design, as in chess
played with men and hors-
      es. Yes, the thus medievally
two-colored sea-pie-patterned semi-swan-
necked magpie-pigeon, gamecock-legged
with long-clawed toes, and all
extremes—head neck back tail
   and feet—coal black, the
rest snow white, has a surpris-
ing modernness and fanciness
      and stateliness and. . . . Yes indeed;
developed by and humbly dedicated to
the Gentlemen of the
   Feather Club, this is a dainty breed.

See in the Midst of Fair Leaves

and much fruit, the swan—
    one line of the mathematician's
sign greater-than, drawn
    to an apex where the lake is
met by the weight on it; or an angel
standing in the sun, how well
    armed, how manly;

and promenading
    in sloughs of despond, a monster—
man when human nothing
    more, grown to immaturity,
punishing debtors, seeking his due—as
an arrow turned inward has
    no chance of peace.

Walking-Sticks and Paperweights and Watermarks

Walking among scepter-headed
weeds and daisies swayed by wind, they said,
  "Don't scatter your
stick, on account of the souls." Led
from sun-spotted
    paths, we went "where leafy trees meet
    overhead and noise of traffic is unknown"—
the mind exhilarated
      by life all round, so stirringly

alive. The root-handled cudgel
with the bark left on, the woodbine smell-
  ing of the rain,
the very stones, have life. Little
scars on church-bell
    tongues put there by the Devil's claws—
    authentic phantoms, ghosts, and witches, transformed
into an invisible
      fabric of inconsistency

motheaten by self-subtractives—
now as outright murderers and thieves,
  thrive openly.
An epigraph before it leaves
the wax, receives
    to give, and giving must itself
    receive, "difficulty is ordained to check
poltroons," and courage achieves
      despaired of ends. Oppositely

jointed against indecision,
the three legs of the triskelion
  meeting in the
middle between triangles, run
in unison
    without assistance. Yet, trudging
    on two legs that move contradictorily,
irked by ghosts and witches, one
      does not fear to ask for beauty

that is power devoid of fear.
A bold outspoken gentleman, cheer-
    ful, plodding, to-
the-point, used to the atmosphere
of work—who here
    appropriate to the thought of
    permanence, says, "this is my taste, it might not
be another man's"—makes clear
        that stark sincere unflattery,

sine cera, is both farthest
from self-defensiveness and nearest;
    as when a seal
without haste, slowly is impressed
and forms a nest
    on which the raised device reversed,
    shows round. It must have been an able workman,
studious and self-possessed,
        a liker of solidity,

who gave a greenish Waterford
glass fool's cap with summit curled down toward
    itself as the
glass grew, the look of tempered sword-
steel, and three-ore-d
    fishscale-burnished antimony-
    tin-and-lead's smoky water-drop type-metal
smoothness emery-armored
        against rust. Its subdued glossy

splendor leaps out at the eye as
form dramatizes thought, in the glass
    witchball and air-
twist cane. This paperweight, in mass
a stone, surpass-
    ing it in tint, enlarges the
    fine chain-lines in the waterleaf weighted by
its hardened raindrop surface.
        The paper-mould's similarly

once unsolid waspnest-blue, snow-
white, or seashell-gray rags, seen through, show
    sheepcotes, turkey-

mills, acorns, and anvils. "Stones grow,"
then stop, and so
    do gardens. "Plants grow and live; men
    grow and live and think." *Utilizey la poste
aerienne*, trade will follow
        the telephone. The post's jerky

cancellings ink the stamp, relet-
tering stiltedly, as a puppet-
    acrobat walks
about with high steps on his net,
an alphabet
    of words and animals where the
    wire-embedded watermark's more integral
expressiveness had first set
        its alabaster effigy.

In bark silverer than the swan,
esparto grass, or so-called Titan
    parchment tougher
than Hercules' lion-skin—Span-
ish, Umbrian,
    eastern, open, and jeweled crowns,
    corroborate the dolphin, crane, and ox; sealed
with wax by a pelican
        studying affectionately

a nest's three-in-one cartwheel tri-
legged face. "For those we love, live and die"
    the motto says.
And we do. Part pelican, I,
doubting the high-
    way's wide giant trivia where
    three roads meet in artificial openness,
am obliged to justify
        outspoken cordiality.

Firm-feathered juniper springing
from difficult ground, the sky trembling
    with power, the rain
falling upon the bird singing,
modest printing,
    on honest paper properly

trimmed, are gifts addressed to memory, and a
gift is permanent, shining
    like the juniper's trinity

of spines. An unburdensomely
worthy officer of charity,
    the evergreen
with awlshaped leaves in whorls of three—
successively
    firm. "On the first day of Christmas
    my true love he sent unto me, part of a
bough of a juniper-tree,"
    javelin-ed consecutively.

THE PANGOLIN AND OTHER VERSE
(1936)

The Old Dominion

Virginia Britannia

Pale sand edges England's old
dominion. The air is soft, warm, hot,
    above the cedar-dotted emerald shore
known to the redbird,
        the redcoated musketeer,
        the trumpet-flower, the cavalier,
the parson, and the
        wild parishioner. A deer-
    track in a church-floor
brick and Sir George Yeardley's
coffin-tacks and tomb remain.
The now tremendous vine-en-
compassed hackberry
        starred with the ivy-flower,
        shades the church tower.
And "a great sinner lyeth here" under
    the sycamore.

A fritillary zigzags
toward the seemly resting-place of this
    unusual man and pleasing sinner who
"waits for a joyful
        resurrection." We-re-wo-
    comoco's fur crown could be no
odder than we were
        with ostrich, Latin motto,
        and small gold horse-shoe,
as arms for an able
sting-ray-hampered pioneer,
painted as a Turk it seems,
the incessantly
        exciting Captain Smith
        who patient with
his inferiors, was a pugnacious
    equal; and to

Powhatan obliged, but not
a flatterer. Rare Indian, crowned by

Christopher Newport! The Old Dominion has
all-green grass-hoppers
   in all-green, box-sculptured grounds;
   an almost English green surrounds
them. Care has formed a-
     mong unEnglish insect sounds,
   the white wall-rose. As
thick as Daniel Boone's grape-
vine, the stem has wide-spaced great
blunt alternating ostrich-
skin warts that were thorns.
     Care has formed walls of yew
     since Indians knew
the Fort Old Field and narrow neck of land
   that Jamestown was.

Observe the terse Virginian,
the mettlesome gray one that drives the
   owl from tree to tree and imitates the call
of whippoorwill or
     lark or katydid—the lead-
     gray lead-legged mocking-bird with head
held half away, and
     meditative eye as dead
   as sculptured marble
eye, alighting noiseless,
muses in the semi-sun,
standing on tall thin legs as
if he did not see,
     conspicuous, alone,
     on the round stone-
topped table with lead cupids grouped to form
   the pedestal.

Narrow herring-bonelaid bricks,
a dusty pink beside the dwarf box-
   bordered pansies, share the ivy-arbor shade
with cemetery
     lace settees, one at each side,
     and with the bird: box-bordered tide-
water gigantic
     jet black pansies (splendor; pride;)

not for a decade
dressed, but for a day, in
overpowering velvet; and
gray blue-Andalusian
cock-feather pale ones
          ink-lined on the edge, fur-
          eyed, with ochre
on the cheek. The slowmoving glossy, tall
   quick cavalcade

of buckeye-brown surprising
jumpers, the contrasting work-mule and
   show-mule & witch-cross door & "strong sweet prison"
are part of what
          has come about, in the Black
          idiom, from advancing back-
ward in a circle;
          from taking The Potomac
          cowbirdlike; and on
The Chickahominy
establishing the Negro, opportunely brought, to strength-
en protest against
          tyranny. Rare unscent-
          ed, provident-
ly hot, too sweet, inconsistent flowerbed!
   Old Dominion

earth makes sunflower-heads grow large;
hibiscus and so-called mimosa
   close at night; the scarlet peculiarly-quilled
pomegranate-petals,
          the African violet,
          and camellia, perfumeless. Yet
house-high glistening green
          magnolia-trees with velvet-
          textured flower, are filled
with anaesthetic scent
enough to make one die; as
the gardenia is, though its
two-toned green-furled buds
          and dark leaf-vein on green-
          er leaf when seen

against the light attract no pigmy bees
    such as the frilled

silk substanceless faint flower of
the crape-myrtle does. Odd Pamunkey
    princess, birdclaw-earringed; with a pet raccoon
from The Mattapo-
        ni (what a bear!) Feminine
        odd Indian young lady! Odd thin-
gauze-and-taffeta-
        dressed English one! Terrapin
    meat and crested spoon
feed the mistress of French
plum-and-turquoise-piped chaise-longue;
of brass-knobbed slat front-door and
everywhere open
        shaded house on Indian-
        named Virginian
streams, in counties named for English lords. The
    rattlesnake soon

said from our once dashingly
undiffident first flag, "don't tread on
    me," tactless symbol of a new republic.
Priorities were
        cradled in this region not
        noted for humility; spot
that has high-singing
        frogs, cotton-mouth snakes and cot-
    ton-fields; clay for brick,
Lawrence jugs with Persian
loping wolf design; and hounds.
Here the poor unpoisonous
terrapin likes to
        idle near the sea-top;
        tobacco-crop
gains have church tablets; Devil's woodyard swamps
    and one-brick-thick-

wall serpentine shadows star-
tle strangers. The strangler fig, the dwarf-
    fancying Egyptian, the American,

the Dutch, the noble
    Roman, in taking what they
    pleased—colonizing as we say—
were not all intel-
    lect and delicacy. A
  black savage or such
as was subject to the
deer-fur Crown is not all brawn
and animality. The
limestone tea-table,
      the mandolin-shaped big
      and little fig,
and the now disused silkworm-trees, imply
  amity; much

kind tyranny made ha-has
that kept back cows; clock-strengthened stocking
  and drooping cotton dress with handmade edge, mark
tyrant taste; the song-
    bird wakes too soon, to enjoy
    excellent idleness, destroy-
ing legitimate
    laziness, this unbought toy
  even in the dark
risking loud whee whee whee
of joy, the caraway-seed-
spotted sparrow perched in the
dew-drenched juniper
      beside the window-ledge;
      the little hedge-
sparrow that wakes up seven minutes soon-
  er than the lark

they say. The live oak's rounded
mass of undulating boughs, the white
  pine, the agèd hackberry—handsomest vis-
itor of all—the
    cedar's etched solidity,
    the cypress, lose identity
and are one tree, as
    sunset flames increasingly

against their leaf-chis-
elled blackening ridge of green;
and the redundantly wind-
widened clouds expanding to
earth size above the
           town's bothered with wages
           childish sages,
are to the child an intimation of
    what glory is.

Bird-Witted

With innocent wide penguin eyes, three
    grown fledgling mocking-birds below
the pussy-willow tree,
    stand in a row,
wings touching, feebly solemn,
    till they see
           their no longer larger
           mother bringing
something which will partially
feed one of them.
    Towards the high-keyed intermittent squeak
    of broken carriage-springs, made by
the three similar, meek-
    coated bird's-eye
freckled forms she comes; and when
    from the beak
           of one, the still living
           beetle has dropped
out, she picks it up and puts
it in again.
    Standing in the shade till they have dressed
    their thickly-filamented, pale
pussy-willow-surfaced
    coats, they spread tail
and wings, showing one by one,
    the modest
           white stripe lengthwise on the
           tail and crosswise
on the under wing, and the
accordion

is closed again. What delightful note
    with rapid unexpected flute-
sounds leaping from the throat
    of the astute
grown bird comes back to one from
the remote
        unenergetic sun-
        lit air before
the brood was here? Why has the
bird's voice become
    harsh? A piebald cat observing them,
        is slowly creeping toward the trim
trio on the tree-stem.
        Unused to him
the three make room—uneasy
    new problem.
        A dangling foot that missed
        its grasp, is raised
and finds the twig on which it
planned to perch. The
    parent darting down, nerved by what chills
        the blood, and by hope rewarded—
of toil—since nothing fills
        squeaking unfed
mouths, wages deadly combat,
    and half kills
        with bayonet beak and
        cruel wings, the
intellectual, cautious-
l y   c r e e p i n g   c a t.

Half Deity

half worm. We all, infant and adult, have
    stopped to watch the butterfly—last of the
elves—and learned to spare the wingless worm
        that hopefully ascends the tree. The well-known
silk tiger swallowtail
        of South America, with body light-
ly furred was that bearing pigments which engrave
the lower wings with dragon's blood, weightless.
        They that have wings must not have weights. This more

peninsula-tailed one with a black
    pitchfork-scallop edge on sunburnt zebra-skin,
tired by the trip it made
    with drover-like tenacity, has been
sleeping upright on the elm. Its yellowness,
that of the autumn poplar-leaf, by day
    has been observed. Disguised in butterfly-
    bush Wedgwood-blue, Psyche follows it
        to that small tree, Micromalus, the midget
    crab; to the mimosa;
        and from that, to the flowering pomegranate.
Baffled not by the quick-clouding serene gray
moon but forced by the hot hot sun to pant,
    she stands on rug-soft grass; though "it is not
    permitted to gaze informally
        on majesty in such a manner as might
    well happen here." The blind
        all-seeing butterfly, fearing the slight
finger, wanders, as though it were ignorant,
across the path and lights on Zephyr's palm,
    planting forefeet soberly; then pawing
    like a horse, turns round—apostrophe-
        tipped brown antennae: porcupining out as
    it arranges nervous
        wings. Vexed because curiosity has
been pursuing it, it cannot now be calm.
The butterfly's round unglazed china eyes,
    pale tobacco brown, with the large eyes of
    the Nymph on them—gray eyes that now are
        black, for she with controlled agitated glance
    observes the insect's face
        and all's a-quiver with significance—
enact the scene of cats' eyes on the magpie's
eyes, by Goya. Butterflies do not need
    home advice. As though Zephyr and Psyche
    were patent-leather cricket singing
        loud, and gnat-catching garden-toad, the swallow-
    tail bewitched and danger-
        ous, springs away, zebra half-deified,
trampling the air as it tramples the flowers, feed-
ing where it pivots. Twig-veined irascible
    fastidious stubborn undisciplined

zebra! Sometimes one is grateful to
    a stranger for looking very nice. But free
to leave the outspread hand
    it flies, drunken with triviality
or guided by visions of strength, off until,
diminishing like wreckage on the sea,
    rising and falling easily, it mounts
    the swell and keeping its true course with
        what swift majesty, indifferent to
us, is gone. Deaf to ap-
    proval—magnet-nice, as it flutters through
airs now slack, now fresh. It has strict ears when the
West Wind speaks. It was he, with mirror eyes
    of strong anxiety, who had no net
    or flowering shrewd-scented tropical
        device, or lignum vitae perch in half-shut
hand; for ours is not a
    canely land; nor was it Oberon, but
this quiet young man with piano replies,
named Zephyr, whose hand spread out was enough
    to tempt the fiery tiger-horse to stand,
    eyes staring skyward and chest arching
        bravely out—historic metamorphoser
and saintly animal
    in India, in Egypt, anywhere.
His talk was as strange as my grandmother's muff.

Smooth Gnarled Crape Myrtle

    A brass-green bird with grass-
green throat smooth as a nut, springs from
    twig to twig askew, copying the
Chinese flower piece—businesslike atom
    in the stiff-leafed tree's blue-
    pink, dregs-of-wine, pyramids
    of mathematic
    circularity—one of a
    pair. A redbird with a hatchet
crest lights straight, on a twig
between the two, bending the
    peculiar
    bouquet down; and there are

several black antique
bootjack fireflies touched with weak bright
hunting-pink. "The legendary white-
eared black bulbul that sings
only in pure Sanskrit" should
be here—"tame clever
true nightingale." The cardinal-
bird that is usually a
pair looks somewhat odd, like
"the ambassadorial
    Inverness
    worn by one who dresses

in New York but dreams of
London." It was artifice saw
on a patch-box pigeon-egg, room for
fervent script, and wrote as with a bird's claw
under the pair on the
hyacinth-blue lid—"joined in
friendship, crowned by love."
An aspect may deceive; as the
elephant's columbine-tubed trunk
held waveringly out—
an at will heavy thing—is
    delicate.
    Art is unfortunate.

One may be a blameless
bachelor and it is but a
step to Congreve. A Rosalindless
redbird comes where people are, knowing they
have not made a point of
being where he is—this bird
which says not sings, "with-
out loneliness I should be more
lonely, so I keep it"—half in
Japanese. And what of
our clasped hands that swear "By Peace
    Plenty; as
    by Wisdom Peace." Alas!

The Pangolin

Another armored animal—scale
    lapping scale with spruce-cone regu-
    larity until they
form the uninterrupted central
    tail-row. This near artichoke
        with head and legs and grit-equipped giz-
    zard, the night miniature artist-
        engineer, is   Leonardo's
        indubitable son? Im-
    pressive animal
and toiler, of whom we seldom hear.
        Armor seems extra. But for him,
    the closing ear-
        ridge—or bare
        ear, lacking even this small
        eminence—and similarly safe

contracting nose and eye apertures
    impenetrably closable,
    are not;—a true ant-eat-
er, not cockroach-eater, who endures
    exhausting solitary
        trips through unfamiliar ground at night,
    returning before sunrise; stepping
        in the moonlight,   on the moonlight
        peculiarly, that the out-
    side edges of his
hands may bear the weight and save the claws
        for digging. Serpentined about
    the tree, he draws
        away from
        danger unpugnaciously,
        with no sound but a harmless hiss; keep-

ing the fragile grace of the Thomas-
    of-Leighton-Buzzard Westminster
        Abbey wrought-iron vine, or
rolls himself into a ball that has
    power to defy all effort

to unroll it;—strongly intailed, neat
head for core, on neck not breaking off,
   with curled-in feet.   Nevertheless
      he has sting-proof scales; and nest
of rocks closed with earth
from inside, which he can thus darken.
         Sun and moon & day and night & man and beast
each with a splen-
dor which man
in all his vileness cannot
set aside; each with an excellence!

"Fearful yet to be feared," the armored
   ant-eater met by the driver
   ant does not turn back, but
engulfs what he can, the flattened sword-
      edged leafpoints on the tail and
         artichoke-set leg and body plates
quivering violently when it
      retaliates   and swarms on him.
         Compact like the furled fringed frill
on the hat-brim of
Gargallo's hollow iron head of a
      matador, he will drop and will
then walk away
unhurt, al-
though if unintruded on
he will come slowly down the tree, helped

by his tail. The giant-pangolin
   tail, graceful tool, as prop or hand
   or broom or axe, tipped like
the elephant's trunk with special skin,
      is not lost on this ant and
         stone swallowing uninjurable
artichoke, which simpletons thought a
      living fable   whom the stones had
         nourished whereas ants had done
      so. Pangolins are
not aggressive animals; between
         dusk and day, they have the not un-
chainlike, machine-

like form and
frictionless creep of a thing
made graceful by adversities, con-

versities. To explain grace requires
a curious hand. If that which
is at all were not for
ever, why would those who graced the spires
with animals and gathered
there to rest, on cold luxurious
low stone seats—a monk and monk and monk—
between the thus   ingenious roof-
supports, have slaved to confuse
grace with a kindly
manner, time in which to pay a debt,
the cure for sins, a graceful use
of what are yet
approved stone
mullions branching out across
the perpendiculars? A sailboat

was the first machine. The manis, made
for moving quietly also,
is neither a prisoner
nor a god; on hind feet plantigrade,
with certain postures of a
man. Beneath sun and moon, man slaving
to make his life more sweet, leaves half the
flowers worth having,   needing to choose
wisely how to use the strength;—
a paper-maker
like the wasp; a tractor of food-stuffs,
like the ant; spidering a length
of web from bluffs
above a
stream; in fighting, mechanicked
like the pangolin; capsizing in

disheartenment. Bedizened or stark
naked, man, the self, the being
so-called human, writing-
master to this world, griffons a dark
"Like does not like like that is

obnoxious"; and writes errror with four
r's. Among animals, one has a
sense of humor   then, which saves a
few steps, which saves years—unig-
norant, modest and
unemotional, and all emo-
tion; one with everlasting vig-
or, power to grow
though there are
few of him—who can make one
breathe faster, and make one erecter.

Not afraid of anything is he
and then goes cowering forth, tread paced
to meet an obstacle
at every step. Consistent with the
formula—warm blood, no gills,
two pairs of hands and a few hairs—that
is a mammal; there he sits in his
own habitat,   serge-clad, strong-shod.
The prey of fear; he, always
curtailed, extinguished,
thwarted by the dusk, work partly done,
says to the alternating blaze,
"Again the sun!
anew each
day; and new and new and new,
that comes into and steadies my soul."

from WHAT ARE YEARS (1941)

What are Years?

What is our innocence,
what is our guilt? All are
    naked, none is safe. And whence
is courage: the unanswered question,
the resolute doubt,—
dumbly calling, deafly listening—that
in misfortune, even death,
    encourages others
    and in its defeat, stirs

    the soul to be strong? He
sees deep and is glad, who
    accedes to mortality
and in his imprisonment, rises
upon himself as
the sea in a chasm, struggling to be
free and unable to be,
    in its surrendering
    finds its continuing.

    So he who strongly feels,
behaves. The very bird,
    grown taller as he sings, steels
his form straight up. Though he is captive,
his mighty singing
says, satisfaction is a lowly
thing, how pure a thing is joy.
    This is mortality,
    this is eternity.

Rigorists

"We saw reindeer
browsing," a friend who'd been in Lapland, said:
"finding their own food; they are adapted

to scant *reino*
or pasture, yet they can run eleven
miles in fifty minutes; the feet spread when

the snow is soft,
and act as snow-shoes. They are rigorists
however handsomely cutwork artists

of Lapland and
Siberia elaborate the trace
or saddle-girth with saw-tooth leather lace.

One looked at us
with its firm face part brown, part white,—a queen
of alpine flowers. Santa Claus' reindeer, seen

at last, had gray-
brown fur, with a neck like edelweiss or
lion's foot,—*leontopodium* more

exactly." And
this candelabrum-headed ornament
for a place where ornaments are scarce, sent

to Alaska,
was a gift preventing the extinction
of the Esquimo. The battle was won

by a quiet man,
Sheldon Jackson, evangel to that race
whose reprieve he read in the reindeer's face.

Light is Speech

One can say more of sunlight
   than of speech; but speech
   and light, each
aiding each—when French—
have not disgraced that still un-
extirpated adjective.
Yes light is speech. Free frank
impartial sunlight, moonlight,
starlight, lighthouse light,
   are language. The Creach'h
d'Ouessant light-
house on its defenseless dot of
rock, is the descendant of Voltaire

whose flaming justice reached a
   man already harmed;
   of unarmed
Montaigne whose balance,
maintained despite the bandit's
hardness, lit remorse's saving
spark; of Émile Littré,
philology's determined,
ardent eight-volume
   Hippocrates-charmed
editor. A
man on fire, a scientist of
freedoms, was firm Maximilien

Paul Émile Littré. England
   guarded by the sea,
   we with re-
enforced Bartholdy's
Liberty holding up her
torch beside the port, hear France
demand, "'Tell me the truth,
especially when it is
   unpleasant.'" And we
cannot but reply,

"The word France means
enfranchisement; means one who can
'animate whoever thinks of her.'"

He "Digesteth Harde Yron"

Although the aepyornis
or roc that lived in Madagascar, and
   the moa are extinct,
    the camel-sparrow, linked
with them in size—the large sparrow
Xenophon saw walking by
      a stream—was and is
      a symbol of justice.

This bird watches his chicks with
a maternal concentration, after
   he has sat on the eggs
    at night six weeks, his legs
their only weapon of defense.
He is swifter than a horse;
      he has a foot hard
      as a hoof; the leopard

is not more suspicious. How
could he, prized for plumes and eggs and young, used
   even as a riding-
    beast, respect men hiding
actorlike in ostrich-skins, with
the right hand making the neck move
      as if alive and
      from a bag the left hand

strewing grain, that ostriches
might be decoyed and killed! Yes this is he
   whose plume was anciently
    the plume of justice; he
whose comic duckling head on its
great neck, revolves with compass-
      needle nervousness,
      when he stands guard, in S-

like foragings as he is
preening the down on his leaden-skinned back.
   The egg piously shown
    as Leda's very own

from which Castor and Pollux hatched,
was an ostrich-egg. And what
    could have been more fit
    for the Chinese lawn it

grazed on, as a gift to an
emperor who admired strange birds, than this
    one who builds his mud-made
    nest in dust yet will wade
in lake or sea till only the
head shows. A nervous restless
    bird that flees at sight
    of danger, he feigns flight

to save his chicks, decoying
his decoyers; never known to hide his
    head in sand, yet lagging
    when he must, and dragging
an as-if-wounded wing. The friend
of hippotigers and wild
    asses, it is as
    though schooled by them he was

the best of the unflying
pegasi, since the Greeks "caught a few wild
    asses but no ostrich";
    quadrupedlike bird which
flies on feet not wings,—his moth-silk
plumage wilted by his speed;
    mobile wings and tail
    behaving as a sail.

Six hundred ostrich-brains served
at one banquet, the ostrich-plume-tipped tent
    and desert spear, jewel-
    gorgeous ugly egg-shell
goblets, eight pairs of ostriches
in harness, dramatize a
    meaning always missed
    by the externalist.

The power of the visible
is the invisible; as even where

no tree of freedom grows,
so-called brute courage knows.
Heroism is exhausting, yet
it contradicts a greed that
   did not wisely spare
   the harmless solitaire

or great auk in its grandeur;
unsolicitude having swallowed up
   all giant birds but an
   alert gargantuan
little-winged, magnificently
speedy running-bird. This one
   remaining rebel
   is the sparrow-camel.

Spenser's Ireland

has not altered;—
   the kindest place I've never been,
   the greenest place I've never seen.
Every name is a tune.
Denunciations do not affect
     the culprit;   nor blows, but it
is torture to him to not be spoken to.
They're natural,—
     the coat, like Venus'
mantle lined with stars,
buttoned close at the neck,—the
     sleeves new from disuse.

If in Ireland
   they play the harp backward at need,
   and gather at midday the seed
of the fern, eluding
their "giants all covered with iron," might
     there be fern   seed for unlearn-
ing obduracy and for reinstating
the enchantment?
     Hindered characters
seldom have mothers—
in Irish stories—
     but they all have grandmothers.

It was Irish;
   a match not a marriage was made
   when my great great grandmother'd said
with native genius for
disunion, "although your suitor be
     perfection,   one objection
is enough; he is not
Irish." Outwitting
     the fairies, befriending the furies,
whoever again
and again says, "I'll never
     give in," never sees

that you're not free
   until you've been made captive by
   supreme belief,—credulity
you say? When large dainty
fingers tremblingly divide the wings
      of the fly   for mid-July
with a needle and wrap it with peacock-tail,
or tie wool and
         buzzard's wing, their pride,
like the enchanter's
is in care, not madness. Con-
      curring hands divide

flax for damask
   that when bleached by Irish weather
   has the silvered chamois-leather
water-tightness of a
skin. Twisted torcs and gold new-moon-shaped
      lunulae   aren't jewelry
like the purple-coral fuchsia-tree's. If Eire—
the guillemot
         so neat and the hen
of the heath and the
linnet spinet-sweet—bespeak
      relentlessness, then

they are to me
   like enchanted Earl Gerald who
   changed himself into a stag, to
a great green-eyed cat of
the mountain. Discommodity makes
      them invis   ible; they've dis-
appeared. The Irish say your trouble is their
trouble and your
         joy their joy? I wish
I could believe it;
I am troubled, I'm dissat-
      isfied, I'm Irish.

Four Quartz Crystal Clocks

There are four vibrators, the world's exactest clocks;
    and these quartz time-pieces that tell
time intervals to other clocks,
    these worksless clocks work well;
and all four, independently the
    same, are there in the cool Bell
        Laboratory time

vault. Checked by a comparator with Arlington,
    they punctualize the "radio,
cinéma," and "presse,"—a group the
    Giraudoux truth-bureau
of hoped-for accuracy has termed
    "instruments of truth." We know—
        as Jean Giraudoux says

certain Arabs have not heard—that Napoleon
    is dead; that a quartz prism when
the temperature changes, feels
    the change and that the then
electrified alternate edges
    oppositely charged, threaten
        careful timing; so that

this water-clear crystal as the Greeks used to say,
    this "clear ice" must be kept at the
same coolness. Repetition, with
    the scientist, should be
synonymous with accuracy.
    The lemur-student can see
        that an aye-aye is not

an angwan-tíbo, potto, or loris. The sea-
    side burden should not embarrass
the bell-boy with the buoy-ball
    endeavoring to pass
hotel patronesses; nor could a
    practiced ear confuse the glass
        eyes for taxidermists

with eye-glasses from the optometrist. And as
  MEridian-7 1, 2
1, 2 gives, each fifteenth second
  in the same voice, the new
data—"The time will be" so and so—
  you realize that "when you
    hear the signal," you'll be

hearing Jupiter or jour pater, the day god—
  the salvaged son of Father Time—
telling the cannibal Chronos
  (eater of his proxime
newborn progeny) that punctual-
  ity is not a crime.

The Paper Nautilus

For authorities whose hopes
are shaped by mercenaries?
   Writers entrapped by
   teatime fame and by
commuters' comforts? Not for these
   the paper nautilus
   constructs her thin glass shell.

   Giving her perishable
souvenir of hope, a dull
   white outside and smooth-
   edged inner surface
glossy as the sea, the watchful
   maker of it guards it
   day and night; she scarcely

   eats until the eggs are hatched.
Buried eight-fold in her eight
   arms, for she is in
   a sense a devil-
fish, her glass ramshorn-cradled freight
   is hid but is not crushed.
   As Hercules, bitten

   by a crab loyal to the hydra,
was hindered to succeed,
   the intensively
   watched eggs coming from
the shell free it when they are freed,—
   leaving its wasp-nest flaws
   of white on white, and close-

   laid Ionic chiton-folds
like the lines in the mane of
   a Parthenon horse,
   round which the arms had
wound themselves as if they knew love
   is the only fortress
   strong enough to trust to.

NEVERTHELESS (1944)

Nevertheless

you've seen a strawberry
    that's had a struggle; yet
    was, where the fragments met,

a hedgehog or a star-
    fish for the multitude
    of seeds. What better food

than apple-seeds—the fruit
    within the fruit—locked in
    like counter-curved twin

hazel-nuts? Frost that kills
    the little rubber-plant-
    leaves of *kok-saghyz*-stalks, can't

harm the roots; they still grow
    in frozen ground. Once where
    there was a prickly-pear-

leaf clinging to barbed wire,
    a root shot down to grow
    in earth two feet below;

as carrots form mandrakes
    or a ram's-horn root some-
    times. Victory won't come

to me unless I go
    to it; a grape-tendril
    ties a knot in knots till

knotted thirty times,—so
    the bound twig that's under-
    gone and over-gone, can't stir.

The weak overcomes its
    menace, the strong over-
    comes itself. What is there

like fortitude! What sap
    went through that little thread
    to make the cherry red!

The Wood-Weasel

emerges daintily, the skunk—
don't laugh—in sylvan black and white chipmunk
regalia. The inky thing
adaptively whited with glistening
goat-fur, is wood-warden. In his
ermined well-cuttlefish-inked wool, he is
determination's totem. Out-
lawed? His sweet face and powerful feet go about
in chieftain's coat of Chilcat cloth.
He is his own protection from the moth,

noble little warrior. That
otter-skin on it, the living pole-cat,
smothers anything that stings. Well,—
this same weasel's playful and his weasel
associates are too. Only
WOOD-weasels shall associate with me.

Elephants

Uplifted and waved until immobilized
wistarialike, the opposing opposed
mouse-gray twined proboscises' trunk formed by two
trunks, fights itself to a spiraled inter-nosed

deadlock of dyke-enforced massiveness. It's a
knock-down drag-out fight that asks no quarter? Just
a pastime, as when the trunk rains on itself
the pool it siphoned up; or when—since each must

provide his forty-pound bough dinner—he broke
the leafy branches. These templars of the Tooth,
these matched intensities, take master care of
master tools. One, sleeping with the calm of youth,

at full length in the half dry sun-flecked stream-bed,
rests his hunting-horn-curled trunk on shallowed stone.
The sloping hollow of the sleeper's body
cradles the gently breathing eminence's prone

mahout, asleep like a lifeless six-foot
frog, so feather light the elephant's stiff
ear's unconscious of the crossed feet's weight. And the
defenseless human thing sleeps as sound as if

incised with hard wrinkles, embossed with wide ears,
invincibly tusked, made safe by magic hairs!
As if, as if, it is all ifs; we are at
much unease. But magic's masterpiece is theirs,—

Houdini's serenity quelling his fears.
Elephant ear-witnesses-to-be of hymns
and glorias, these ministrants all gray or
gray with white on legs or trunk, are a pilgrims'

pattern of revery not reverence,—a
religious procession without any priests,
the centuries-old carefullest unrehearsed
play. Blessed by Buddha's Tooth, the obedient beasts

themselves as toothed temples blessing the street, see
the white elephant carry the cushion that
carries the casket that carries the Tooth.
Amenable to what, matched with him, are gnat

trustees, he does not step on them as the white-
canopied blue-cushioned Tooth is augustly
and slowly returned to the shrine. Though white is
the color of worship and of mourning, he

is not here to worship and he is too wise
to mourn,—a life-prisoner but reconciled.
With trunk tucked up compactly—the elephant's
sign of defeat—he resisted, but is the child

of reason now. His straight trunk seems to say: when
what we hoped for came to nothing, we revived.
As loss could not ever alter Socrates'
tranquillity, the elephant has contrived

equanimity. With the Socrates of
animals as with Sophocles the Bee, on whose
tombstone a hive was incised, sweetness tinctures
his gravity. His held up fore-leg for use

as a stair, to be climbed or descended with
the aid of his ear, expounds the brotherhood
of creatures to man the encroacher by the
small word with the dot, meaning know,—the verb bùd.

These knowers, these distinct rememberers
like Bùd, of what they have experienced, are
"unable to pierce by one dart from the bow
four plaintain-leaves laid at the points of a square";

and cannot, like Buddha, change missiles to wreaths,
alter their shape, bisect hairs in the dark, make
their wisdom apparent in rays of all hues,
or turn heat, exasperated, to earthquake-

fire. Yet they "arouse the feeling that they are
allied to man" and can change roles with their trustees.
Hardship makes the soldier; then teachableness
makes him the philosopher—as Socrates,

prudently testing the suspicious thing, knew
the wisest is he who's not sure that he knows.
Who rides on a tiger can never dismount;
asleep on an elephant, that is repose.

A Carriage from Sweden

They say there is a sweeter air
    where it was made, than we have here;
    a Hamlet's castle atmosphere.
At all events there is in Brooklyn
something that makes me feel at home.

No one may see this put-away
    museum-piece, this country cart
    that inner happiness made art;
and yet, in this city of freckled
integrity it is a vein

of resined straightness from north-wind
    hardened Sweden's once-opposed-to-
    compromise archipelago
of rocks. Washington and Gustavus
Adolphus, forgive our decay.

Seats, dashboard and sides of smooth gourd-
    rind texture, a flowered step, swan-
    dart brake, and swirling crustacean-
tailed equine amphibious creatures
that garnish the axle-tree! What

a fine thing! What unannoying
    romance! And how beautiful, she
    with the natural stoop of the
snowy egret, gray-eyed and straight-haired,
for whom it should come to the door,—

of whom it reminds me. The split
    pine fair hair, steady gannet-clear
    eyes and the pine-needled-path deer-
swift step; that is Sweden, land of the
free and the soil for a spruce-tree—

vertical though a seedling—all
    needles: from a green trunk, green shelf
    on shelf fanning out by itself.

The deft white-stockinged dance in thick-soled
shoes! Denmark's sanctuaried Jews!

The puzzle-jugs and hand-spun rugs,
        the root-legged kracken shaped like dogs,
        the hanging buttons and the frogs
that edge the Sunday jackets! Sweden,
you have a runner called the Deer, who

when he's won a race, likes to run
        more; you have the sun-right gable-
        ends due east and west, the table
spread as for a banquet; and the put-
in twin vest-pleats with a fish-fin

effect when you need none. Sweden,
        what makes the people dress that way
        and those who see you wish to stay?
The runner, not too tired to run more
at the end of the race? And that

cart, dolphin-graceful? A Dalén
        light-house, self-lit?—responsive and
        responsible. I understand;
it's not pine-needle-paths that give spring
when they're run on, it's a Sweden

of moated white castles,—the bed
        of densely grown flowers in an S
        meaning Sweden and stalwartness,
skill, and a surface that says
Made in Sweden: carts are my trade.

The Mind is an Enchanting Thing

is an enchanted thing
    like the glaze on a
katydid-wing
        subdivided by sun
        till the nettings are legion.
Like Gieseking playing Scarlatti;

like the apteryx-awl
    as a beak, or the
kiwi's rain-shawl
        of haired feathers, the mind
        feeling its way as though blind,
walks along with its eyes on the ground.

It has memory's ear
    that can hear without
having to hear.
        Like the gyroscope's fall,
        truly unequivocal
because trued by regnant certainty,

it is a power of
    strong enchantment. It
is like the dove-
        neck animated by
        sun; it is memory's eye;
it's conscientious inconsistency.

It tears off the veil; tears
    the temptation, the
mist the heart wears,
        from its eyes,—if the heart
        has a face; it takes apart
dejection. It's fire in the dove-neck's

iridescence; in the
    inconsistencies
of Scarlatti.

Unconfusion submits
its confusion to proof; it's
not a Herod's oath that cannot change.

In Distrust of Merits

Strengthened to live, strengthened to die for
    medals and position victories?
They're fighting, fighting, fighting the blind
    man who thinks he sees,—
who cannot see that the enslaver is
enslaved; the hater, harmed. O shining O
       firm star, O tumultuous
          ocean lashed till small things go
    as they will, the mountainous
       wave makes us who look, know

depth. Lost at sea before they fought! O
    star of David, star of Bethlehem,
O black imperial lion
    of the Lord—emblem
of a risen world—be joined at last, be
joined. There is hate's crown beneath which all is
       death; there's love's without which none
         is king; the blessed deeds bless
    the halo. As contagion
       of sickness makes sickness,

contagion of trust can make trust. They're
    fighting in deserts and caves, one by
one, in battalions and squadrons;
    they're fighting that I
may yet recover from the disease, My
Self; some have it lightly, some will die. "Man's
    wolf to man" and we devour
       ourselves. The enemy could not
    have made a greater breach in our
    defenses. One pilot-

ing a blind man can escape him, but
    Job disheartened by false comfort knew
that nothing can be so defeating
    as a blind man who
can see. O alive who are dead, who are
proud not to see, O small dust of the earth

that walks so arrogantly,
        trust begets power and faith is
an affectionate thing. We
        vow, we make this promise

to the fighting—it's a promise—"We'll
    never hate black, white, red, yellow, Jew,
Gentile, Untouchable." We are
    not competent to
make our vows. With set jaw they are fighting,
fighting, fighting,—some we love whom we know,
        some we love but know not—that
            hearts may feel and not be numb.
        It cures me; or am I what
            I can't believe in? Some

in snow, some on crags, some in quicksands,
    little by little, much by much, they
are fighting fighting fighting that where
    there was death there may
be life. "When a man is prey to anger,
he is moved by outside things; when he holds
        his ground in patience patience
            patience, that is action or
        beauty," the soldier's defense
            and hardest armor for

the fight. The world's an orphans' home. Shall
    we never have peace without sorrow?
without pleas of the dying for
    help that won't come? O
quiet form upon the dust, I cannot
look and yet I must. If these great patient
        dyings—all these agonies
            and woundbearings and bloodshed—
        can teach us how to live, these
            dyings were not wasted.

Hate-hardened heart, O heart of iron,
    iron is iron till it is rust.
There never was a war that was
    not inward; I must
fight till I have conquered in myself what

causes war, but I would not believe it.
    I inwardly did nothing.
        O Iscariotlike crime!
    Beauty is everlasting
        and dust is for a time.

POEMS 1944–1951

"Keeping Their World Large"

All too literally, their flesh
and their spirit are our shield
New York Times, 7th June, 1944

I should like to see that country's tiles, bedrooms,
stone patios
and ancient wells: Rinaldo
Caramonica's the cobbler's, Frank Sblendorio's
and Dominick Angelastro's country—
the grocer's, the iceman's, the dancer's—the
beautiful Miss Damiano's; wisdom's

and all angels' Italy, this Christmas Day
this Christmas year.
A noiseless piano, an
innocent war, the heart that can act against itself. Here,
each unlike and all alike, could
so many—stumbling, falling, multiplied
till bodies lay as ground to walk on—say

"If Christ and the apostles died in vain, I'll
die in vain with them"?
When the very heart was a prayer
against this way of victory. Stem after stem
of what we call the tree—set, row
on row; that forest of white crosses; the
vision makes us faint. My eyes won't close to it. While

the knife was lifted, Isaac the offering
lay mute.
These, laid like animals for sacrifice,
like Isaac on the mount, were their own substitute.
And must they all be harmed by those
whom they have saved. Tears that don't fall are what
they wanted. Belief in belief marching

marching marching—all alone, all similar,
spurning pathos,
clothed in fear—marching to death
marching to life; it was like the cross, is like the cross.
Keeping their world large, that silent

marching marching marching and this silence
for which there is no description, are

the voices of fighters with no rests between,
who would not yield;
whose spirits and whose bodies
all too literally were our shield, are still our shield.
They fought the enemy, we fight
fat living and self-pity. Shine, O shine
unfalsifying sun, on this sick scene.

His Shield

The pin-swin or spine-swine
    (the edgehog miscalled hedgehog) with all his edges out,
  echidna and echinoderm in distressed-
pin-cushion thorn-fur coats, the spiny pig or porcupine,
    the rhino with horned snout—
  everything is battle-dressed.

Pig-fur won't do, I'll wrap
    myself in salamander-skin like Presbyter John.
  A lizard in the midst of flames, a firebrand
that is life, asbestos-eyed asbestos-eared, with tattooed nap
    and permanent pig on
  the instep; he can withstand

fire and won't drown. In his
    unconquerable country of unpompous gusto,
  gold was so common none considered it; greed
and flattery were unknown. Though rubies large as tennis-
    balls conjoined in streams so
  that the mountain seemed to bleed,

the inextinguishable
    salamander styled himself but presbyter. His shield
  was his humility. In Carpasian
linen coat, flanked by his household lion-cubs and sable
    retinue, he revealed
  a formula safer than

an armorer's: the power of relinquishing
    what one would keep; that is freedom. Become dinosaur-
  skulled, quilled or salamander-wooled, more ironshod
and javelin-dressed than a hedgehog battalion of steel, but be
    dull. Don't be envied or
  armed with a measuring-rod.

Propriety

is some such word
    as the chord
        Brahms had heard
        from a bird,
sung down near the root of the throat;
it's the little downy woodpecker
                spiraling up a tree—
                up up up like mercury;

    a not long
    sparrow-song
        of hayseed
        magnitude—
a tuned reticence with rigor
from strength at the source. Propriety is
            Bach's Solfegietto—
            harmonica and basso.

    The fish-spine
    on firs, on
        somber trees
        by the sea's
walls of wave-worn rock—have it; and
a moonbow and Bach's cheerful firmness
            in a minor key.
            It's an owl-and-a-pussy-

    both-content
    agreement.
        Come, come. It's
        mixed with wits;
it's not a graceful sadness. It's
resistance with bent head, like foxtail
            millet's. Brahms and Bach,
            no; Bach and Brahms. To thank Bach

    for his song
    first, is wrong.
        Pardon me;
        both are the

unintentional pansy-face
uncursed by self-inspection; blackened
    because born that way.

Voracities and Verities Sometimes are Interacting

I don't like diamonds;
the emerald's "grass-lamp glow" is better;
   and unobtrusiveness is dazzling,
      upon occasion.
      Some kinds of gratitude are trying.

Poets, don't make a fuss;
the elephant's "crooked trumpet" "doth write";
   and to a tiger-book I am reading—
      I think you know the one—
      I am under obligation.

      One may be pardoned, yes I know
      one may, for love undying.

A Face

"I am not treacherous, callous, jealous, superstitious,
supercilious, venomous, or absolutely hideous":
    studying and studying its expression,
    exasperated desperation
        though at no real impasse,
        would gladly break the glass;

when love of order, ardor, uncircuitous simplicity,
with an expression of inquiry, are all one needs to be!
    Certain faces, a few, one or two—or one
    face photographed by recollection—
        to my mind, to my sight,
        must remain a delight.

By Disposition of Angels

Messengers much like ourselves? Explain it.
Steadfastness the darkness makes explicit?
Something heard most clearly when not near it?
    Above particularities,
These unparticularities praise cannot violate.
    One has seen, in such steadiness never deflected,
    How by darkness a star is perfected.

Star that does not ask me if I see it?
Fir that would not wish me to uproot it?
Speech that does not ask me if I hear it?
    Mysteries expound mysteries.
Steadier than steady, star dazzling me, live and elate,
    No need to say, how like some we have known; too like her,
    Too like him, and a-quiver forever.

Efforts of Affection

Genesis tells us of Jubal and Jabal.
One handled the harp and one herded the cattle.

Unhackneyed Shakespeare's
"Hay, sweet hay, which hath no fellow,"
Love's extraordinary-ordinary stubbornness
Like La Fontaine's done
by each as if by each alone,
smiling and stemming distraction;
          How welcome:

Vermin-proof and pilfer-proof integration
In which unself-righteousness humbles inspection.

"You know I'm not a saint!" Sainted obsession.
The bleeding-heart's—that strange rubber fern's attraction

Puts perfume to shame.
Unsheared sprays of elephant-ears
Do not make a selfish end look like a noble one.
Truly as the sun
can rot or mend, love can make one
bestial or make a beast a man.
          Thus wholeness—

wholesomeness? best say efforts of affection—
attain integration too tough for infraction.

The Icosasphere

"In Buckinghamshire hedgerows
  the birds nesting in the merged green density,
    weave little bits of string and moths and feathers and
        thistledown,
      in parabolic concentric curves"
  and, working for concavity, leave spherical feats of rare efficiency;
    whereas through lack of integration,

avid for someone's fortune,
  three were slain and ten committed perjury,
    six died, two killed themselves, and two paid fines for risks
        they'd run.
    But then there is the icosasphere
  in which at last we have steel-cutting at its summit of economy,
    since twenty triangles conjoined, can wrap one

ball or double-rounded shell
  with almost no waste, so geometrically
    neat, it's an icosahedron. Would the engineers making one,
      or Mr. J. O. Jackson tell us
  how the Egyptians could have set up seventy-eight-foot solid
        granite vertically?
    We should like to know how that was done.

Pretiolae

The dutiful, the firemen of Hartford,
Are not without a reward—
A temple of Apollo on a velvet sward

And legend has it that small pretzels come,
Not from Reading but from Rome:
A suppliant's folded arms twisted by a thumb.

Armor's Undermining Modesty

At first I thought a pest
must have alighted on my wrist.
It was a moth almost an owl,
its wings were furred so well,
with backgammon-board wedges interlacing
on the wing—

like cloth of gold in a pattern
of scales with a hair-seal Persian
sheen. Once, self-determination
made an axe of a stone
and hacked things out with hairy paws. The consequence—
our mis-set
alphabet.

Arise, for it is day.
Even gifted scholars lose their way
through faulty etymology.
No wonder we hate poetry,
and stars and harps and the new moon. If tributes cannot
be implicit,

give me diatribes and the fragrance of iodine,
the cork oak acorn grown in Spain;
the pale-ale-eyed impersonal look
which the sales-placard gives the bock beer buck.
What is more precise than precision? Illusion.
Knights we've known,

like those familiar
now unfamiliar knights who sought the Grail, were
ducs in old Roman fashion
without the addition
of wreaths and silver rods, and armor gilded
or inlaid.

They did not let self bar
their usefulness to others who were
different. Though Mars is excessive
is being preventive,

heroes need not write an ordinall of attributes to enumerate
what they hate.

I should, I confess,
like to have a talk with one of them about excess,
and armor's undermining modesty
instead of innocent depravity.
A mirror-of-steel uninsistence should countenance
continence,

objectified and not by chance,
there in its frame of circumstance
of innocence and altitude
in an unhackneyed solitude.
There is the tarnish; and there, the imperishable wish.

Quoting An Also Private Thought

Some speak of things we know, as new;
    And you, of things unknown as things forgot.

A similar coral invades the apple, dyed
    Inside as by infusion of the rind,

Or the poem that chanced to be prose,
    Disclosing the signature in an interior

Mathematician's parenthesis—
    Astute device quite different from the autograph.

Somehow the accident of pleasure—a dedication qualitied
    Indeed. It is at the opposite pole from the miser's

Escutcheon, three vises hard-screwed;
    Three padlocks clodhopping upon sensibility

That devastating asset antipodal to pride,
    That would not for the world intrude.

We Call Them the Brave

who likely were reluctant to be brave.
Sitting by a slow fire on a waste
of snow, I would last about an hour.
Better not euphemize the grave.

In this fashionable town, endearments are the mode
though generals are appraised—not praised—
and one is not forced to walk about
where a muddy slough serves as a road.

"What are these shadows barely
visible, which radar fails to scan?"
Ships "keeping distance on the gentle swell."
And "what is a free world ready

to do, for what it values most?"
Bestow little discs the bereaved may touch?
Can I ever forget it even when dead—
that congressionally honored ghost

mourned by a friend whose shoulder sags—
weeping on the shoulder of another
for another; with another sitting near,
filling out casualty-tags.

What of it? We call them the brave
perhaps? Yes; what if the time should come
when no one will fight for anything
and there's nothing of worth to save.

LIKE A BULWARK (1956)

Bulwarked against Fate

Affirmed. Pent by power that holds it fast—
a paradox. Pent. Hard pressed,
    you take the blame and are inviolate.
        Abased at last;
        not the tempest-tossed.
Compressed; firmed by the thrust of the blast
    till compact, like a bulwark against fate;
        lead-saluted,
        saluted by lead?
As though flying Old Glory full mast.

Apparition of Splendor

Partaking of the miraculous
    since never known literally,
Dürer's rhinoceros
    might have startled us equally
    if black-and-white-spined elaborately.

Like another porcupine, or fern,
    the mouth in an arching egret
was too black to discern
    till exposed as a silhouette;
    but the double-embattled thistle of jet—

disadvantageous supposedly—
    has never shot a quill. Was it
some joyous fantasy,
    plain eider-eared exhibit
    of spines rooted in the sooty moss,

or "train supported by porcupines—
    a fairy's eleven yards long"? . . .
as when the lightning shines
    on thistlefine spears, among
    prongs in lanes above lanes of a shorter prong,

"with the forest for nurse," also dark
    at the base—where needle-debris
springs and shows no footmark;
    the setting for a symmetry
    you must not touch unless you are a fairy.

Maine should be pleased that its animal
    is not a waverer, and rather
than fight, lets the primed quill fall.
    Shallow oppressor, intruder,
    insister, you have found a resister.

Then the Ermine:

"rather dead than spotted"; and believe it
    despite reason to think not,
I saw a bat by daylight;
hard to credit

but I knew that I was right. It charmed me—
    wavering like a jack-in-
the-green, weaving about me
insecurely.

Instead of hammer-handed bravado
    adopting force for fashion,
momentum with a motto:
Mutare sperno

vel timere—I don't change, am not craven;
    although on what ground could I
say that I am hard to frighten?
Nothing's certain.

Fail, and Lavater's physiography
    has another admirer
of skill in obscurity—
now a novelty.

So let the *palissandre* settee express
    change, "ebony violet,"
Master Corbo in full dress,
and shepherdess,

at once; exhilarating hoarse crow-note
    and dignity with intimacy.
Foiled explosiveness is yet
a kind of prophet,

a perfecter, and so a concealer—
    with the power of implosion;
like violets by Dürer;
even darker.

Tom Fool at Jamaica

Look at Jonah embarking from Joppa, deterred by
the whale; hard going for a statesman whom nothing could detain,
    although one who would not rather die than repent.
    Be infallible at your peril, for your system will fail,
and select as a model the schoolboy in Spain
        who at the age of six, portrayed a mule and jockey
        who had pulled up for a snail.

"There is submerged magnificence, as Victor Hugo
said." *Sentir avec ardeur*; that's it; magnetized by feeling.
    Tom Fool "makes an effort and makes it oftener
        than the rest"—out on April first, a day of some significance
in the ambiguous sense—the smiling
        Master Atkinson's choice, with that mark of a champion, the extra
        spurt when needed. Yes, yes. "Chance

is a regrettable impurity"; like Tom Fool's
left white hind foot—an unconformity; though judging by
    results, a kind of cottontail to give him confidence.
        Up in the cupola comparing speeds, Signor Capossela
            keeps his head.
"It's tough," he said; "but I get 'em; and why shouldn't I?
I'm relaxed, I'm confident, and I don't bet." Sensational.
            He does not
        bet on his animated

valentines—his pink and black-striped, sashed or dotted silks.
Tom Fool is "a handy horse," with a chiseled foot. You've the beat
    of a dancer to a measure or harmonious rush
        of a porpoise at the prow where the racers all win easily—
like centaurs' legs in tune, as when kettledrums compete;
        nose rigid and suede nostrils spread, a light left hand on the rein,
            till
        well—this is a rhapsody.

Of course, speaking of champions, there was Fats Waller
with the feather touch, giraffe eyes, and that hand alighting in
    Ain't Misbehavin'! Ozzie Smith and Eubie Blake
        ennoble the atmosphere; you recall the Lippizan school;

the time Ted Atkinson charged by on Tiger Skin—
   no pursuers in sight—cat-loping along. And you may have seen a
            monkey
   on a greyhound. "But Tom Fool . . ."

The Web One Weaves of Italy

grows till it is not what but which,
blurred by too much. The very blasé alone could
    choose the contest or fair to which to go.
    The crossbow tournament at Gubbio?

For quiet excitement, canoe-ers
or peach fairs? or near Perugia, the mule-show;
    if not the Palio, slaying the Saracen.
    One salutes—on reviewing again

this modern *mythologica*
esopica—its nonchalances of the mind,
    that "fount by which enchanting gems are spilt."
    And are we not charmed by the result?—

quite different from what goes on
at the Sorbonne; but not entirely, since flowering
    in more than mere talent for spectacle.
    Because the heart is in it all is well.

The Staff of Aesculapius

A symbol from the first, of mastery,
    experiments such as Hippocrates made
        and substituted for vague
    speculation, stayed
        the ravages of a plague.

A "going on"; yes, *anastasis* is the word
    for research a virus has defied,
        and for the virologist
    with variables still untried—
        too impassioned to desist.

Suppose that research has hit on the right one
    and a killed vaccine is effective
        say temporarily—
    for even a year—although a live
        one could give lifelong immunity,

knowledge has been gained for another attack.
    Selective injury to cancer
        cells without injury to
    normal ones—another
        gain—looks like prophecy come true.

Now, after lung resection, the surgeon fills space.
    To sponge implanted, cells following
        fluid, adhere and what
    was inert becomes living—
        that was framework. Is it not

like the master-physician's Sumerian rod?—
    staff and effigy of the animal
        which by shedding its skin
    is a sign of renewal—
        the symbol of medicine.

The Sycamore

             Against a gun-metal sky
    I saw an albino giraffe. Without
             leaves to modify,
chamois-white as
said, though partly pied near the base,
        it towered where a chain of
             stepping-stones lay in a stream nearby;
             glamour to stir the envy

             of anything in motley—
Hampshire pig, the living lucky-stone; or
             all-white butterfly.
A commonplace:
there's more than just one kind of grace.
        We don't like flowers that do
             not wilt; they must die, and nine
             she-camel-hairs aid memory.

             Worthy of Imami,
        the Persian—clinging to a stiffer stalk
             was a little dry
thing from the grass,
in the shape of a Maltese cross,
        retiringly formal
             as if to say: "And there was I
             like a field-mouse at Versailles."

Rosemary

Beauty and Beauty's son and rosemary—
Venus and Love, her son, to speak plainly—
born of the sea supposedly,
at Christmas each, in company,
braids a garland of festivity.
        Not always rosemary—

since the flight to Egypt, blooming differently.
With lancelike leaf, green but silver underneath,
its flowers—white originally—
turned blue. The herb of memory,
imitating the blue robe of Mary,
        is not too legendary

to flower both as symbol and as pungency.
Springing from stones beside the sea,
the height of Christ when thirty-three—
not higher—it feeds on dew and to the bee
"hath a dumb language"; is in reality
        a kind of Christmas-tree.

Style

revives in Escudero's constant of the plumbline,
axis of the hairfine moon—his counter-camber of the skater.
no more fanatical adjuster
of the tilted hat
than Escudero; of tempos others can't combine.
And we—besides evolving
the classic silhouette, Dick Button whittled slender—

have an Iberian-American champion yet
the deadly Etchebaster. Entranced, were you not, by Solidad?
black-clad solitude that is not sad;
like a letter from
Casals; or perhaps say literal alphabet-
S soundholes in a 'cello
set contradictorily; or should we call her

la lagarta? or bamboos with fireflies a-glitter;
or glassy lake and the whorls which a vertical stroke brought about,
of the paddle half-turned coming out.
As if bisecting
a viper, she can dart down three times and recover
without a disaster, having
been a bull-fighter. Well; she has a forgiver.

Etchebaster's art, his catlike ease, his mousing pose,
his genius for anticipatory tactics, preclude envy
as the traditional unwavy
Sandeman sailor
is Escudero's; the guitar, Rosario's—
wrist-rest for a dangling hand
that's suddenly set humming fast fast fast and faster.

There is no suitable simile. It is as though
the equidistant three tiny arcs of seeds in a banana
had been conjoined by Palestrina;
it is like the eyes,
or say the face, of Palestrina by El Greco.
O Escudero, Solidad,
Rosario Escudero, Etchebaster!

Logic and "The Magic Flute"

Up winding stair,
here, where, in what theater lost?
was I seeing a ghost—
a reminder at least
of a sunbeam or moonbeam
that has not a waist?
By hasty hop
or accomplished mishap,
the magic flute and harp
somehow confused themselves
with China's precious wentletrap.

Near Life and Time
in their peculiar catacomb,
abalonean gloom
and an intrusive hum
pervaded the mammoth cast's
small audience-room.
Then out of doors,
where interlacing pairs
of skaters raced from rink
to ramp, a demon roared
as if down flights of marble stairs:

"'What is love and
shall I ever have it?'" The truth
is simple. Banish sloth,
fetter-feigning uncouth
fraud. Trapper Love with noble
noise, the magic sleuth,
as bird-notes prove—
first telecolor-trove—
illogically wove
what logic can't unweave:
you need not shoulder, need not shove.

Blessed is the Man

who does not sit in the seat of the scoffer—
   the man who does not denigrate, depreciate, denunciate;
   who is not "characteristically intemperate,"
who does not "excuse, retreat, equivocate; and will be heard."

(Ah, Giorgione! there are those who mongrelize
   and those who heighten anything they touch; although it
      may well be
   that if Giorgione's self-portrait were not said to be he,
it might not take my fancy. Blessed the geniuses who know

that egomania is not a duty.)
   "Diversity, controversy; tolerance"—in that "citadel
   of learning" we have a fort that ought to armor us well.
Blessed is the man who "takes the risk of a decision,"—asks

himself the question: "Would it solve the problem?
   Is it right as I see it? Is it in the best interests of all?"
   Alas. Ulysses' companions are now political—
living self-indulgently until the moral sense is drowned,

having lost all power of comparison,
   thinking license emancipates one, "slaves whom they
      themselves have bound."
   Brazen authors, downright soiled and downright spoiled,
      as if sound
and exceptional, are the old quasi-modish counterfeit,

Mitin-proofing conscience against character.
   Affronted by "private lies and public shame," blessed is
      the author
   who favors what the supercilious do not favor—
who will not comply. Blessed, the unaccommodating man.

Blessed is the man whose faith is different
   from possessiveness—of a kind not framed by "things which
      do appear"—
   who will not visualize defeat, too intent to cower;
whose illumined eye has seen the shaft that gilds the sultan's tower.

from O TO BE A DRAGON (1959)

O to Be a Dragon

    If I, like Solomon, . . .
    could have my wish—

    my wish . . . O to be a dragon,
a symbol of the power of Heaven—of silkworm
size or immense; at times invisible.
    Felicitous phenomenon!

I May, I Might, I Must

If you will tell me why the fen
appears impassable, I then
will tell you why I think that I
can get across it if I try.

A Jellyfish

Visible, invisible,
  a fluctuating charm
an amber-tinctured amethyst
  inhabits it, your arm
approaches and it opens
  and it closes; you had meant
to catch it and it quivers;
  you abandon your intent.

Values in Use

I attended school and I liked the place—
grass and little locust-leaf shadows like lace.

Writing was discussed. They said, "We create
values in the process of living, daren't await

their historic progress." Be abstract
and you'll wish you'd been specific; it's a fact.

What was I studying? Values in use,
"judged on their own ground." Am I still abstruse?

Walking along, a student said offhand,
"'Relevant' and 'plausible' were words I understand."

A pleasing statement, anonymous friend.
Certainly the means must not defeat the end.

Hometown Piece for Messrs. Alston and Reese

To the tune:
"Li'l baby, don't say a word: Mama goin' to buy you a mocking-bird.
Bird don't sing: Mama goin' to sell it and buy a brass ring."

"Millennium," yes; "pandemonium"!
Roy Campanella leaps high. Dodgerdom

crowned, had Johnny Podres on the mound.
Buzzie Bavasi and the Press gave ground;

the team slapped, mauled, and asked the Yankees' match,
"How did you feel when Sandy Amoros made the catch?"

"I said to myself"—pitcher for all innings—
"as I walked back to the mound I said, 'Everything's

getting better and better.'" (Zest, they've zest.
"'Hope springs eternal in the Brooklyn breast.'"

And would the Dodger Band in 8, row 1, relax
if they saw the collector of income tax?

Ready with a tune if that should occur:
"Why Not Take All of Me—All of Me, Sir?")

Another series. Round-tripper Duke at bat,
"Four hundred feet from home-plate"; more like that.

A neat bunt, please; a cloud-breaker, a drive
like Jim Gilliam's great big one. Hope's alive.

Homered, flied out, fouled? Our "stylish stout"
so nimble Campanella will have him out.

A-squat in double-headers four hundred times a day,
he says that in a measure the pleasure is the pay:

catcher to pitcher, a nice easy throw
almost as if he'd just told it to go.

Willie Mays should be a Dodger. He should—
a lad for Roger Craig and Clem Labine to elude;

but you have an omen, pennant-winning Peewee,
on which we are looking superstitiously.

Ralph Branca has Preacher Roe's number; recall?
and there's Don Bessent; he can really fire the ball.

As for Gil Hodges, in custody of first—
"He'll do it by himself." Now a specialist versed

in an extension reach far into the box seats—
he lengthens up, he leans, and gloving the ball defeats

expectation by a whisker. The modest star,
irked by one misplay, is no hero by a hair;

in a strikeout slaughter when what could matter more,
he lines a homer to the signboard and has changed the score.

Then for his nineteenth season, a home run—
with four of six runs batted in—Carl Furillo's the big gun;

almost dehorned the foe—has fans dancing in delight.
Jake Pitler and his Playground "get a Night"—

Jake, that hearty man, made heartier by a harrier
who can bat as well as field—Don Demeter.

Shutting them out for nine innings—a hitter too—
Carl Erskine leaves Cimoli nothing to do.

Take off the goat-horns, Dodgers, that egret
which two very fine base-stealers can offset.

You've got plenty: Jackie Robinson
and Campy and big Newk, and Dodgerdom again
watching everything you do. You won last year. Come on.

Enough

Jamestown, 1607–1957

Some in the Godspeed, the Susan C.,
others in the Discovery,

found their too earthly paradise.
Dazzled, the band, with grateful cries

clutched the soil; then worked upstream,
safer if landlocked, it would seem;

to pests and pestilence instead—
the living outnumbered by the dead.

Their namesake ships traverse the sky
as jets to Jamestown verify.

The same reward for best and worst
doomed communism, tried at first.

Three acres each, initiative,
six bushels paid back, they could live.

Captain Dale became kidnapper—
the master—lawless when the spur

was desperation, even though
his victim had let her victim go—

Captain John Smith. Poor Powhatan
had to make peace, embittered man.

Then teaching—insidious recourse—
enhanced Pocahontas and flowered of course

in marriage. John Rolfe fell in love
with her and she—in rank above

what she became—renounced her name
yet found her status not too tame.

The crested moss-rose casts a spell;
its bud of solid green, as well,

and the Old Pink Moss—with fragrant wings
imparting balsam scent that clings

where redbrown tanbark holds the sun,
resilient beyond comparison.

Not to begin with. No select
artlessly perfect French effect

mattered at first. (Small point to rhymes
for maddened men in starving-times.)

Tested until unnatural,
one became a cannibal.

Marriage, tobacco, and slavery,
initiated liberty

when the Deliverance brought seed
of that now controversial weed—

a blameless plant Red-Ridinghood.
Who, after all, knows what is good!

A museum of the mind "presents";
one can be stronger than events.

The victims of a search for gold
cast yellow soil into the hold.

With nothing but the feeble tower
to mark the site that did not flower,

could the most ardent have been sure
that they had done what would endure?

It was enough; it is enough
if present faith mend partial proof.

Melchior Vulpius
c. 1560–1615

a contrapuntalist—
             composer of chorales
and wedding-hymns to Latin words
but best of all an anthem:
  "God be praised for conquering faith
  which feareth neither pain nor death."

We have to trust this art—
             this mastery which none
can understand. Yet someone has
acquired it and is able to
  direct it. Mouse-skin-bellows'-breath
  expanding into rapture saith

"Hallelujah." Almost
             utmost absolutist
and fugue-ist, Amen; slowly building
from miniature thunder,
  crescendos antidoting death—
  love's signature cementing faith.

No better than "a withered daffodil"

Ben Johnson said he was? "O I could still
Like melting snow upon some craggy hill,
　　　Drop, drop, drop, drop."

I too until I saw that French brocade
blaze green as though some lizard in the shade
　　　became exact—

set off by replicas of violet—
like Sidney, leaning in his striped jacket
　　　against a lime—

a work of art. And I too seemed to be
an insouciant rester by a tree—
　　　no daffodil.

In the Public Garden

Boston has a festival—
compositely for all—
and nearby, cupolas of learning
(crimson, blue, and gold) that
    have made education individual.

My first—an exceptional,
an almost scriptural—
taxi-driver to Cambridge from Back Bay said
as we went along, "They
    make some fine young men at Harvard." I recall

the summer when Faneuil Hall
had its weathervane with gold ball
and grasshopper, gilded again by
a -leafer and -jack
    till it glittered. Spring can be a miracle

there—a more than usual
bouquet of what is vernal—
"pear blossoms whiter than the clouds," pin-
oak leaves barely showing
    when other trees are making shade, besides small

fairy iris suitable
for Dulcinea del
Toboso; O yes, and snowdrops
in the snow, that smell like
    violets. Despite secular bustle,

let me enter King's Chapel
to hear them sing: "My work be praise while
others go and come. No more a stranger
or a guest but like a child
    at home." A chapel or a festival

means giving what is mutual,
even if irrational:
black sturgeon-eggs—a camel

from Hamadan, Iran;
   a jewel, or, what is more unusual,

   silence—after a word-waterfall of the banal—
   as unattainable
as freedom. And what is freedom for?
For "self-discipline," as our
   hardest-working citizen has said—a school;

   it is for "freedom to toil"
   with a feel for the tool.
Those in the trans-shipment camp must have
a skill. With hope of freedom hanging
   by a thread—some gather medicinal

   herbs which they can sell.
   Ineligible if they ail.
         Well?

There are those who will talk for an hour
without telling you why they have
   come. And I? This is no madrigal—

   no medieval gradual—
   but it is a grateful tale.
Without that radiance which poets
are supposed to have—
   unofficial, unprofessional, still one need not fail

   to wish poetry well
   where intellect is habitual—
glad that the Muses have a home and swans—
that legend can be factual;
   happy that Art, admired in general,
   is always actually personal.

The Arctic Ox (or Goat)

Derived from "Golden Fleece of the Arctic," by John J. Teal, Jr., who rears musk oxen on his farm in Vermont, as set forth in the March 1958 issue of the Atlantic Monthly.

To wear the arctic fox
you have to kill it. Wear
   qiviut—the underwool of the arctic ox—
pulled off it like a sweater;
your coat is warm; your conscience, better.

I would like a suit of
qiviut, so light I did not
   know I had it on; and in the
course of time, another
since I had not had to murder

the "goat" that grew the fleece
that made the first. The musk ox
   has no musk and it is not an ox—
illiterate epithet.
Bury your nose in one when wet.

It smells of water, nothing else,
and browses goatlike on
   hind legs. Its great distinction
is not egocentric scent
but that it is intelligent.

Chinchillas, otters, water rats,
and beavers keep us warm
   but think! a "musk ox" grows six pounds
of *qiviut*; the cashmere ram,
three ounces—that is all—of pashm.

Lying in an exposed spot,
basking in the blizzard,
   these ponderosos could dominate
the rare-hairs market in Kashan and yet
you could not have a choicer pet.

They join you as you work;
love jumping in and out of holes,

play in water with the children,
learn fast, know their names,
    will open gates and invent games.

While not incapable
of courtship, they may find its
    servitude and flutter, too much
like Procrustes' bed;
so some decide to stay unwed.

Camels are snobbish
and sheep, unintelligent;
    water buffaloes, neurasthenic—
even murderous.
Reindeer seem over-serious,

whereas these scarce *qivies*,
with golden fleece and winning ways,
    outstripping every fur-bearer—
there in Vermont quiet—
could demand Bold Ruler's diet:

Mountain Valley water,
dandelions, carrots, oats—
    encouraged as well—by bed
made fresh three times a day,
to roll and revel in the hay.

Insatiable for willow
leaves alone, our goatlike
    qivi-curvi-capricornus
sheds down ideal for a nest.
Song-birds find *qiviut* best.

Suppose you had a bag
of it; you could spin a pound
    into a twenty-four-or-five-
mile thread—one, forty-ply—
that will not shrink in any dye.

If you fear that you are
reading an advertisement,
    you are. If we can't be cordial
to these creatures' fleece,
I think that we deserve to freeze.

Saint Nicholas,

might I, if you can find it, be given
a chameleon with tail
that curls like a watch spring; and vertical
on the body—including the face—pale
  tiger-stripes, about seven;
    (the melanin in the skin
    having been shaded from the sun by thin
      bars; the spinal dome
        beaded along the ridge
        as if it were platinum).

If you can find no striped chameleon,
might I have a dress or suit—
I guess you have heard of it—of *qiviut*?
and to wear with it, a taslon shirt, the drip-dry fruit
  of research second to none;
    sewn, I hope, by Excello;
    as for buttons to keep down the collar-points, no.
      The shirt could be white—
        and be "worn before six,"
        either in daylight or at night.

But don't give me, if I can't have the dress,
a trip to Greenland, or grim
trip to the moon. The moon should come here. Let him
make the trip down, spread on my dark floor some dim
  marvel, and if a success
    that I stoop to pick up and wear,
    I could ask nothing more. A thing yet more rare,
      though, and different,
        would be this: Hans von Marées'
        St. Hubert, kneeling with head bent,

form erect—in velvet, tense with restraint—
hand hanging down: the horse, free.
Not the original, of course. Give me
a postcard of the scene—huntsman and divinity—
  hunt-mad Hubert startled into a saint

by a stag with a Figure entined.
But why tell you what you must have divined?
   Saint Nicholas, O Santa Claus,
      would it not be the most
   prized gift that ever was!

For February 14th

Saint Valentine,
although late, would "some interested law
impelled to plod in the poem's cause"
        be unwelcome with a line?

Might you have liked a stone
from a De Beers Consolidated Mine?
or badger-neat saber-thronged thistle
        of Palestine—the leaves alone

down'd underneath,
worth a touch? or that mimosa-leafed vine
called an "Alexander's armillary
        sphere" fanning out in a wreath?

Or did the ark
preserve paradise-birds with jet-black plumes,
whose descendants might serve as presents?
        But questioning is the mark

of a pest! Why think
only of animals in connection
with the ark or the wine Noah drank?
        but that the ark did not sink.

Combat Cultural

One likes to see a laggard rook's high
speed at sunset to outfly the dark,
    or a mount well schooled for a medal—
front legs tucked under for the barrier,
    or team of leapers turned aerial.

I recall a documentary
of Cossacks: a visual fugue, a mist
    of swords that seemed to sever
heads from bodies—feet stepping as through
    harp-strings in a scherzo. However,

the quadrille of Old Russia for me:
with aimlessly drooping handkerchief
    snapped like the crack of a whip;
a deliriously spun-out-level
    frock-coat skirt, unswirled and a-droop

in remote promenade. Let me see . . .
Old Russia, did I say? Cold Russia
    this time: the prize bunnyhug
and platform-piece of experts in the
    trip-and-slug of wrestlers in a rug.

"Sacked" and ready for bed apparently—
with a jab, a kick, pinned to the wall,
    they work toward the edge and stick;
stagger off, and one is victim of a
    flipflop—leg having circled leg as thick.

Some art, because of high quality,
is unlikely to command high sales;
    yes, no doubt; but here, oh no;
not with the frozen North's Nan-ai-ans
    of the sack in their tight touch-and-go.

These battlers, dressed identically—
just one person—may, by seeming twins,
    point a moral, should I confess;
we must cement the parts of any
    objective symbolic of *sagesse*.

Leonardo da Vinci's

Saint Jerome and his lion
  in that hermitage
  of walls half gone,
    share sanctuary for a sage—
joint-frame for impassioned ingenious
    Jerome versed in language—
and for a lion like one on the skin of which
    Hercules' club made no impression.

The beast, received as a guest,
  although some monks fled—
  with its paw dressed
    that a desert thorn had made red—
stayed as guard of the monastery ass . . .
    which vanished, having fed
its guard, Jerome assumed. The guest then, like an ass,
    was made carry wood and did not resist,

but before long, recognized
  the ass and consigned
  its terrorized
    thieves' whole camel-train to chagrined
Saint Jerome. The vindicated beast and
    saint somehow became twinned;
and now, since they behaved and also looked alike,
    their lionship seems officialized.

Pacific yet passionate—
  for if not both, how
  could he be great?
    Jerome—reduced by what he'd been through—
with tapering waist no matter what he ate,
    left us the Vulgate. That in *Leo*,
the Nile's rise grew food checking famine,
    made lion's-mouth fountains appropriate,

if not universally,
  at least not obscure.
  And here, though hardly a summary, astronomy—
    or pale paint—makes the golden pair

in Leonardo da Vinci's sketch, seem
    sun-dyed. Blaze on, picture,
saint, beast; and Lion Haile Selassie, with household
    lions as symbol of sovereignty.

from THE ARCTIC OX (1964)

Blue Bug

Upon seeing Dr. Raworth Williams' Blue Bug with seven other ponies,
photographed by Thomas McAvoy: Sports Illustrated.

In this camera shot,
from that fine print in which you hide
(eight-pony portrait from the side),
    you seem to recognize
    a recognizing eye,
        limber Bug.
Only partly said, perhaps, it has been implied
that you seem to be the one to ride.

I don't know how you got your name
    and don't like to inquire.
        Nothing more punitive than the pest
    who says, "I'm trespassing," and
does it just the same.
        I've guessed, I think.
        I like a face that seems a nest,

a "mere container for the eye"—
    triangle-cornered—and
        pitchfork-pronged ears stiffly parallel:
    bug brother to an Arthur
Mitchell dragonfly,
    speeding to left,
        speeding to right; reversible,

like "turns in an ancient Chinese
    melody, a thirteen
        twisted silk-string three-finger solo."
    There they are, Yellow River-
scroll accuracies
    of your version
        of something similar—polo.

            Restating it:
            pelo, I turn,
        on *polos*, a pivot.

If a little elaborate,
Redon (Odilon) brought it to mind,
    his thought of the eye,
of revolving—combined somehow with pastime—
    pastime that is work,
muscular docility,
    also mentality,

as in the acrobat Li Siau Than,
    gibbonlike but limberer,
  defying gravity,
    nether side arched up,
    cup on head not upset—
China's very most ingenious man.

To Victor Hugo of My Crow Pluto

Even when the bird is walking, we know that it has wings.
Victor Hugo

Of:

my crow
Pluto,

the true
Plato,

azzuro-
negro

green-blue
rainbow.

Victor Hugo,
it is true:

we know
that the crow

"has wings," how
ever pigeon-toe-

inturned on grass. We do.
   (adagio)

Vivo-
roso

"corvo,"
although

con dizio-
nario

io parlo
Italiano

this pseudo
esperanto

which, savio
uccello, you

speak too—
my vow and motto

(beto e totto)
io giuro,

è questo
credo:

lucro
è peso morto.

And so
dear crow—

gioiello
mio—

I have to
let you go;

a bel bosco
generoso,

tottuto
vagabondo,

serafino
uvacceo.

Sunto,
oltramarino

verecondo
Plato, *addio*.

impromptu equivalents for *esperanto madinusa* (Made in U.S.A.) for
those who might not resent them:

azzuro-negro: blue-black
vivoroso: lively

gioiello mio: my jewel
a bel bosco: to lovely woods

con dizionario: with the
  dictionary
savio uccello: knowing bird
beto e totto: vow and motto
io giuro: I swear
è questo credo: is this credo
lucro è peso morto: Profit is a
  dead weight

tottuto vagabondo: the complete
  gypsy
serafino uvacceo: grape-black
  seraph
sunto: in short
verecondo: modest

Baseball and Writing

(Suggested by post-game broadcasts)

Fanaticism? No. Writing is exciting
and baseball is like writing.
   You can never tell with either
     how it will go
     or what you will do;
     generating excitement—
     a fever in the victim—
     pitcher, catcher, fielder, batter.
          Victim in what category?
*Owl*man watching from the press box?
       To whom does it apply?
       Who is excited? Might it be I?

It's a pitcher's battle all the way—a duel—
a catcher's, as, with cruel
    puma paw, Elston Howard lumbers lightly
      back to plate. (His spring
      de-winged a bat swing.)
    They have that killer instinct;
    yet Elston—whose catching
    arm has hurt them all with the bat—
       when questioned, says, unenviously,
    "I'm very satisfied. We won."
       Shorn of the batting crown, says, "We";
       robbed by a technicality.

When three players on a side play three positions
and modify conditions,
    the massive run need not be everything.
      "Going, going . . ." Is
      it? Roger Maris
    has it, running fast. You will
    never see a finer catch. Well . . .
    "Mickey, leaping like the devil"—why
       gild the cliché, deer sounds better—
    snares what was speeding towards its treetop nest,
      one-handing the souvenir-to-be
      meant to be caught by you or me.

Assign Yogi Berra to Cape Canaveral;
he could handle any missile.
   He is no feather. "Strike! . . . Strike *two!*"
   Fouled back. A blur.
   It's gone. You would infer
   that the bat had eyes.
   He put the wood to that one.
Praised, Skowron says, "Thanks, Mel.
   I think I helped a *little* bit."
         All business, each, and modesty.
Blanchard, Richardson, Kubek, Boyer.
      Who in that galaxy
      of nine won the pennant? Each. It was he.

Those two magnificent saves from the knee—throws
by Boyer, finesses in twos—
   like Whitey's three kinds of pitch and pre-
      diagnosis
      with pick-off psychosis.
   Pitching is a large subject.
   Your arm, too true at first, can learn to
   catch the corners—even trouble
         Mickey Mantle. ("Grazed a Yankee!
   My baby pitcher, Montejo!
      With some pedagogy,
      you'll be tough, premature prodigy.")

They crowd him and curve him and aim for the knees. Trying
indeed! The secret implying:
   "I can stand here, bat held steady."
      One may suit him;
      none has hit him.
   Imponderables smite him.
   Muscle kinks, infections, spike wounds
   require *food*, rest, respite from ruffians. (Drat it!
      Celebrity costs privacy!)
   Cow's milk, "tiger's milk," soy milk, carrot juice,
      brewer's yeast (high-potency)—
      concentrates presage victory

sped by Luis Arroyo, Hector Lopez—
deadly in a pinch. And "Yes,
   it's work; I want you to bear down,

but enjoy it
while you're doing it."
Mr. Houk and Mr. Sain,
if you have a rummage sale,
don't sell Roland Sheldon or Tom Tresh.
    Studded with stars in belt and crown,
the Stadium is an adastrium.
    O flashing Orion,
        your stars are muscled like the lion.

To a Giraffe

If it is unpermissible, in fact fatal
to be personal and undesirable

to be literal—detrimental as well
if the eye is not innocent—does it mean that

one can live only on top leaves that are small
reachable only by a beast that is tall?—

of which the giraffe is the best example—
the unconversational animal.

When plagued by the psychological
a creature can be unbearable

that could have been irresistible;
or to be exact exceptional

since less conversational
than some emotionally-tied-in-knots animal.

> After all
> consolations of the metaphysical
> can be profound. In Homer, existence

> is flawed; transcendence, conditional;
> the journey from sin to redemption, perpetual.

Arthur Mitchell

Slim dragonfly
too rapid for the eye
   to cage—
contagious gem of virtuosity—
make visible, mentality.
Your jewels of mobility

  reveal
    and veil
      a peacock-tail

Tell Me, Tell Me

where might there be a refuge for me
from egocentricity
and its propensity to bisect,
misstate, misunderstand,
and obliterate continuity?
Why, oh why, one ventures to ask, set
flatness on some cindery pinnacle
as if on Lord Nelson's revolving diamond rosette?

It appeared; gem, burnished rarity,
and peak of delicacy—
in contrast with grievance touched off on
any ground—the absorbing
geometry of a fantasy:
a James, Miss Potter, Chinese
"passion for the particular," of a
tired man who yet, at dusk,
cut a masterpiece of cerise—

for no tailor-and-cutter jury,
only a few mice to see—
who "breathed inconsistency and drank
contradiction," dazzled
not by the sun but by "shadowy
possibility." (I'm referring
to James, and Beatrix Potter's tailor.)
I vow, rescued tailor
of Gloucester, I am going

to flee; by engineering strategy—
the viper's traffic knot—flee
to metaphysical new-mown hay,
honeysuckle, or woods fragrance.
Might one say or imply T.S.V.P.—
Taisez-vous? "Please" does not make sense
to a refugee from verbal ferocity; I am
perplexed. Even so, "deference,"
yes, deference may be my defense.

A *précis*?
          In this told-backward biography
          of how the cat's mice, when set free
by the tailor of Gloucester, finished
the Lord Mayor's cerise coat,
          the tailor's tale ended captivity
               in two senses. Besides having told
of a coat which made the tailor's fortune,
it rescued a reader
               from being driven mad by a scold.

Rescue with Yul Brynner

*Appointed Special Consultant to the United Nations High Commissioner
for Refugees, 1959–60.*

"Recital? 'Concert' is the word,"
and stunning, by the Budapest Symphony—
    displaced but not deterred—
listened to by me,
        though with detachment then,
            like a grasshopper that did not
            know it missed the mower, a pigmy citizen;
            a case, I'd say, of too slow a grower.
There were thirty million; there are thirteen still—
healthy to begin with, kept waiting till they're ill.
History judges. It will
salute Winnipeg's incredible
conditions: "Ill; no sponsor; and no kind of skill."
    Odd—a reporter with guitar—a puzzle.
    Mysterious Yul did not come to dazzle.

    Magic bird with multiple tongue—
five tongues—equipped for a crazy twelve-month tramp
    (a plod), he flew among
the damned, found each camp
        where hope had slowly died
            (some had never seen a plane).
            Instead of feathering himself, he exemplified
                the rule that, self-applied, omits the gold.
He said, "You may feel strange; nothing matters less.
Nobody notices; you'll find some happiness.
No new 'big fear'; no distress."
Yul can sing—twin of an enchantress—
elephant-borne dancer in silver-spangled dress,
    swirled aloft by trunk, with star-tipped wand, Tamara,
    as true to the beat as Symphonia Hungarica.

    Head bent down over the guitar,
he barely seemed to hum; ended "all come home";
    did not smile; came by air;
did not have to come.
        The guitar's an event.

Guests of honor can't dance; don't smile.
"Have a home?" a boy asks. "Shall we live in a tent?"
"In a house," Yul answers. His neat cloth hat
has nothing like the glitter reflected on the face
of milkweed-witch seed-brown dominating a palace
that was nothing like the place
where he is now. His deliberate pace
is a king's, however. "You'll have plenty of space."
Yule—Yul log for the Christmas-fire tale-spinner—
of fairy tales that can come true: Yul Brynner.

Carnegie Hall: Rescued

It spreads, the campaign—carried on
by long-distance telephone,
    with Saint Diogenes
        supreme commander.
At the fifty-ninth minute
    of the eleventh hour, a rescuer

makes room for Mr. Carnegie's
music hall, which by degrees
    became (becomes)
        our music stronghold
    (accented on the "né," as
        perhaps you don't have to be told).

Paderewski's "palladian
majesty" made it a fane;
    Tchaikovsky, of course,
        on the opening
    night, 1891;
        and Gilels, a master, playing.

With Andrew C. and Mr. R.,
"our spearhead, Mr. Star"—
    in music, Stern—
        has grown forensic,
    and by civic piety
        has saved our city panic;

rescuer of a music hall
menaced by the "cannibal
    of real estate"—bulldozing potentate,
        land-grabber, the human crab
    left cowering like a neonate.

As Venice "in defense of children"
has forbidden for the citizen,
    by "a tradition of
        noble behavior,
    dress too strangely shaped or scant,"
        posterity may impute error

to our demolishers of glory. Cocteau's "Preface
to the Past" contains the phrase
   "When very young my dream
      was of pure glory."
   Must he say "was" of his "light
      dream," which confirms our glittering story?

They need their old brown home. Cellist,
violinist, pianist—
   used to unmusical
      impenetralia's
   massive masonry—have found
      reasons to return. Fantasias

of praise and rushings to the front
dog the performer. We hunt
   you down, Saint Diogenes—
      are thanking you for glittering,
   for rushing to the rescue
      as if you'd heard yourself performing.

An Expedient—Leonardo da Vinci's—and a Query

It was patience
  protecting the soul as clothing the body
from cold, so that "great wrongs
      were powerless to vex"—
      and problems that seemed to perplex
  him bore fruit, memory
making past present—
like "the grasp of the gourd,
          sure and firm."

"None too dull to
  be able to do one thing well. Unworthy
of praise, an orator
      who knows only one word,
      lacking variety." Height deterred
  from his verdure, any
polecat or snake that
might have burdened his vine:
          it kept them away.

With a passion,
  he drew flowers, acorns, rocks—intensively,
like Giotto, made Nature
      the test, Imitation—
      Rome's taint—did not taint what he'd done.
  He saw as treachery
the all-in-one-mould.
Peerless, venerated
          by all, he succumbed

to dejection. Could not
  the Leda with face matchless minutely—
      have lightened the blow?
      "Sad" . . . Could not Leonardo
  have said, "I agree; proof refutes me.
If all is mobility,
      mathematics won't do":
instead of, "Tell me if any thing
          at all has been done?"

from TELL ME, TELL ME (1966)

Granite and Steel

Enfranchising cable, silvered by the sea,
  of woven wire, grayed by the mist,
  and Liberty dominate the Bay—
  her feet as one on shattered chains,
  once whole links wrought by Tyranny.

Caged Circe of steel and stone,
  her parent German ingenuity.
  "O catenary curve" from tower to pier,
  implacable enemy of the mind's deformity,
  of man's uncompunctious greed,
  his crass love of crass priority,
      just recently
  obstructing acquiescent feet
  about to step ashore when darkness fell
      without a cause,
  as if probity had not joined our cities
      in the sea.

"O path amid the stars
  crossed by the seagull's wing!"
"O radiance that doth inherit me!"
  —affirming inter-acting harmony!

Untried expedient, untried; then tried;
  sublime elliptic two-fold egg—
  way out; way in; romantic passageway
  first seen by the eye of the mind,
  then by the eye. O steel! O stone!
  Climactic ornament, double rainbow,
  as if inverted by French perspicacity,
      John Roebling's monument,
      German tenacity's also;
      composite span—an actuality.

In Lieu of the Lyre

One debarred from enrollment at Harvard,
may have seen towers and been shown the Yard—
animated by Madame de Boufflers's choice rhymes:
Sentir avec ardeur: with fire; yes, with passion;
rime-prose revived also by word-wizard Achilles—
      Chinese Dr. Fang.

The *Harvard Advocate*'s formal-informal craftly rare
invitation to Harvard made grateful, Brooklyn's (or Mexico's)
      ineditos—
one whose "French aspect" was invented by
      Professor Levin,
a too outspoken outraged refugee from clichés particularly,
      who was proffered redress
      by the Lowell House Press—
Vermont Stinehour Press, rather. (No careless statements
to Kirkland House; least of all inexactness in quoting a fact.)

      To the *Advocate, gratia sum*
    unavoidably lame as I am, verbal pilgrim
like Thomas Bewick, drinking from his hat-brim,
drops spilled from a waterfall, denominated later by him
    a crystalline Fons Bandusian miracle.

It occurs to the guest—if someone had confessed it in time—
that you might have preferred to the waterfall, pilgrim and hat-brim,
    a nutritive axiom such as
"a force at rest is at rest because balanced by some other force,"
or "catenary and triangle together hold the span in place"
    (of a bridge),

or a too often forgotten surely relevant thing, that Roebling cable
    was invented by John A. Roebling.

    These reflections, Mr. Davis,
      in lieu of the lyre.

The mind, intractable thing

even with its own ax to grind, sometimes
helps others. Why can't it help me?

O imagnifico,
wizard in words—poet, was it, as
Alfredo Panzini defined you?
Weren't you refracting just now
on my eye's half-closed triptych
the image, enhanced, of a glen—
"the foxgrape festoon as sere leaves fell"
on the sand-pale dark byroad, one leaf adrift
from the thin-twigged persimmon; again,

a bird—Arizona
caught-up-with, uncatchable cuckoo
after two hours' pursuit, zigzagging
road-runner, stenciled in black
stripes all over, the tail
windmilling up to defy me?
You understand terror, know how to deal
with pent-up emotion, a ballad, witchcraft.
I don't. O Zeus and O Destiny!

Unafraid of what's done,
undeterred by apparent defeat,
you, imagnifico, unafraid
of disparagers, death, dejection,
have out-wiled the Mermaid of Zennor,
made wordcraft irresistible:
reef, wreck, lost lad, and "sea-foundered bell"—
as near a thing as we have to a king—
craft with which I don't know how to deal.

Dream

*(After coming on Jerome S. Shipman's comment concerning
academic appointments for artists)*

The committee—now a permanent body—
formed to do but one thing,
discover positions for artists, was worried, then happy;
rejoiced to have magnetized Bach and his family
    "to Northwestern," besides five harpsichords
    without which he would not leave home.
For his methodic unmetronomic melodic diversity
contrapuntally appointedly persistently
    irresistibly Fate-like Bach—find me words.

Expected to create for university
    occasions, inventions with wing,
was no problem after master-classes (stiffer in Germany),

each week a cantata; chorales, fugues, concerti!
    Here, students craved a teacher and each student worked.
    Jubilation! Re-rejoicings! Felicity!
    Repeated fugue-like, all of it, to infinity.
    (Note too that over-worked Bach was not irked.)

Haydn, when he had heard of Bach's billowing sail,
begged Prince Esterházy to lend him to Yale.
Master-mode expert fugue-al forms since, prevail.

    Dazzling nonsense . . . I imagine it? Ah! nach
    enough. J. Sebastian—born at Eisenach:
    its coat-of-arms in my dream: BACH PLAYS BACH!

Old Amusement Park

Before it became LaGuardia Airport

Hurry, worry, unwary
visitor, never vary
  the pressure till nearly bat-blind.
    A predicament so dire could not
    occur in this rare spot—

where crowds flock to the tramcar,
rattling greenish caterpillar,
  as bowling-ball thunder
    quivers the air. The park's elephant
    slowly lies down aslant;

then pygmy replica rides
the mound the back provides.
  Jet black, a furry pony sits
    down like a dog, has an innocent air—
    no tricks—the best act there.

It's all like the never-ending
Ferris-wheel ascending
  picket-fenced pony-rides (ten cents).
    A businessman, the pony-paddock boy
    locks his equestrian toy—

flags flying, fares collected,
shooting gallery neglected—
  half-official, half-sequestered,
    limber-slouched against a post,
    and tells a friend what matters least.

It's the old park in a nutshell,
like its tame-wild carrousel—
  the exhilarating peak
    when the triumph is reflective
    and confusion, retroactive.

W. S. Landor

There
is someone I can bear—
  "a master of indignation . . .
meant for a soldier
  converted to letters," who could

throw
a man through the window
  yet, "tender toward plants," say "Good God,
the violets!" (below).
  "Accomplished in every

style
and tint"—considering meanwhile
  infinity and eternity,
he could only say, "I'll
  talk about them when I understand them."

Charity Overcoming Envy

(Late-fifteenth-century tapestry, Flemish or French, in the Burrell
Collection, Glasgow Art Gallery and Museum)

Have you time for a story
(depicted in tapestry)?
Charity, riding an elephant,
on a "mosaic of flowers," faces Envy,
the flowers "bunched together, not rooted."
Envy, on a dog, is worn down by obsession,
his greed (since of things owned by others
he can only take *some*). Crouching uneasily
in the flowered filigree, among wide weeds
    indented by scallops that swirl,
little flattened-out sunflowers,
thin arched coral stems, and—ribbed horizontally—
slivers of green, Envy, on his dog,
    looks up at the elephant,
cowering away from her, his cheek scarcely scratched.
    He is saying, "O Charity, pity me, Deity!
O pitiless Destiny,
    what will become of me,
maimed by Charity—*Caritas*—sword unsheathed
over me yet? Blood stains my cheek. I am hurt."
In chest armor over chain mail, a steel shirt
to the knee, he repeats, "I am hurt."
The elephant, at no time borne down by self-pity,
    convinces the victim
that Destiny is not devising a plot.

The problem is mastered—insupportably
tiring when it was impending.

Deliverance accounts for what sounds like an axiom.

    The Gordian knot need not be cut.

Saint Valentine,

permitted to assist you, let me see . . .
   If those remembered by you
are to think of you and not me,
      it seems to me that the memento
      or compliment you bestow
should have a name beginning with "V,"

such as Vera, El Greco's only
   daughter (though it has never been
proved that he had one), her starchy
   veil, inside chiffon; the stone in her
   ring, like her eyes; one hand on
her snow-leopard wrap, the fur widely

dotted with black. It could be a vignette—
   a replica, framed oval—
bordered by a vine or vinelet.
   Or give a mere flower, said to mean the
   love of truth or truth of
love—in other words, a violet.

Verse—unabashedly bold—is appropriate;
   and always it should be as neat
as the most careful writer's "8."
   Any valentine that is *written*
Is as the *vendange* to the vine.
   Might verse not best confuse itself with fate?

POEMS 1963–1970

I've been Thinking . . .

Make a fuss
and be tedious.

I'm annoyed?
yes; am—avoid

"adore"
and "bore";

am, I
say, by

the word
bore, bored;

refuse
to use

"divine"
to mean

something
pleasing;

"terrific color"
for some horror.

Though flat,
myself, I'd say that

"Atlas"
(pressed glass)

looks best
embossed.

I refuse
to use

"enchant,"
"dement";

even "fright-
ful plight"
(however justified)

or "frivol-
ous fool"
(however suitable).

I've escaped?
am still trapped

by these
word diseases.

No pauses—
the phrases

lack lyric
force; sound capric-

like Attic
capric-Alcaic,

or freak
calico-Greek.

(Not verse
of course)
I'm sure of this:

Nothing mundane is divine;
Nothing divine is mundane.

Love in America?

Whatever it is, it's a passion—
a benign dementia that should be
engulfing America, fed in a way
   the opposite of the way
in which the Minotaur was fed.
It's a Midas of tenderness;
   from the heart;
nothing else. From one with ability
to bear being misunderstood—
   take the blame, with "nobility
   that is action," identifying itself with
   pioneer unperfunctoriness

   without brazenness or
   bigness of overgrown
   undergrown shallowness.

Whatever it is, let it be without
   affectation.

Yes, yes, yes, *yes.*

Tippoo's Tiger

The tiger was his prototype.
The forefeet of his throne were tiger's feet.
He mounted by a four-square pyramid of silver stairs converging
        as they rose.

The jackets of his infantry and palace guard
    bore little woven stripes incurved like buttonholes.

Beneath the throne an emerald carpet lay.
Approaching it, each subject kissed nine times
the carpet's velvet face of meadow-green.

Tipu owned sixteen hunting-cats to course the antelope
until his one great polecat ferret with exciting tail
escaped through its unlatched hut-door along a plank
above a ditch; paused, drank, and disappeared—
    precursor of its master's fate.

His weapons were engraved with tiger claws and teeth
in spiral characters that said the conqueror is God.
The infidel claimed Tipu's helmet and cuirasse
and a vast toy, a curious automaton—
a man killed by a tiger; with organ pipes inside
from which blood-curdling cries merged with inhuman groans.
The tiger moved its tail as the man moved his arm.

    This ballad still awaits a tiger-hearted bard.
      Great losses for the enemy
    cannot make one's own loss less hard.

The Camperdown Elm

Gift of Mr. A. G. Burgess to Prospect Park, Brooklyn, 1872.

I think, in connection with this weeping elm,
of "Kindred Spirits" at the edge of a rockledge
      overlooking a stream:
Thanatopsis-invoking tree-loving Bryant
conversing with Timothy Cole
in Asher Durand's painting of them
under the filigree of an elm overhead.

No doubt they had seen other trees—lindens,
maples and sycamores, oaks and the Paris
street-tree, the horse-chestnut; but imagine
their rapture, had they come on the Camperdown elm's
massiveness and "the intricate pattern of its branches,"
arching high, curving low, in its mist of fine twigs.
The Bartlett tree-cavity specialist saw it
and thrust his arm the whole length of the hollowness
of its torso and there were six small cavities also.

Props are needed and tree-food. It is still leafing;
still there; *mortal* though. We must save it. It is
      our crowning curio.

Mercifully,

I am hard to disgust,
but a pretentious poet can do it;
a person without a taproot; and
impercipience can do it; did it.

But why talk about it—
offset by Musica Antiqua's
"legendary performance"
of impassioned exactitude.

What an elate tongue is music,
the plain truth—complex truth—
in which unnatural emphases,
"passi-on" and "divis-i-on,"
sound natural. Play it all; *do*—
except in uproars of conversation.

Celestial refrain. My mind
hears it again. Without music
life is flat—bare existence.
Dirgelike David and Absalom. That.
     Let it be that.

"Like a Wave at the Curl"

On a kind of Christmas Day—
big flakes blurring everything,

cat-power matching momentum,

each kitten having capsized the other,

    one kitten fell;

the other's hind leg planted hard

on the eye that had guided the onslaught—

ears laid back, both tails lashing—

a cynic might have said, "Sir Francis

    Bacon defined it:

'Foreign war is like the heat of exercise;
civil war, like the heat of a fever.'"

Not at all. The expert would say,

    "Rather hard on the fur."

Enough

Am I a fanatic? The opposite.
    And where would I like to be?
    Sitting under Plato's olive tree
or propped against its thick old trunk,

        away from controversy
        or anyone choleric.

If you would see stones set right, unthreatened
    by mortar (masons say "mud"),
    squared and smooth, let them rise as they should,
Ben Jonson said, or he implied.

        In "Discoveries" he then said,
        "Stand for truth, and 'tis enough."

The Magician's Retreat

of moderate height.
(I have seen it)
cloudy but bright inside
like a moonstone,
while a yellow glow
from a shutter-crack shone,
a cat's-eye yellow crack in the shutter,
and a blue glow from the lamppost
close to the front door.
It left nothing of which to complain,
nothing more to obtain,
consummately plain.

A black tree mass rose at the back
almost touching the eaves
with the definiteness of Magritte,
was above all discreet.

APPENDIX: POEMS 1915–1918

To a Man Working his Way through the Crowd

To Gordon Craig: Your lynx's eye
Has found the men most fit to try
   To serve you. Ingenious creatures follow in your wake.

Your speech is like Ezekiel's;
You make one feel that wrath unspells
   Some mysteries—some of the cabals of the vision.

The most propulsive thing you say,
Is that one need not know the way,
   To be arriving. That foreword smacks of retrospect.

Undoubtedly you overbear,
But one must do that to come where
   There is a space, a fit gymnasium for action.

To the Soul of "Progress"

You use your mind
Like a mill stone to grind
    Chaff.

You polish it
And with your warped wit
    Laugh

At your torso,
Prostrate where the crow—
    Falls

On such kind hearts
As its God imparts—
    Calls,

And claps its wings
Till the tumult brings
    More

Black minute-men
To revive again,
    War

At little cost
They cry for the lost
    Head

And seek their prize
Till the evening sky's
    Red.

That Harp You Play So Well

O David, if I had
Your power, I should be glad—
  In harping, with the sling,
  In patient reasoning!

Blake, Homer, Job, and you,
Have made old wine-skins new.
  Your energies have wrought
  Stout continents of thought.

But, David, if the heart
Be brass, what boots the art
  Of exorcising wrong,
  Of harping to a song?

The scepter and the ring
And every royal thing
  Will fail. Grief's lustiness
  Must cure that harp's distress.

Counseil to a Bacheler

Elizabethan Trencher Motto—Bodleian Library:
[with title and modification of second line]

If thou bee younge, then marie not yett;
If thou bee olde, then no wyfe gett;
For younge mens' wyves will not bee taught,
And olde mens' wyves bee good for naught.

Appellate Jurisdiction

Fragments of sin are a part of me.
New brooms shall sweep clean the heart of me.
   Shall they? Shall they?

When this light life shall have passed away,
God shall redeem me, a castaway.
   Shall He? Shall He?

To William Butler Yeats on Tagore

It is made clear by the phrase,
Even the mood—by virtue of which he says

The thing he thinks—that it pays,
To cut gems even in these conscience-less days;

But the jewel that always
Outshines ordinary jewels, is your praise.

To a Friend in the Making

You wild, uncooked young fellow!
  The swinkèd hind will stumble home
    Not looking at the tasks he scorned to shirk.
  Impelled to respite by rough hands,
The labored ox will bellow;
    While you stand there agape before your handiwork.

Not all good men are mellow.
  You savor of a walnut rind,
    Of oak leaves, or plucked mullein on the brae.
  And yet with all your clumsiness,
You give me pleasure, fellow;
    Your candor compensates me for my old bouquet.

Blake

I wonder if you feel as you look at us,
As if you were seeing yourself in a mirror at the end
    Of a long corridor—walking frail-ly.
I am sure that we feel as we look at you,
As if we were ambiguous and all but improbable
    Reflections of the sun—shining pale-ly.

Diogenes

Day's calumnies,
Midnight's translucencies,
  Pride's open book
Of closed humilities—
  With its inflated look;
Shall contrarieties
As feasible as these
   Confound my wit?

Is Persian cloth
One thread with Persian sloth?
  Is gold dust bran?
Though spotted Ashtaroth
  Is not a Puritan,
Must every gorgeous moth
Be calico, and Thoth
   Be thanked for it?

Feed Me, Also, River God

Lest by diminished vitality and abated
  Vigilance, I become food for crocodiles—for that quicksand
  Of gluttony which is legion. It is there—close at hand—
    On either side
    Of me. You remember the Israelites who said in pride

And stoutness of heart: "The bricks are fallen down, we will
  Build with hewn stone, the sycamores are cut down, we will
      change to
  Cedars?" I am not ambitious to dress stones, to renew
    Forts, nor to match
    My value in action, against their ability to catch

Up with arrested prosperity. I am not like
Them, indefatigable, but if you are a god you will
Not discriminate against me. Yet—if you may fulfill
    None but prayers dressed
    As gifts in return for your own gifts—disregard the request.

He Made This Screen

Not of silver nor of coral,
But of weatherbeaten laurel.

Here, he introduced a sea
Uniform like tapestry;

Here, a fig-tree; there, a face;
There, a dragon circling space—

Designating here, a bower;
There, a pointed passion-flower.

Holes Bored in a Workbag by the Scissors

A neat, round hole in the bank of the creek
    Means a rat;
        That is to say, craft, industry, resourcefulness:
        While
These indicate the unfortunate, meek
    Habitat
        Of surgery thrust home to fabricate useless
        Voids.

Apropos of Mice

Come in, Rat, and eat with me;
One must occasionally—
    If one would rate the rat at his true worth—
    Practice catholicity.

Cheeseparings and a porkrind
Stock my house—good of their kind
    But were they not, you would oblige me? Is
    Plenty, multiplicity?

The Just Man And

His pie. "I would be
Repossessed of all the
Superlatives that I have squandered,
That I might use them in praise of it."

The four and twenty
Birds were singing while he
Apportioned it off casually
And found in it nothing for himself.

In "Designing a Cloak to Cloak his Designs," you
Wrested from Oblivion, a Coat of Immortality for
your own Use.

Cowed by his uningenious will
Of dragon-like demeanor, till
    It left them orphans.

His foibles clustered underneath
Him, dominated by a wreath
    Of upright half notes.

Encumbered as he was with pride,
But for that coat he might have died
    So despicably

That kindness might have seemed unkind
Had not the garment been designed
    To serve two masters.

The Past is the Present

Revived bitterness
is unnecessary unless
   One is ignorant.

To-morrow will be
Yesterday unless you say the
   Days of the week back-

Ward. Last weeks' circus
Overflow frames an old grudge. Thus:
   When you attempt to

Force the doors and come
At the cause of the shouts, you thumb
   A brass nailed echo.

You Say You Said

"Few words are best."
    Not here. Discretion has been abandoned in this part of the
                world too lately
    For it to be admired. Disgust for it is like the
Equinox—all things in

One. Disgust is
    No psychologist and has not opportunity to be a hypocrite.
    It says to the saw-toothed bayonet and to the cue
Of blood behind the sub-

Marine—to the
    Poisoned comb, to the Kaiser of Germany and to the intolerant
    gateman at the exit from the eastbound express: "I hate
You less than you must hate

Yourselves: You have
    Accoutred me. 'Without enemies one's courage flags.' Your error
              has been timed
    To aid me, I am in debt to you for you have primed
Me against subterfuge."

Old Tiger

You are right about it; that wary,
presumptuous young baboon is nothing to you; and the chimpanzee?
  An exemplary hind leg hanging like a plummet at the end of a

string—the tufts of fur depressed like grass
on which something heavy has been lying—nominal ears of black
      glass—
  what is there to look at? And of the leopard, spotted underneath
      and on

its toes; of the American rattler,
his eyes on a level with the crown of his head and of the lesser
  varieties, fish, bats, greyhounds and other animals of one thickness,

the same may be said, they are nothing
to you and yet involuntarily you smile; as at the dozing,
  magisterial hauteur of the camel or the facial expression

of the parrot: you to whom a no
is never a no, loving to succeed where all others have failed, so
  constituted that opposition is pastime and struggle is meat, you

see more than I see but even I
see too much; the select many are all but one thing to avoid, my
  prodigy and yours—as well as those mentioned above, who cannot
      commit

an act of self-destruction—the will
apparently having been made part of the constitution until
  it has become subsidiary, but observe; in that exposition

is their passion, concealment, yours, they
are human, you are inhuman and the mysterious look, the way
  in which they comport themselves and the conversation imported
      from the

birdhouse, are one version of culture.
You demur? To see, to realize with a prodigious leap is your
  version and that should be all there is of it. Possibly so, but
      when one

is duped by that which is pleasant, who
is to tell one that it is too much? Attempt to brush away the Foo
    dog and it is forthwith more than a dog, its tail superimposed
                    on its

self in a complacent half spiral—
incidentally so witty. One may rave about the barren wall
    or rave about the painstaking workmanship, the admirable subject;

the little dishes, brown, mulberry
or sea green, are half human and waiving the matter of artistry,
    anything which can not be reproduced, is "divine." It is as with the

book—that commodity inclusive
of the idea, the art object, the exact spot in which to live,
    the favorite item of wearing apparel. You have "read Dante's Hell

till you are familiar with it"—till
the whole surface has become so polished as to afford no little
    seam or irregularity at which to catch. So here, with the wise few;

the shred of superior wisdom
has engaged them for such a length of time as somehow to have
                become
    a fixture, without rags or a superfluous dog's ear by which to seize

it and throw it away before it
is worn out. As for you—forming a sudden resolution to sit
    still—looking at them with that fixed, abstracted lizardlike
            expression of

the eye which is characteristic
of all accurate observers, you are there, old fellow, in the thick
    of the enlightenment along with the cultured, the profusely
            lettered,

the intentionally hirsute—made
just as ludicrous by self appointedly sublime disgust, inlaid
    with wiry, jet black lines of objection. You, however, forbear
            when the

mechanism complains—scorning to
push. You know one thing, an inkling of which has not entered their
minds; you
know that it is not necessary to live in order to be alive.

MOORE'S NOTES

A Note on the Notes

A willingness to satisfy contradictory objections to one's manner of writing, might turn one's work into the donkey that finally found itself being carried by its masters, since some readers suggest that quotation-marks are disruptive of pleasant progress; others, that notes to what should be complete are a pedantry or evidence of an insufficiently realized task. But since in *Observations*, and in anything I have written, there have been lines in which the chief interest is borrowed, and I have not yet been able to outgrow this hybrid method of composition, acknowledgments seem only honest. Perhaps those who are annoyed by provisos, detainments, and postscripts, could be persuaded to take probity on faith, the will for the deed, the poem as a self-sufficiency, and disregard the notes.

M. M.

Observations

To a Prize Bird

Bernard Shaw

Injudicious Gardening

Letters of Robert Browning and Elizabeth Barrett; Harper. Vol. I, p. 513; "the yellow rose? 'Infidelity,' says the dictionary of flowers." Vol. II, p. 38: "I planted a full dozen more rose-trees, all white—to take away the yellow-rose reproach!"

To a Strategist

Disraeli

To a Steam Roller

"impersonal judgment": Lawrence Gilman

To a Snail

"compression is the first grace of style": Democritus
"method of conclusions"; "knowledge of principles": Duns Scotus

"The Bricks are Fallen Down, [. . .]"

Isaiah, 9:10

George Moore

Vale: Appleton, 1914; p. 82. "We certainly pigged it together, pigs no doubt, but aspiring pigs."

"Nothing will Cure the Sick Lion [. . .]"

Carlyle

To the Peacock of France

"taking charge"; "anchorites"; Molière: A Biography; H. C. Chatfield-Taylor; Chatto, 1907

In this Age of Hard Trying, [. . .]

"it is not the business of gods": Dostoyevsky

The Monkey Puzzler

the Chili pine: araucaria imbricata. Arauco—a territory in Araucania which is in the southern part of Chili: imbricatus—crooked like a gutter, or roof-tile; or laid one under another like tiles

"a certain proportion in the skeleton": Lafcadio Hearn; Talks to Writers; Dodd, Mead, 1920; p. 170

Poetry

Diary of Tolstoy; Dutton, p. 84: "Where the boundary between prose and poetry lies, I shall never be able to understand. The question is raised in manuals of style, yet the answer to it lies beyond me. Poetry is verse: prose is not verse. Or else poetry is everything with the exception of business documents and school books."

"literalists of the imagination": Yeats; Ideas of Good and Evil, 1903; William Blake and his Illustrations to The Divine Comedy; p. 182; "The limitation of his view was from the very intensity of his vision; he was a too literal realist of imagination, as others are of nature; and because he believed that the figures seen by the mind's eye, when exalted by inspiration were 'eternal existences,' symbols of divine essences, he hated every grace of style that might obscure their lineaments."

The Past is the Present

"Hebrew poetry is prose": The Reverend Edwin H. Kellogg

Pedantic Literalist

All excerpts from Richard Baxter: The Saints' Everlasting Rest;
Lippincott, 1909

"He Wrote The History Book"

At the age of five or six, John Andrews, son of Dr. C. M. Andrews,
replied when asked his name: "My name is John Andrews. My father
wrote the history book."

To be Liked by You [. . .]

"Attack is more piquant than concord": Hardy

Sojourn in the Whale

"water in motion is far from level": Literary Digest

My Apish Cousins

An old gentleman during a game of chess: "It is difficult to recall the
appearance of what one might call the minor acquaintances twenty
years back."

In the Days of Prismatic Color

"Part of it was crawling": Nestor; Greek Anthology; Loeb Classical
Library; Vol. III, p. 129

Peter

A black-and-white cat owned by Miss Magdalen Hueber and Miss
Maria Weniger

Picking And Choosing

feeling: T. S. Eliot; In Memory; The Little Review; August 1918.
"James's critical genius comes out most tellingly in his mastery over,
his baffling escape from, Ideas; a mastery and an escape which are
perhaps the last test of a superior intelligence. He had a mind so fine
that no idea could violate it . . . In England ideas run wild and pasture

on the emotions; instead of thinking with our feelings (a very different thing) we corrupt our feelings with ideas; we produce the political, the emotional idea, evading sensation and thought."

"sad French greens": The Compleat Angler

"top of a *diligence*": Preparatory school boy translating Caesar; recollected by Mr. E. H. Kellogg

"right good salvo of barks"; "strong wrinkles": Xenophon; Cynegeticus

England

"chrysalis of the nocturnal butterfly": Erté

"I envy nobody": The Compleat Angler

When I Buy Pictures

snipe legged hieroglyphic: Egyptian low relief in The Metropolitan Museum

"A silver fence was erected by Constantine to enclose the grave of Adam": Literary Digest, Jan. 5, 1918; a descriptive paragraph with photograph

Michael taking Adam: wash drawing by Blake; "Adam and Eve taken by Michael out of Eden."

"lit by piercing glances": A. R. Gordon; The Poets of The Old Testament; Hodder and Stoughton, 1912

The Labors of Hercules

the piano: someone writes of the smooth polished case of the piano offering temptation to one as a child, to draw on it with a pin

"charming tadpole notes": Review in the London Spectator

"the Negro is not brutal": The Reverend J. W. Darr

New York

fur trade: in 1921, New York succeeded St. Louis as the center of the wholesale fur trade

"as satin needlework": The Literary Digest, March 30, 1918, quotes Forest and Stream, March 1918—an article by George Shiras, 3rd:

"Only once in the long period that I have hunted or photographed these animals (white-tailed deer) in this region, have I seen an albino, and that one lingered for a year and a half about my camp, which is situated midway between Marquette and Grand Island. Signs were put up in the neighborhood reading: 'Do not shoot the white deer—it will bring you bad luck.' But tho the first part of the appeal stayed the hand of the sportsman, and the latter that of most pot-hunters, it was finally killed by an unsuperstitious homesteader, and the heretofore unsuccessful efforts to photograph it naturally came to an end.

"Some eight years ago word came that a fine albino buck had been frequently seen on Grand Island and that it came to a little pond on the easterly part of the island. Taking a camping outfit, a canoe, and my guide, several days and nights were spent watching the pond; . . . the white buck did not appear.

"The next year the quest was no more successful, and when I heard that on the opening of the season the buck had been killed by a lumberjack, it was satisfactory to know that the body had been shipped to a taxidermist in Detroit, preparatory to being added to the little museum of the island hotel.

"About the middle of June, 1916, a white fawn only a few days old was discovered in a thicket and brought to the hotel. Here, in the company of another fawn, it grew rapidly. During the earlier months this fawn had the usual row of white spots on the back and sides, and altho there was no difference between these and the body color, they were conspicuous in the same way that satin needlework in a single color may carry a varied pattern. . . . In June, 1917, one of these does bore an albino fawn, which lacked, however, the brocaded spots which characterized the previous one.

"It may be of interest to note that the original buck weighed 150 pounds and possessed a rather extraordinary set of antlers, spreading twenty-six inches, with terminal points much further apart than any I have ever seen. The velvet on the antlers . . . was snow-white, giving them a most statuesque appearance amid the green foliage of the forest. The eyes of the three native albinos are a very light gray-blue, while the doe has the usual red eyeballs; . . . and in the absence of accident or disease, there should soon be a permanent herd of these interesting animals."

picardel: an Elizabethan ruff

if the fur is not finer: Isabella, Duchess of Gonzaga. Frank Alvah Parsons; The Psychology of Dress; Doubleday, p. 68. "I wish black cloth even if it cost ten ducats a yard. If it is only as good as that

which I see other people wear, I had rather be without it."
"accessibility to experience": Henry James

People's Surroundings

"natural promptness": Ward's English Poets. Webbe—"a witty gentleman and the very chief of our late rhymers. Gifts of wit and natural promptness appear in him abundantly."

1420 pages. Advertisement; New York Times, June 13, 1921: "Paper—As Long as a Man, As Thin as a Hair. One of the Lindenmeyr Lines was selected by Funk & Wagnalls Company, publishers of The Literary Digest, and The Standard Dictionary, for their twelve page pamphlet on India Paper. India Paper is so extremely thin that many grew fearful of the results when the unwieldly size, 45 x 65 inches, was mentioned. No mill ever made so large a sheet of India Paper; no printer ever attempted to handle it. But S. D. Warren Company produced the paper and Charles Francis Press printed it—printed it in two colors with perfect register. Warren's India is so thin that 1420 pages make only one inch."

Persian velvet: Exhibition of Persian objects, Bush Terminal Building, December, 1919, under the auspices of the Persian Throne. Descriptive label—piece of 16th century brocaded velvet: "The design consists of single rose bushes in pearl white and pale black outline posed on a field of light brown ivory so that the whole piece bears the likeness of the leopard's spots."

Waterford: Irish glass

"a good brake": advertisement

municipal bat roost: experiment in San Antonio, Texas, to combat mosquitoes

"instant beauty": advertisement

Bluebeard's tower: limestone tower at St. Thomas, Virgin Islands; purports to be the castle of the traditional Bluebeard

"chessmen carved out of moonstones": Anatole France

"as an escalator cuts the nerve of progress": The Reverend J. W. Darr

"a setting": The Perfect Host; Vogue, August 1, 1921

captains of armies: Raphael; Horary Astrology

Snakes, Mongooses [. . .]

"the slight snake": George Adam Smith

plastic animal: Hegel: Philosophy of History; The Greek state was plastic, i.e. all of a piece

Bowls

"appear the first day": advertisement in French magazine

Novices

"Is it the buyer or the seller who gives the money?": Anatole France; Petit Pierre. Pierre's inquiry upon first visiting a chocolate shop

"dracontine cockatrices": Southey; The Young Dragon

"lit by the half lights of more conscious art": A. R. Gordon; The Poets of the Old Testament

"the smell of the cypress": Landor; Imaginary Conversations; Camelot Series, Walter Scott Publishing Company; page 52. Petrarca: "The smell of box, although not sweet, is more agreeable to me than many that are. . . . The cypress too seems to strengthen the nerves of the brain."

"that tinge of sadness": Arthur Hadyn; Illustrated London News, February 26, 1921. "The Chinese objects of art and porcelain dispersed by Messrs. Puttick and Simpson on the 18th, had that tinge of sadness which a reflective mind always feels; it is so little and so much."

"the authors are wonderful people": Leigh Hunt

"much noble vagueness": James Harvey Robinson; The Mind in the Making

"split like a glass against a wall": The Decameron; introduction by Morley; Cassell, 1908. Freaks of Fortune

"precipitate of dazzling impressions": W. R. Gordon; The Poets of the Old Testament

"fathomless suggestions of color": P. T. Forsyth; Christ on Parnassus; Hodder and Stoughton

"ocean of hurrying consonants": George Adam Smith; Expositor's Bible

"great livid stains": Faguet; Gustave Flaubert; Houghton, Mifflin

"flashing lances"; "molten fires": Leigh Hunt; Autobiography

"with foam on its barriers": George Adam Smith; Expositor's Bible

"crashing itself out": George Adam Smith; Expositor's Bible

Marriage

"of circular traditions": Francis Bacon

write simultaneously: Scientific American; January, 1922; Multiple Consciousness or Reflex Action of Unaccustomed Range. "Miss A—— will write simultaneously in three languages, English, German, and French, talking in the meantime. (She) takes advantage of her abilities in everyday life, writing her letters simultaneously with both hands; namely, the first, third, and fifth words with her left and the second, fourth, and sixth with her right hand. While generally writing outward, she is able as well to write inward with both hands."

"See her, see her in this common world": "George Shock"

"unlike flesh, stones": Richard Baxter; The Saints' Everlasting Rest; Lippincott, 1909

"something feline, something colubrine": Philip Littell; Books and Things; Santayana's Poems; New Republic, March 21, 1923. "We were puzzled and we were fascinated, as if by something feline, by something colubrine."

"treading chasms": Hazlitt; Essay on Burke's style

"past states": Baxter

"he experiences a solemn joy": Anatole France; Filles et Garçons; Hachette. A Travers Champs; "le petit Jean comprend qu'il est beau et cette idée le pénètre d'un respect profond de lui-même. . . . Il goûte une joie pieuse à se sentir devenu une idole."

"it clothes me with a shirt of fire": Hagop Boghossian; The Nightingale

"he dares not clap his hands": Edward Thomas; Feminine Influence on the Poets; Martin Secker, 1910. "The Kingis Quair—To us the central experience is everything—the strong unhappy king, looking out of the prison window and seeing the golden-haired maiden in rich attire trimmed with pearls, rubies, emeralds and sapphires, a chaplet of red, white and blue feathers on her head, a heart-shaped ruby on a chain of fine gold hanging over her white throat, her dress looped up carelessly to walk in that fresh morning of nightingales in the new-leaved thickets—her little dog with his bells at her side."

"illusion of a fire": Baxter

"as high as deep": Baxter

"very trivial object": Godwin: "marriage is a law and the worst of all laws . . . a very trivial object indeed."

"a kind of overgrown cupid": Brewer; Dictionary of Phrase and Fable

"the crested screamer": remark in conversation; Glenway Wescott

"for love that will gaze an eagle blind": Anthony Trollope; Barchester Towers, Vol. II

"No truth can be fully known": Robert of Sorbonne

"darkeneth her countenance as a bear doth": Ecclesiasticus; Women Bad and Good—An Essay; Modern Reader's Bible; Macmillan

"seldom and cold": Baxter

"Married people often look that way": C. Bertram Hartmann

"Ahasuerus tête à tête banquet": George Adam Smith; Expositor's Bible

"Good monster, lead the way": The Tempest

"Four o'clock does not exist": la Comtesse de Noailles; Femina, December, 1921. le Thè: "Dans leur impérieuse humilité elles jouent instinctivement leurs rôles sur le globe."

"What monarch": "The Rape of the Lock"; a satire in verse by Mary Frances Nearing with suggestions by M. Moore

"the sound of the flute": A. Mitram Rhibany; The Syrian Christ. Silence on the part of women—"to an Oriental, this is as poetry set to music" although "in the Orient as here, husbands have difficulty in enforcing their authority"; "it is a common saying that not all the angels in heaven could subdue a woman."

"men are monopolists": Miss M. Carey Thomas, President Emeritus of Bryn Mawr College. Founders address, Mount Holyoke College, 1921: "Men practically reserve for themselves stately funerals, splendid monuments, memorial statues, membership in academies, medals, titles, honorary degrees, stars, garters, ribbons, buttons and other shining baubles, so valueless in themselves and yet so infinitely desirable because they are symbols of recognition by their fellow craftsmen of difficult work well done."

"the crumbs from a lion's meal": Amos: 3; 12. Translation by George Adam Smith: Expositor's Bible

"a wife is a coffin": quoted by John Cournos from Ezra Pound

"settle on my hand": Charles Reade; Christie Johnston

"some have rights": Morley; Burke; English Men of Letters Series

"leaves her peaceful husband": Simone A. Puget; Change of Fashion; advertisement, English Review, June, 1914. "Thus proceed pretty dolls when they leave their old home to renovate their frame, and dear others who may abandon their peaceful husband only because they have seen enough of him."

"Everything to do with love is mystery": F. C. Tilney; The Original Fables of La Fontaine; Dutton. Love and Folly: Book XII, No. 14.

"I am such a cow": remark in conversation; Miss M. H. Tolman

"Liberty and Union": Daniel Webster

Silence

My father used to say: a remark in conversation; Miss A. M. Homans, Professor Emeritus of Hygiene, Wellesley College. "My father used to say, 'superior people never make long visits, then people are not so glad when you've gone.' When I am visiting, I like to go about by myself. I never had to be shown Longfellow's grave nor the glass flowers at Harvard."

"Make my house your inn": Edmund Burke to a stranger with whom he had fallen into conversation in a bookshop. Life of Burke: James Prior; "'Throw yourself into a coach,' said he. 'Come down and make my house your inn.'"

An Octopus

glass that will bend: Sir William Bell of the British Institute of Patentees has made a list of inventions which he says the world needs. The list includes glass that will bend; a smooth road surface that will not be slippery in wet weather; a furnace that will conserve 95 percent of its heat; a process to make flannel unshrinkable; a noiseless airplane; a motor engine of one pound weight per horse-power; methods to reduce friction; a process to extract phosphorus from vulcanized India rubber so that it can be boiled up and used again; practical ways of utilizing the tides

"Picking periwinkles": M. C. Carey; London Graphic, August 25, 1923

"spider fashion": W. P. Pycraft; Illustrated London News, June 28, 1924

"ghostly pallor": Francis Ward; Illustrated London News, August 11, 1923 "magnitude of their root systems": John Muir

"creepy to behold": W. P. Pycraft

"each like the shadow of the one beside it": Ruskin

"conformed to an edge": W. D. Wilcox; The Rockies of Canada; Putnam, 1903

"thoughtful beavers": Clifton Johnson; What to See in America; Macmillan

"blue stone forests": Clifton Johnson; What to See in America

"grottoes": W. D. Wilcox; The Rockies of Canada

"two pairs of trousers": W. D. Wilcox. "My old packer, Bill Peyto. He usually wears two pairs of trousers, one over the other, the outer pair about six months older. Every once in a while, Peyto would give one or two nervous yanks at the fringe and tear off the longer pieces, so that his outer trousers disappeared day by day from below upwards."

"deliberate wide eyed wistfulness": Olivia Howard Dunbar; review of Alice Meynell's prose; Post Literary Review, June 16, 1923. "There is no trace here of deliberate wide eyed wistfulness."

marmot: W. P. Taylor, Assistant Biologist, Bureau of Biological Survey, U. S. Department of Agriculture; "The clear and penetrating whistle of the hoary marmot is perhaps the best wild music of the mountains."

"glass eyes": W. D. Wilcox. A colorless condition of the retina, characteristic of the Indian pony or cayuse

"business men": W. D. Wilcox: "A crowd of the business men of Banff, who usually take about 365 holidays every year, stands around to offer advice."

"menagerie of styles": W. M.; The Mystery of an Adjective and of Evening Clothes; London Graphic, June 21, 1924: "Even in the Parisian menagerie of styles there remains this common feature that evening dress is always evening dress in men's wear. With women there is no saying whether a frock is meant for tea, dinner, or for breakfast in bed."

"bristling, puny, swearing men": Clifton Johnson

"They make a nice appearance, don't they?": Comment overheard at the circus

"Greek, that pride-producing language": Anthony Trollope; An Autobiography; Oxford University Press

"rashness is rendered innocuous": Cardinal Newman; Historical Sketches

"Like happy souls in hell": Richard Baxter; The Saints' Everlasting Rest

"so noble and so fair": Cardinal Newman; Historical Sketches

"complexities . . . an accident": Richard Baxter

"The Greeks were emotionally sensitive": W. D. Hyde; The Five Great Philosophies; Macmillan

"creeping slowly": Francis Ward

"tear the snow"; "flat on the ground"; "bent in a half circle": Clifton Johnson

"with a sound like the crack of a rifle": W. D. Wilcox

Quoted descriptions of scenery and of animals, of which the source is not given, have been taken from government pamphlets on our national parks

Sea Unicorns and Land Unicorns

"mighty monoceroses": Spenser

"disquiet shippers": Violet A. Wilson—Queen Elizabeth's Maids of Honour, (Lane)—quotes Olaus Magnus; History of the Goths and Swedes: "The sea serpent: he hath commonly hair hanging from his neck a cubit long, and sharp scales and is black, and he hath flameling shining eyes. This snake disquiets shippers and he puts up his head like a pillar, and catcheth away men."

a voyager: Violet A. Wilson; Queen Elizabeth's Maids of Honour. Thomas Cavendish: "He sailed up the Thames in splendour, the sails of his ship being cloth of gold and his seamen clad in rich silks. Many were the curiosities which the explorers brought home as presents for the ladies. The Queen naturally had first choice and to her fell the unicorn's horn valued at a hundred thousand pounds, which became one of the treasures of Windsor."

"abounding in land unicorns": Violet A. Wilson; "Hawkins affirmed the existence of land unicorns in the forests of Florida, and from their presence deducted abundance of lions because of the antipathy between the two animals, so that 'where the one is the other cannot be missing.'"

"in politics, in trade": Henry James; English Hours

"polished garlands"; "myrtle rods": J. A. Symonds

"cobwebs, and knotts, and mulberries": Queen Elizabeth's dresses. Violet A. Wilson; Queen Elizabeth's Maids of Honour: "a forepart of white satten, embrodered all over with pansies, little roses, knotts, and a border of mulberries, pillars, and pomegranets, of Venice golde, sylver, and sylke of sondrye colours. One forepart of green satten embrodered all over with sylver, like beasts, fowles, and fishes." "A petticoat embrodered all over slightly with snakes of Venice gold and silver and some O's, with a faire border embrodered like seas, cloudes, and rainbowes."

the long tailed bear of Ecuador: In his Adventures in Bolivia (Lane, 1922), p. 193, C. H. Prodgers tells of a strange animal that he bought: "It was stuffed with long grass and cost me ten shillings, turning out eventually to be a bear with a tail. In his book on wild life, Rowland Ward says, 'Amongst the rarest animals is a bear with a tail; this animal is known to exist, is very rare, and only to be found in the forest of Ecuador,' and this was where the man who sold it to me said he got it."

"deriving agreeable terror": Leigh Hunt. "The lover of reading will derive agreeable terror from Sir Bertram and The Haunted Chamber."

"moonbeam throat": Medieval—anonymous poem in Punch, April 25, 1923

an unmatched device: Bulfinch's Mythology. "Some described the horn as movable at the will of the animal, a kind of small sword in short, with which no hunter who was not exceedingly cunning in fence could have a chance. Others maintained that all the animal's strength lay in its horn, and that when hard pressed in pursuit it would throw itself from the pinnacle of the highest rocks horn foremost, so as to pitch on it, and then quietly march off not a whit the worse for its fall."

Herodotus says of the phoenix: "I have not seen it myself except in a picture."

"impossible to take alive": Pliny

"as straight": Charles Cotton, "An Epitaph on M. H.

As soft, and snowy, as that down
Adorns the Blow-ball's frizzled crown;
As straight and slender as the crest,
Or antlet of the one-beam'd beast;"

"improved all over": see "cobwebs"

"with pavon high"; "upon her lap": Medieval—anonymous poem in Punch, April 25, 1923

Poems 1932–1936

The Student

"In America." Les Ideals de l'Éducation Française; lecture, December 3, 1931, by M. Auguste Desclos, Director-adjoint. Office National des Universités et Écoles Françaises de Paris.

The singing tree. Each leaf was a mouth, and every leaf joined in concert. *Arabian Nights.*

Lux et veritas (Yale); *Christo et ecclesiae* (Harvard); *sapiet felici.* —

"Science is never finished." Professor Einstein to an American student; *New York Times.*

Jack Bookworm, in Goldsmith's *The Double Transformation.*

A variety of hero: Emerson in *The American Scholar*: "there can be no scholar without the heroic mind"; "let him hold by himself; . . . patient of neglect, patient of reproach."

The wolf. Edmund Burke, November, 1781, in reply to Fox: "there is excellent wool on the back of a wolf and therefore he must be sheared. . . . But will he comply?"

"Gives his opinion." Henry McBride in the *New York Sun,* December 12, 1931: "Dr. Valentiner . . . has the typical reserve of the student. He does not enjoy the active battle of opinion that invariably rages when a decision is announced that can be weighed in great sums of money. He gives his opinion firmly and rests upon that."

No Swan So Fine

"There is no water so still as the dead fountains of Versailles." Percy Phillip, *New York Times Magazine,* 10th May, 1931.

A pair of Louis XV candelabra with Dresden figures of swans belonging to Lord Balfour.

The Jerboa

The Popes' colossal fir-cone of bronze. "Perforated with holes, it served as a fountain. Its inscription states 'P. Cincius P. l. Salvius fecit.' See Duff's *Freedmen in the Early Roman Empire. The Periodical,* February, 1929 (Oxford University Press).

Stone locusts. Toilet-box dating from about the twenty-second Egyptian Dynasty. *Illustrated London News,* 26th July, 1930.

The king's cane. Description by J. D. S. Pendlebury. *Illustrated London News,* 19th March, 1932.

Folding bedroom. The portable bed-chamber of Queen Hetepheres presented to her by her son, Cheops. Described by Dr. G. A. Reisner. *Illustrated London News,* 7th May, 1932.

"There are little rats called jerboas which run on long hind-legs as thin as a match. The forelimbs are mere tiny hands." Dr. R. L. Ditmars: p. 274, *Strange Animals I Have Known.*

Camellia Sabina

The Abbé Berlèse; Monographie du Genre Camellia (H. Cousin).

Bordeaux merchants have spent a great deal of trouble. *Encyclopaedia Britannica.*

The French are a cruel race, etc. J. S. Watson, Jr.

A food grape. In Vol. I, *The Epicure's Guide to France* (Thornton Butterworth), Curnonsky and Marcel Rouff quote Monselet: "Everywhere else you eat grapes which have ripened to make wine. In France you eat grapes which have ripened for the table. They are a product at once of nature and of art." . . . The bunch "is covered and uncovered alternately, according to the intensity of the heat, to gild the grapes without scorching them. Those which refuse to ripen—and there are always some—are delicately removed with special scissors, as are also those which have been spoiled by the rain."

Wild parsnip. Edward W. Nelson, "Smaller Mammals of North America," *National Geographic Magazine,* May, 1918.

Mouse with a grape. Photograph by Spencer R. Atkinson, *National Geographic Magazine,* February, 1932. "Carrying a baby in her mouth and a grape in her right forepaw, a round-tailed wood rat took this picture."

The wire cage. Photograph by Alvin E. Worman of Attleboro, Massachusetts.

The Plumet Basilisk

Basiliscus Americanus Gray.

Guatavita Lake. Associated with the legend of El Dorado, the Gilded One. The king, painted with gums and powdered with gold-dust as symbolic of the sun, the supreme deity, was each year escorted by his nobles on a raft, to the center of the lake, in a ceremonial of tribute to the goddess of the lake. Here he washed off his golden coat by plunging into the water while those on the raft and on the shores chanted and threw offerings into the waters—emeralds or objects of gold, silver, or platinum. See A. Hyatt Verrill, *Lost Treasure* (Appleton-Century).

Frank Davis: *The Chinese Dragon. Illustrated London News;* 23rd August, 1930. "He is the god of Rain, and the Ruler of Rivers, Lakes, and Seas. For six months of the year he hibernates in the depths of the sea, living in beautiful palaces. . . .

"We learn from a book of the T'ang Dynasty that 'it may cause itself to become visible or invisible at will, and it can become long or short, and coarse or fine, at its own good pleasure.'"

A dragon "is either born a dragon (and true dragons have nine sons) or becomes one by transformation." There is a "legend of the carp that try to climb a certain cataract in the western hills. Those that succeed become dragons."

The Malay Dragon and the "basilisks". W. P. Pycraft, *Illustrated London News,* 6th February, 1932. The basilisk "will when alarmed drop to the water and scuttle along the surface on its hind-legs. . . . An allied species (Deiropteryx) can not only run along the surface of the water, but can also dive to the bottom, and there find safety till danger is past."

The Tuatera or Ngarara. In appearance a lizard—with characteristics of the tortoise; on the ribs, uncinate processes like a bird's; and crocodilian features—it is the only living representative of the order Rhynchocephalia. Shown by Captain Stanley Osborne in motion pictures. Cf. *Animals of New Zealand,* by F. W. Hutton and James Drummond (Whitcombe and Tombs).

A fox's bridge. The South American vine suspension bridge.

A seven-hundred-foot chain of gold weighing more than ten tons was being brought from Cuzco, as part of the ransom for Atahualpa. When news of his murder reached those in command of the convoy, they ordered that the chain be hidden, and it has never been found. See A. Hyatt Verrill, *Lost Treasure* (Appleton-Century).

The Frigate Pelican

Fregata aquila. The Frigate Pelican of Audubon.

Giant tame armadillo. Photograph and description by W. Stephen Thomas of New York.

Red-spotted orchids. The blood, supposedly, of natives slain by Pizarro.

"If I do well, I am blessed," etc. Hindu saying.

Nine Nectarines and Other Porcelain

Alphonse de Candolle: *Origin of Cultivated Plants* (Appleton, 1886). "The Chinese believe the oval peaches which are very red on one side, to be a symbol of long life. . . . According to the work of Chin-noug-king, the peach *Yu* prevents death. If it is not eaten in time, it at least preserves the body from decay until the end of the world."

"Brown beaks and cheeks." Anderson Catalogue 2301, to Karl Freund collection sale, 1928.

New York Sun, 2nd July, 1932. *The World To-day,* by Edgar Snow, from Soochow, China; "An old gentleman of China, whom I met when I first came to this country, volunteered to name for me what he called the 'six certainties.' He said: 'You may be sure that the clearest jade comes from Yarkand, the prettiest flowers from Szechuen, the most fragile porcelain from Kingtehchen, the finest tea from Fukien, the sheerest silk from Hangchow, and the most beautiful women from Soochow'. . ."

The kylin (or Chinese unicorn). Frank Davis: *Illustrated London News,* 7th March, 1931. 'It has the body of a stag, with a single horn, the tail of a cow, horse's hoofs, a yellow belly, and hair of five colours.'

See in the Midst of Fair Leaves

The leaves thereof were fair, and the fruit thereof much. *Daniel,* IV: 12.

Walking-Sticks and Paperweights and Watermarks

"Where leafy trees meet overhead." Travel page, *New York Sun.*

Little scars on churchbell-tongues. In *Little Known England,* Harold Donaldson Eberlein quotes John Leland: "there is the spire and choir of Saint Alkmund's where 'in the year 1533, uppon Twelffe daye, in Shrowsburie, the Dyvyll appeared . . . when the Preest was at High Masse, with great tempeste and Darknesse, soe that as he pasyd through, he mounted upp the Steeple in the sayd churche, tering the wyers of the clocke, and put the prynt of his clawes uppon the 4th bell, and tooke one of the pynnacles away with him, and for the Tyme stayde all the Bells in the churches within the sayd Towne, that they could neither toll nor ringe.'"

"Difficulty is ordained to check poltroons." Giordano Bruno.

"Stones grow," etc. Quotation in the *Vest Pocket Manual of Printing;* Inland Printer Co., Chicago.

Water marks: in book paper; oxhead (Van Gelder), swan (1411 and earlier), dolphin (Auvergne and earlier), crown (B. Cramer, Van Gelder, various Dutch papers, Kelmscott), eagle (Basle mill 1633), Umbrian crown (Umbria handmade), anvil (Kelmscott). Machine-made paper: eastern crown (Papyrus Regia), open crown (Eaton's [Berkshire] Souvenir Bond), jeweled crown (Lion Ledger), leopard (Florian); eagle (U. S. Government), quill (Crane's Post), acorn (Whiting).

"For those we love live and die:" motto surrounding pelican and young on an 18th century seal.

The fugue's reiterated chain: exposition, development, conclusion.

"On the first day of Christmas." "The Twelve Presents" in *Welcome Christmas: Legends, Carols, Stories* collected by Eleanor Graham (Dutton).

The Pangolin and Other Verse

Virginia Britannia

Virginia Britannia. See William Strachey: *Travaile into Virginia Britannia.*

a great sinner. Here lyeth the body of Robert Sherwood who was born in the Parish of Whitechapel near London, a great sinner who waits for a joyful resurrection.

Werewocomoco. Powhatan's capitol

strong sweet prison. Of Middle Plantation, now Williamsburg.

serpentine shadows. Of the University of Virginia's one-brick-thick wall designed by Thomas Jefferson.

deer-fur crown. Worn by Powhatan's werowances and, it is said, by Powhatan, who presented a deer-skin mantle—now in the Ashmolean—to Captain Christopher Newport when crowned by him and by Captain John Smith.

the lark. The British Empire Naturalists' Association has found that the hedge-sparrow sings seven minutes earlier than the lark.

Half Deity

tiger swallowtail of South America. *Papilio filesilans.*

this more peninsula-tailed one. *Papilio podalirius.*

it is not permitted. Edmund Gilligan: *The New York Sun,* December 1, 1934; Meeting the Emperor Pu Yi.

Zephyr's palm. Carved Marble Group by Jean Baptiste Boyer (Psyche trying to capture the butterfly held out on Zephyr's palm).

Goya. The portrait of Don Manuel Osorio De Zuñiga in which he stands to the left of three cats, holding in his hand a thread attached to the leg of a magpie.

Smooth Gnarled Crape Myrtle

See J. I. Lawrence: *The New York Sun,* June 23, 1934. "Bulbul is a broadly generic term like sparrow, warbler, bunting. . . . The legendary nightingale of Persia is the white-eared bulbul, *Pycnonotus leucotis,* richly garbed in black velvet, trimmed with brown, white, and saffron yellow; and it is a true bulbul, . . .

Edward FitzGerald told what Omar meant: that the speech of man changes and coarsens, but the bulbul sings eternally in the 'high-piping Pehlevi,' the pure heroic Sanskrit of the ancient poets."

"those who sleep in New York, but dream of London." Beau Nash: *The Playbill* January 1935.

"Joined in friendship, crowned by love." Battersea-box motto.

"without loneliness." Yoné Noguchi,—paraphrasing Saigyo. *The (London) Spectator,* February 15, 1935.

"By Peace Plenty By Wisdom Peace." Encircling two horns of plenty, one at either side of the caduceus, above clasped hands, on the title-page of the first edition of the Thomas Lodge *Rosalynde.*

The Pangolin

The "closing ear-ridge," and certain other detail, from "Pangolins," by Robert T. Hatt; *Natural History,* December, 1935—American Museum of Natural History.

stepping peculiarly. See Lyddeker's *Royal Natural History.*

Thomas of Leighton Buzzard vine. A fragment of ironwork in Westminster Abbey.

"'Fearful yet to be feared.'" See above, "Pangolins," by R. T. Hatt.

"A sailboat was the first machine." See *Power,* by F. L. Morse.

What Are Years

Rigorists

Sheldon Jackson (1834–1909). Dr. Jackson felt that to feed the Esquimo at government expense was not advisable, that whales having been almost exterminated, the ocean could not be restocked as a river can be with fish, and having prevailed on the Government to authorize the importing of reindeer from Siberia, he made an expedition during the summer of 1891, procured 16 reindeer—by barter—and later brought others. *Report on Introduction of Domestic Reindeer into Alaska, 1895; 1896; 1897; 1899,* by Sheldon Jackson, General Agent of Education in Alaska. U.S. Educ. Bureau, Washington.

Light is Speech

A man already harmed: Jean Calas, unjustly accused of murdering his son, and put to death, March 9, 1762. In vindicating him and his household, Voltaire "fut le premier qui S'éleva en sa faveur. Frapé de l'impossibilité du crime dont on acusait Calas le pere, ce fut lûy qui engagea le veuve a venir demander justice au Roy . . ." *The History of the Misfortunes of John Calas, a Victim to Fanaticism, to which is added a Letter from M. Calas To His Wife and Children; Written by M. De Voltaire.* Printed by P. Williamson. Edinburgh, M, DCC, LXXVI.

Creach'h d'Ouessant aeromaritime lighthouse, the first observable— as planned—by ships and planes approaching the continent from North or South America.

Montaigne, captured by bandits and unexpectedly released, says "I was told that I owed my deliverance to my bearing and the uncowed resoluteness of my speech, which showed that I was too good a fellow to hold up."

Littré (1801–1881) devoted the years 1839–1862 to translating and editing Hippocrates.

Bartholdy's Liberty.

"Tell me the truth," etc. Marshal Pétain.

"Animate whoever thinks of her." "Paradise Lost" by Janet Flanner in *Decision*, January, 1941.

He "Digesteth Harde Yron"

Lyly's *Euphues*: "the estrich digesteth harde yron to preserve his health."

The large sparrow. "Xenophon (Anabasis, I, 5, 2) reports many ostriches in the desert on the left . . . side of the middle Euphrates, on the way from North Syria to Babylonia." *Animals for Show and Pleasure in Ancient Rome* by George Jennison.

A symbol of justice, men in ostrich-skins, Leda's egg, and other allusions: *Ostrich Egg-shell Cups from Mesopotamia* by Berthold Laufer, The Open Court, May, 1926. "An ostrich plume symbolized truth and justice, and was the emblem of the goddess Ma-at, the patron saint of judges. Her head is adorned with an ostrich feather, her eyes are closed, . . . as Justice is blind-folded."

Six hundred ostrich brains. At a banquet given by Elagabalus. See above: *Animals for Show and Pleasure.*

Egg-shell goblets, e.g., the painted ostrich-egg cup mounted in silver-gilt by Elias Geier of Leipzig about 1589. *Antiques in and About London* by Edward Wenham; *New York Sun*, May 22, 1937.

Eight pairs of ostriches. See above: *Animals for Show and Pleasure.*

Sparrow-camel: στρουθοκάμελος.

Spenser's Ireland

Every name is a tune; it is torture; ancient jewelry; your trouble is their trouble: See *Ireland: The Rock Whence I Was Hewn* by Don Byrne; *National Geographic Magazine*, March, 1927.

The sleeves. In Maria Edgeworth—*Castle Rackrent* as edited by Professor Morley—Thady Quirk says, "I wear a long greatcoat . . . ; it holds on by a single button round my neck, cloak fashion."

Venus' mantle. Footnote, *Castle Rackrent*: "The cloak, or mantle, as described by Thady is of high antiquity. See Spenser, in his 'View of the State of Ireland.'"

"The sad-yellow-fly, made with the buzzard's wings"; and "the shell-fly, for the middle of July," Maria Edgeworth: *The Absentee.*

The guillemot; the linnet. *Happy Memories of Glengarry* by Denis O'Sullivan.

Earl Gerald. From a lecture by Padraic Colum.

Four Quartz Crystal Clocks

Bell T. leaflet, 1939, *"The World's Most Accurate Clocks*: In the Bell Telephone Laboratories in New York, in a 'time vault' whose temperature is maintained within 1/100 of a degree, at 41° Centigrade, are the most accurate clocks in the world—the four quartz crystal clocks. . . . When properly cut and inserted in a suitable circuit, they will control the rate of electric vibration to an accuracy of one part in a million. . . . When you call MEridian 7—1212 for correct time you get it every 15 seconds."

Jean Giraudoux: "Appeler à l'aide d'un camouflage ces instruments fait pour la vérité qui sont la radio, le cinéma, la presse?" "J'ai traversé voila un an des pays arabes où l'on ignorait encore que Napoleon était mort." *Une allocation radiodiffusée de M. Giraudoux aux Françaises à propos de Sainte Catherine*; the *Figaro*, November, 1939.

The cannibal Chronos. Rhea, mother of Zeus, hid him from Chronos who "devoured all his children except Jupiter (air), Neptune (water), and Pluto (the grave). These Time cannot consume." Brewer's *Dictionary of Phrase and Fable*.

Nevertheless

Elephants

For data incorporated in the above stanzas I am indebted to a lecture-film entitled *Ceylon, the Wondrous Isle* by Charles Brooke Elliott. And Cicero deploring the sacrifice of elephants in the Roman Games, said they "aroused both pity and a feeling that the elephant was somehow allied with man—" (p. 52, *Animals for Show and Pleasure in Ancient Rome* by George Jennison).

Poems 1944–1951

"Keeping Their World Large"

Title: The Reverend James Gordon Gilkey.

Propriety

Line 16: Bach's *Solfeggietto*. Karl Philipp Emanuel's (C minor).

Voracities and Verities [. . .]

Line 2: "*Grass-lamp glow.*" V. Locke-Ellis.

Line 7: "The elephant's crooked trumpet doth write."

> "*Elephants*
> . . . Yea (if the Grecians doe not mis-recite)
> With's crooked trumpet he doth sometimes write."

Du Bartas: "The Sixth Day of the First Weeke."

Dance Index-Ballet Caravan Inc.: *Clowns, Elephants, and Ballerinas,* June 1946.

Line 8: "To a tiger-book." *Man-Eaters of Kumaon* by Jim Corbett.

Line 12: *With love undying.* As the closing words of the sixth chapter of Ephesians, the phrase lingered in my mind. I wrote this piece, came upon Mr. V. Locke-Ellis's "grass-lamp glow," substituted it for my less good equivalent; upon rereading his poems later, I noticed the phrase "with love undying," used by him also.

The Icosasphere

The Mellon Institute is responsible for a steel globe of a design invented by J. O. Jackson. Waldemar Kaempffert in the *New York Times,* February 5, 1950, says: "Jackson has solved a problem which has long baffled draftsmen and engineers. Anybody who has tried to wrap a rubber ball without wrinkling or waste . . . will understand the nature of the problem." "Steel, like wrapping-paper, is delivered in rectangles . . . Mr. Jackson discovered that plexiglass . . . has the same plastic flow as steel and . . . will writhe back into its exact original shape if placed under proper heat. So he moulded a four-inch sphere out of flat plexiglass, studied the flat pattern" and worked out a design whereby "twenty equilateral triangles—the greatest number of regular sides geometrically possible—could be grouped into five parallelograms and cut from rectangular sheets with negligible scrap loss."

Pretiolae

The Hartford Fire Insurance Company and Hartford Accident and Indemnity Company building—690 Asylum Avenue, Hartford, Connecticut—as part of its classic facade, has six granite columns supporting the pediment; all of solid granite.

Pretiolae are thought by the *New York Times* to have been originally Roman—little pieces of baked dough, symbolizing the folded arms of a supliant, presented to children for dutifully said prayers. "Little pretzels" were introduced to America in the 18th Century from Germany, by bakeries in Lititz and Reading, Pennsylvania, in accordance with a secret recipe—hand-twisted for factory ovens.

Armor's Undermining Modesty

Line 11: *Hacked things out with hairy paws.* "The very oldest relics of man's early ancestors are crudely chipped stone. He gripped them in his hairy paw and used them to hammer and chop with." Oscar Ogg, *The 26 Letters*, p. 6.

Line 13: *Arise for it is day.* Motto of The John Day Company.

Line 22: *The bock beer buck.* Porter unsigned, distributed by Eastern Beverage Corporation, Hammonton, New Jersey.

Line 27: *Ducs.* "In England, in the Saxon times, the officers or commanders of armies, after the old Roman fashion, were called *dukes,* without any addition, but after the Norman conquest, the title was no longer used; till, in 1358, Edward III created his son, who was first called the Black Prince, Duke of Cornwall. . . . After Edward the Black Prince, more were made. . . . The Black Prince was created by a wreath on his head, a ring on his finger, and a silver rod." *The Book of the Ranks and Dignities of British Society,* attributed in the press and elsewhere to Charles Lamb (New York: Charles Scribners Sons, 1924).

Like a Bulwark

Apparition of Splendor

Lines 16–17: "*train . . . long.*" Oliver Goldsmith in one of his essays refers to "a blue fairy with a train eleven yards long, supported by porcupines."

Line 21: "*with . . . nurse.*" "All over spines, with the forest for nurse." "The Hedgehog, the Fox, and the Flies," Book Twelve, Fable XIII, *The Fables of La Fontaine* (New York: The Viking Press, 1954).

Then the Ermine:

Line 2: "*rather . . . spotted*" Clitophon; "his device was the Ermion, with a speach that signified, Rather dead than spotted." Sidney's *Arcadia*, Book 1, Chapter 17, paragraph 4. Cambridge Classics, Volume I, 1912, edited by Albert Feuillerat.

Line 12: *motto.* Motto of Henry, Duke of Beaufort: *Mutare vel timere sperno.*

Line 18: *Lavater:* John Kaspar Lavater (1741–1801), a student of physiography. His system includes morphological, anthropological, anatomical, histrionical, and graphical studies. Kurt Seligmann: *The Mirror of Magic* (New York: Pantheon Books, 1948, page 332).

Tom Fool at Jamaica

Line 6: *mule and jockey.* A mule and jockey by "Giulio Gomez 6 años" from a collection of drawings by Spanish school children, solicited on behalf of a fund-raising committee for Republican Spain, sold by Lord and Taylor; given to me by Miss Louise Crane.

Lines 8–9: *"There . . . said."* The Reverend David C. Shipley, July 20, 1952.

Line 9: *Sentir avec ardeur.* By Madame Boufflers—Marie-Françoise-Catherine de Beauveau, Marquise de Boufflers (1711–1786). See note by Dr. Achilles Fang, annotating Lu Chi's "Wên Fu" (A.D. 261–303)— his "Rhymeprose on Literature" ("rhyme-prose" from "Reimprosa" of German medievalists): "As far as notes go, I am at one with a contemporary of Rousseau's: 'Il faut dire en deux mots/Ce qu'on veut dire'; . . . But I cannot claim 'J'ai réussi,' especially because I broke Mme. de Boufflers' injunction ('Il faut éviter l'emploi/Du moi, du moi.')" *Harvard Journal of Asiatic Studies,* Volume 14, Number 3, December 1951, page 529 (revised, *New Mexico Quarterly,* September 1952).

Air: *Sentir avec ardeur*

Il faut dire en deux mots
   Ce qu'on veut dire;
   Les long propos
     Sont sots.

Il faut savoir lire
Avant que d'écrire,
Et puis dire en deux mots
   Ce qu'on veut dire.
   Les long propos
     Sont sots.

Il ne faut pas toujours conter,
   Citer,
   Dater,
   Mais écouter.
Il faut éviter l'emploi
   Du moi, du moi,
   Voici pourquoi:

Il est tyrannique,
Trop académique;
   L'ennui, l'ennui
   Marche avec lui.
Je me conduis toujours ainsi
   Ici,
   Aussi
   J'ai réussi.

Il faut dire en deux mots
   Ce qu'on veut dire;
   Les long propos
     Sont sots.

Line 13: *Master Atkinson.* I opened *The New York Times* one morning (March 3, 1952) and a column by Arthur Daley on Ted Atkinson and Tom Fool took my fancy. Asked what he thought of Hill Gail, Ted Atkinson said, "He's a real good horse, . . . real good," and paused a moment. "But I think he ranks only second to Tom Fool. . . . I prefer Tom Fool. . . . He makes a more sustained effort and makes it more often." Reminded that Citation could make eight or ten spurts in a race, "That's it," said Ted enthusiastically. "It's the mark of a champion to spurt 100 yards, settle back and spurt another

100 yards, giving that extra burst whenever needed. From what I've seen of Tom Fool, I'd call him a 'handy horse.'" He mentioned two others. "They had only one way of running. But Tom Fool. . . ." Then I saw a picture of Tom Fool (*New York Times,* April 1, 1952) with Ted Atkinson in the saddle and felt I must pay him a slight tribute; got on with it a little way, then realized that I had just received an award from Youth United for a Better Tomorrow and was worried indeed. I deplore gambling and had never seen a race. Then in the *Times* for July 24, 1952, I saw a column by Joseph C. Nichols about Frederic Capossela, the announcer at Belmont Park, who said when interviewed, "Nervous? No, I'm never nervous. . . . I'll tell you where it's tough. The straightaway at Belmont Park, where as many as twenty-eight horses run at you from a point three quarters of a mile away. I get 'em though, and why shouldn't I? I'm relaxed, I'm confident and I don't bet."

In the way of a sequel, "Money Isn't Everything" by Arthur Daley (*New York Times,* March 1, 1955): "'There's a constant fascination to thoroughbreds,' said Ted, '. . . they're so much like people. . . . My first love was Red Hay . . . a stouthearted little fellow . . . he always tried, always gave his best.' [Mr. Daley: 'The same description fits Atkinson.'] 'There was Devil Diver, . . . the mare Snow Goose. One of my big favorites . . . crazy to get going. . . . But once she swung into stride . . . you could ride her with shoelaces for reins. . . . And then there was Coaltown. . . . There were others of course, but I never met one who could compare with Tom Fool, my favorite of favorites. He had the most personality of all. . . . Just to look at him lit a spark. He had an intelligent head, an intelligent look and, best of all, was intelligent. He had soft eyes, a wide brow and—gee, I'm sounding like a lovesick boy. But I think he had the handsomest face of any horse I ever had anything to do with. He was a great horse but I was fond of him not so much for what he achieved as for what he was.' With that the sprightly Master Theodore fastened the number plate on his right shoulder and headed for the paddock."

Lines 14–15: "*Chance . . . impurity.*" The *I Ching* or *Book of Changes,* translated by Richard Wilhelm and Cary Baynes, Bollingen Series XIX (New York: Pantheon Books, 1950).

Line 29: *Fats Waller.* Thomas Waller, "a protean jazz figure," died in 1943. See *The New York Times,* article and Richard Tucker (Pix) photograph, March 16, 1952.

Line 31: *Ozzie Smith.* Osborne Smith, a Negro chanter and drummer who improvised the music for Ian Hugo's *Ai-Yé.*

Line 31: *Eubie Blake.* The Negro pianist in *Shuffle Along.*

The Web One Weaves of Italy

The greater part of stanzas 1 and 2 is quoted from an article by Mitchell Goodman, "Festivals and Fairs for the Tourist in Italy," *New York Times*, April 18, 1954.

Line 12: *"fount . . . spilt."* "The Monkey and the Leopard," Book Nine, Fable III, *The Fables of La Fontaine* (The Viking Press, 1954).

The Staff of Aesculapius

Line 11: *Suppose . . . one. Time*, March 29, 1954, article on the Salk vaccine.

Lines 17–20: *Selective . . . true.* Sloan–Kettering Institute for Cancer Research, *Progress Report VII*, June 1954; pp. 20–21.

Lines 22–25: *To . . . framework.* Abbott Laboratories, "Plastic Sponge Implants in Surgery," *What's New*, Number 186, Christmas 1954.

The Sycamore

Lines 15–16: *nine . . . hairs.* Imami, the Iranian miniaturist, draws "with a brush made of nine hairs from a newborn she camel and a pencil sharpened to a needle's point. . . . He was decorated twice by the late Riza Shah; once for his miniatures and once for his rugs." *New York Times*, March 5, 1954.

Rosemary

Line 17: *"hath . . . language."* Sir Thomas More (see below).

According to a Spanish legend, rosemary flowers—originally white— turned blue when the Virgin threw her cloak over a rosemary bush, while resting on the flight into Egypt. There is in Trinity College Library, Cambridge, a manuscript sent to Queen Philippa of Hainault by her mother, written by "a clerk of the school of Salerno" and translated by "danyel bain." The manuscript is devoted entirely to the virtues of rosemary, which, we are told, never grows higher than the height of Christ; after thirty-three years the plant increases in breadth but not in height. See "Rosemary of Plesant Savour," by Eleanour Sinclair Rohde, *The Spectator*, July 7, 1930.

Style

Line 8: *Dick Button*. See photograph, *New York Times*, January 2, 1956.

Line 10: *Etchebaster*. Pierre Etchebaster, a machine-gunner in the First World War; champion of France in chistera (jai alai), pala, and mainnues. He took up court tennis in 1922, won the American championship in 1928, and retired in 1954. (*New York Times*, February 13, 1954 and February 24, 1955). *New York Times*, January 19, 1956: "Pierre Etchebaster, retired world champion, and Frederick S. Moseley won the pro–amateur handicap court tennis tournament at the Racquet and Tennis Club yesterday. . . . The score was 5–6, 6–5, 6–5. Moseley, president of the club, scored the last point of the match with a railroad ace. Johnson and McClintock had pulled up from 3–5 to 5–all in this final set."

Line 10: *Solidad*. Danced in America, 1950–1951.

Line 27: *Rosario's*. Rosario Escudero, one of the company of Vincente Escudero, but not related to him.

Logic and "The Magic Flute"

The Magic Flute. Colorcast by NBC Opera Theater, January 15, 1956.

Line 11: *precious wentletrap*. "wen´tle·trap´ (wen´t'l·trap´), *n*. [D. *wenteltrap* a winding staircase; cf. G. *wendeltreppe*.] Any of numerous elegant, usually white, marine shells of the genus *Epitonium*, or the family Epitoniidae. The shell of *E. pretiosa* was formerly highly valued."—*Webster's New International Dictionary*.

Lines 23–24: "'*What . . . it?*'" *Demon in Love* by Horatio Colony (Cambridge, Massachusetts: Hampshire Press, 1955).

Line 25: *Banish sloth.* "Banish sloth; you have defeated Cupid's bow," Ovid, *Remedia Amoris.*

Blessed is the Man

Lines 1–2: *Blessed . . . scoffer.* Psalm 1:1.

Line 4: "*characteristically intemperate.*" Campaign manager's evaluation of an attack on the Eisenhower Administration.

Line 5: "*excuse . . . heard.*" Charles Poore reviewing James B. Conant's *The Citadel of Learning* (New Haven: Yale University Press)—quoting Lincoln. *New York Times,* April 7, 1956.

Line 8: *Giorgione's self-portrait.* Reproduced in *Life,* October 24, 1955.

Lines 11–12: "*Diversity . . . learning.*" James B. Conant, *The Citadel of Learning.*

Line 13: "*takes . . . decision.*" Louis Dudek: "poetry . . . must . . . take the risk of a decision"; "to say what we know, loud and clear—and if necessary ugly—that would be better than to say nothing with great skill." "The New Laocoön," *Origin,* Winter–Spring 1956.

Lines 14–15: "*Would . . . all?*" "President Eisenhower Vetoes Farm Compromise [Agricultural Act of 1956]," *New York Times,* April 17, 1956: "We would produce more of certain crops at a time when we need less of them. . . . If natural resources are squandered on crops that we cannot eat or sell, all Americans lose."

Line 19: *Ulysses' companions.* "The Companions of Ulysses," Book Twelve, Fable I, *The Fables of La Fontaine* (The Viking Press, 1954).

Line 22: Mitin (From *la mite,* moth). Odorless, non-toxic product of Geigy Chemical Corporation research scientists (Swiss). *New York Times,* April 7, 1956.

Line 23: "*private . . . shame.*" See note for line 13.

Line 27: "*things . . . appear.*" Hebrews 11:3.

O to Be a Dragon

O to Be a Dragon

Dragon: see secondary symbols, Volume II of *The Tao of Painting,* translated and edited by Mai-mai Sze, Bollingen Series 49 (New York: Pantheon, 1956).
Solomon's wish: "an understanding heart." 1 Kings 3:9.

Values in Use

Philip Rahv, July 30, 1956, at the Harvard Summer School Conference on the Little Magazine, Alston Burr Hall, Cambridge, Massachusetts, gave as the standard for stories accepted by the *Partisan Review* "maturity, plausibility, and the relevance of the point of view expressed." "A work of art must be appraised on its own ground; we produce values in the process of living, do not await their historic progress in history." See *Partisan Review,* Fall 1956.

Hometown Piece for Messrs. Alston and Reese

Messrs. Alston and Reese: Walter Alston, manager of the Brooklyn Dodgers; Harold (Peewee) Reese, captain of the Dodgers.

Line 1: *millennium.* "The millennium and pandemonium arrived at approximately the same time in the Brooklyn Dodgers' clubhouse at the Yankee Stadium yesterday." Roscoe McGowen, *New York Times,* October 5, 1955.

Line 2: *Roy Campanella.* Photograph: "Moment of Victory," *New York Times,* October 5, 1955.

Line 4: *Buzzie Bavasi.* "The policemen understood they were to let the players in first, but Brooklyn officials—Walter O'Malley, Arthur (Red) Patterson, Buzzie Bavasi and Fresco Thompson—wanted the writers let in along with the players. This, they felt, was a different occasion and nobody should be barred." Roscoe McGowen, *New York Times,*

October 5, 1955. E. J. Bavasi: Vice President of the Dodgers. William J. Briordy, "Campanella Gets Comeback Honors," *New York Times,* November 17, 1955.

Line 6: *when Sandy Amoros made the catch.* [Joe Collins to Johnny Podres]: "'The secret of your success was the way you learned to control your change-up . . .' 'I didn't use the change-up much in the seventh game of the world series,' said Johnny. 'The background was bad for it. So I used a fast ball that really had a hop on it.' . . . 'Hey, Johnny,' said Joe, 'how did you feel when Amoros made that catch?' 'I walked back to the mound,' said Podres, 'and I kept saying to myself, "everything keeps getting better and better."'" Arthur Daley, "Sports of the Times: Just Listening," *New York Times,* January 17, 1956.

Line 10: *"Hope springs eternal."* Roscoe McGowen, "Brooklyn against Milwaukee," *New York Times,* July 31, 1956.

Line 11: *8, Row 1.* The Dodgers' Sym-Phoney Band sits in Section 8, Row 1, Seats 1 to 7, conducted by Lou Soriano (who rose by way of the snare-drum). "The Sym-Phoney is busy rehearsing a special tune for the Brooklyn income tax collector: It's 'All of Me—Why Not Take All of Me?'" William R. Conklin, "Maestro Soriano at Baton for 18th Brooklyn Season," *New York Times,* August 12, 1956.

Line 16: *"Four hundred feet . . ."* "Gilliam opened the game with a push bunt for a hit, and with one out Duke Snider belted the ball more than 400 feet to the base of the right-center-field wall. Gilliam came home but had to return to base when the ball bounced high into the stands for a ground-rule double." Roscoe McGowen, "Dodgers against Pittsburgh." Duke Snider "hit twenty-three homers in Ebbets Field for four successive years." John Drebinger, *New York Times,* October 1, 1956.

Line 19: *"stylish stout."* [A catcher]: "He crouches in his wearying squat a couple of hundred times a day, twice that for double-headers." Arthur Daley, "At Long Last," *New York Times Magazine,* July 9, 1956.

Line 29: *Preacher Roe's number.* 28. Venerated left-handed pitcher for Brooklyn who won 22 games in the season of 1951.

Line 42: *Jake . . .* "He's a Jake of All Trades—Jake Pitler, the Dodgers' first-base coach and cheer-leader." Joseph Sheehan, *New York Times,* September 16, 1956, "Dodgers Will Have a Night for Jake"—an honor accepted two years ago "with conditions": that contributions be for Beth-El Hospital Samuel Strausberg Wing. Keepsake for the

"Night": a replica of the plaque in the Jake Pitler Pediatric Playroom (for underprivileged children).

Line 44: *Don Demeter.* Center fielder, a newcomer from Fort Worth, Texas. "Sandy Amoros whacked an inside-the-park homer—the third of that sort for the Brooks this year—and Don Demeter, . . . hit his first major league homer, also his first hit, in the eighth inning." Roscoe McGowen, *New York Times*, September 20, 1956.

Lines 45–46: *Shutting . . . do.* Carl Erskine's no-hitter against the Giants at Ebbets Field, May 12, 1956. *New York Times*, May 27, 1956.

Enough: Jamestown, 1607–1957

On May 13, 1957—the 350th anniversary of the landing at Jamestown of the first permanent English settlers in North America— three United States Air Force Super Sabre jets flew non-stop from London to Virginia. They were the Discovery, the Godspeed, and the Susan Constant—christened respectively by Lady Churchill, by Mrs. Whitney (wife of Ambassador John Hay Whitney), and by Mrs. W. S. Morrison (wife of the speaker of the House of Commons). *New York Times*, May 12 and 13, 1957.

The colonists entered Chesapeake Bay, having left England on New Year's Day, almost four months before, "fell upon the earth, embraced it, clutched it to them, kissed it, and, with streaming eyes, gave thanks unto God . . ." Paul Green, "The Epic of Old Jamestown," *New York Times Magazine*, March 31, 1957.

Line 54: *if present faith mend partial proof.* Dr. Charles Peabody, chaplain at Yale, 1896, author of *Mornings in College Chapel*, said past gains are not gains unless we in the present complete them.

Melchior Vulpius

"And not only is the great artist mysterious to us but is that to himself. The nature of the power he feels is unknown to him, and yet he has acquired it and succeeds in directing it." Arsène Alexander, *Malvina Hoffman—Critique and Catalogue* (Paris: J. E. Pouterman, 1930).

Line 11: *Mouse-skin-bellows'-breath.* "Bird in a Bush . . . The bird flies from stem to stem while he warbles. His lungs, as in all automatons, consist of tiny bellows constructed from mouse-skin." Daniel Alain, *Réalités*, April 1957, page 58.

No better than "a withered daffodil"

Line 2: "Slow, Slow, fresh Fount" by Ben Jonson, from *Cynthia's Revels*.

Line 11: *a work of art*. Sir Isaac Oliver's miniature on ivory of Sir Philip Sidney. (Collection at Windsor.)

In the Public Garden

Originally entitled "A Festival." Read at the Boston Arts Festival, June 15, 1958.

Lines 11–15: *Faneuil Hall ... glittered*. "Atop Faneuil Hall, ... market-place hall off Dock Square, Boston, Laurie Young, Wakefield gold-leafer and steeple-jack, applies ... finishing paint on the steeple rod after ... gilding the dome and the renowned 204-year-old grasshopper." *Christian Science Monitor,* September 20, 1946.

Line 13: *grasshopper*. "Deacon Shem Drowne's metal grasshopper, placed atop old Faneuil Hall by its creator in 1749, ... still looks as if it could jump with the best of its kind ... thought to be an exact copy of the vane on top of the Royal Exchange in London." *Christian Science Monitor,* February 16, 1950, quoting *Crafts of New England,* by Allen H. Eaton (New York: Harper, 1949).

Line 27: "*My work be praise.*" Psalm 23—traditional Southern tune, arranged by Virgil Thomson. "President Eisenhower attributed to Clemenceau ... the observation, 'Freedom is nothing ... but the opportunity for self-discipline.'. . . 'And that means the work that you yourselves lay out for yourselves is worthwhile doing—doing without hope of reward.'" *New York Times,* May 6, 1958.

Saint Nicholas,

Line 3: *a chameleon*. See photograph in *Life,* September 15, 1958, with a letter from Dr. Doris M. Cochran, curator of reptiles and amphibians, National Museum, Washington, D.C.

For February 14th

Line 2: "*some interested law ...*" From a poem to M. Moore by Marguerite Harris.

Combat Cultural

Line 29: *Nan-ai-ans.* The Nanaians inhabit the frigid North of the Soviet Union.

Line 32: *one person.* Lev Golanov: "Two Boys in a Fight." Staged by Igor Moiseyev, Moiseyev Dance Company, presented in New York, 1958, by Sol Hurok.

Leonardo da Vinci's

See *Time,* May 18, 1959, page 73: "Saint Jerome," an unfinished picture by Leonardo da Vinci, in the Vatican; and *The Belles Heures of Jean, Duke of Berry, Prince of France,* with an Introduction by James J. Rorimer (New York: Metropolitan Museum of Art, 1958).

The Arctic Ox

To a Giraffe

Ennis Rees summarizes the Odyssey, I feel, when he finds expressed in it, the conditional nature of existence, the consolations of the metaphysical: the journey from sin to redemption.

Arthur Mitchell

Puck in Lincoln Kirstein's and George Balanchine's New York City Center's Music and Drama Inc. production of *A Midsummer Night's Dream*.

Tell Me, Tell Me

Line 9: *Lord Nelson's revolving diamond rosette*. In the museum at Whitehall.

Lines 21–22: "The literal played in our education as small a part as it perhaps ever played in any and we wholesomely breathed inconsistency and ate and drank contradictions." Henry James, *Autobiography* (*A Small Boy and Others*, *Notes of a Son and Brother*, *The Middle Years*), edited by F. W. Dupee (New York: Criterion, 1958).

Rescue With Yul Brynner

See *Bring Forth the Children* by Yul Brynner (New York: McGraw-Hill, 1960).

Line 30: *Symphonia Hungarica*. By Zoltán Kodály.

Carnegie Hall: Rescued

Nelson Rockefeller.

An Expedient—Leonardo da Vinci's—and a Query

See Sir Kenneth Clark: *Leonardo da Vinci: An Account of His Development as an Artist.* "Continuous energy. If everything was continuous in movement it could not be controlled by mathematics in which Leonardo had placed his faith."

Line 21: *Nature the test.* See *Leonardo da Vinci's Notebooks,* translated by Edward McCurdy.

Lines 31–36: *"Sad"* . . . *"Tell me if anything at all has been done?"* To Dr. Henry W. Moss, Associate Professor of History, New York University.

Tell Me, Tell Me

Granite and Steel

See *Brooklyn Bridge: Fact and Symbol* by Alan Trachtenberg (New York: Oxford University Press, 1965).

Line 7: *Caged Circe*. See Meyer Berger's story (retold in *Brooklyn Bridge: Fact and Symbol*) of a young reporter who in the 1870s was unaccountably drawn to climb one of the cables to the top of the bridge's Manhattan tower, became spellbound, couldn't come down, and cried for help; none came till morning.

Line 9: *O catenary curve*. The curve formed by a rope or cable hanging freely between two fixed points of support. "Engineering problems of the greatest strength, greatest economy, greatest safety . . . are all solved by the same curve," John Roebling said. (Trachtenberg, p. 69.)

In Lieu of the Lyre

Written in response to a request from Stuart Davis, president of the *Advocate*, for a poem.

Line 4: *Sentir avec ardeur*. By Madame Boufflers—Marie-Françoise-Catherine de Beauveau, Marquise de Boufflers (1711–1786). See note by Dr. Achilles Fang, annotating Lu Chi's "Wên Fu" (A.D. 261–303)— his "Rhymeprose on Literature" ("rhyme-prose" from "Reimprosa" of German medievalists): "As far as notes go, I am at one with a contemporary of Rousseau's: '*Il faut dire en deux mots/Ce qu'on veut dire*'; . . . But I cannot claim '*J'ai réussi*,' especially because I broke Mme. de Boufflers's injunction ('*Il faut éviter l'emploi/Du moi, du moi*')." *Harvard Journal of Asiatic Studies*, Volume 14, Number 3, December 1951, page 529 (revised, *New Mexico Quarterly*, September, 1952).

Line 11: *Professor Levin*. Harry Levin, "A Note on Her French Aspect," p. 40, *Festschrift for Marianne Moore's Seventy-Seventh*

Birthday, edited by T. Tambimuttu. (New York: Tambimuttu and Mass, 1964.)

Line 14: *Lowell House Press.* Referring to a Lowell House *separatum: Occasionem Cognosce* (1963).

Line 17: *gratia sum.* Bewick tailpiece, "a trickle of water from a rock, underlined by heart in outline carved on the rock," p. 53, *Memoir of Thomas Bewick Written by Himself* (Centaur Classics).

Line 27: *a bridge. Brooklyn Bridge: Fact and Symbol,* by Alan Trachtenberg (1965).

The mind, intractable thing

Line 26: *The Mermaid of Zennor.* See "The Ballad of the Mermaid of Zennor," in *Affinities,* by Vernon Watkins (New York: New Directions, 1962).

Dream

Jerome S. Shipman's comment. In *Encounter,* July, 1956.

Old Amusement Park

A Port Authority photograph given to me by Brendan Gill.

W. S. Landor

See introductory note by Havelock Ellis to Landor's *Imaginary Conversations.*

Poems 1963–1970

Love in America?

Line 5: The Minotaur demanded a virgin to devour once a year.

Line 6: Midas, who had the golden touch, was inconvenienced when eating or picking things up.

Lines 10–11: Unamuno said that what we need as a cure for unruly youth is "nobility that is action."

Lines 13–15: *without brazenness or bigness* . . . Winston Churchill: "Modesty becomes a man."

Tippoo's Tiger

Derived from a Victoria and Albert Museum monograph, "Tippoo's Tiger," by Mildred Archer (London: Her Majesty's Stationery Office, 1959).

See Keats's *The Cap and Bells*.

"Tippoo" is the original form of the name used in the eighteenth century; "Tipu" is the accepted modern form.

Lines 17–20: *a vast toy, a curious automaton* . . . A mechanical tiger "captured by the British at Seringapatam in 1799, when Tipu Sultan, ruler of Mysore in Southern India, was defeated and killed." Mildred Archer.

Line 18: *Organ pipes*. Cf. "Technical Aspects of Tipu's Organ" by Henry Willis, Jr., in Mildred Archer's monograph.

Mercifully,

Lines 6–8: *An Evening of Elizabethan Verse and Its Music*—W. H. Auden and the New York Pro Musica Antiqua; Noah Greenberg, Director. *Legendary Performances* (Odyssey 32160171).

"Like a Wave at the Curl"

Kittens owned by Mr. and Mrs. Richard Thoma.

The Magician's Retreat

Drawing by Jean-Jacques Lequeu (1757–1825), *Arts Magazine*, December/January 1967–68.

Line 14: René Magritte, Domain of Lights, 1953–54. *New York Times Magazine*, January 19, 1969, page 69.

EDITOR'S NOTES

EDITING THE POEMS

I. Moore the Editor

Anyone who would like a quick introduction to the ways Marianne Moore edited her own work can infer it from the complaints of her most devoted readers. In 1935 T. S. Eliot edited and wrote the introduction for her *Selected Poems*, describing his work this way:

> The original suggestion was that I should make a selection, from both previously published and more recent poems. But Miss Moore exercised her own rights of proscription first, so drastically, that I have been concerned to preserve rather than abate. (xiv)

In a review of Moore's *Complete Poems*, which she edited herself in 1967, the poet Anthony Hecht lamented,

> while she has occasionally added beautifully to a familiar and well-known poem, more often than not she has cut and trimmed in radical and merciless ways. (Hecht, 208)[1]

Hugh Kenner, reflecting on Moore's lifelong willingness to sacrifice her work when it no longer met her ever-shifting standards, neatly summed the situation up in 1975:

> [Miss Moore's] conscience was her admirers' despair. (Kenner, 112)

Moore's implacable answer to all such expressions of despair is the terse phrase that has been the epigraph to her *Collected Poems* since it was first published in 1967: "Omissions are not accidents." In its broadest terms this edition argues that although Moore's omissions were not accidents, they were nevertheless mistakes.

---

1 Hecht offers no examples of these additions, and I believe he is mistaken in thinking they exist. The only well-known poem Moore lengthened in her *Complete Poems* is "The Steeple-Jack," and in that case Moore was in fact restoring previously published material she had cut for *Selected Poems* and *Collected Poems*.

I think that Moore, in the later decades of her life, did her readers a lasting, and compounding, disservice by altering and suppressing the writing she published as a younger poet. As the first generations of Moore readers have disappeared, so has the Moore they collectively sustained in memory. This edition exists in the service of the Moore her peers witnessed, and as a counter-testimony to the Moore she herself invented to take her place.

Such essentially reconstructive work is not simple. Understanding the puzzle of Moore's published work involves understanding two interlocking categories of her own editorial thinking: that pertaining to her books, and that pertaining to her individual poems.

Comparatively speaking (though only comparatively speaking) the record of her books is less complicated. There are four key books, each overseen or approved by Moore herself, that shaped the Moore canon as most readers have known it. Tracing the history of Moore's decision-making with respect to them illuminates the evolving principles she wanted her work to reflect. It also suggests why many ardent readers have had reason to regret her stewardship of the poems. The books in question are:

> *Observations* (1924)
> *Selected Poems*, ed. T. S. Eliot (1935)
> *Collected Poems* (1951)
> *Complete Poems* (1967)

Observations was Moore's first authorized trade publication in the United States. It came about when, in 1924, the editors of the *Dial*, New York's foremost magazine of literature and the arts, gave her the *Dial* Award for distinguished service to American letters. The prize, which had gone two years earlier to T. S. Eliot for *The Waste Land*, was prestigious and practical, including $2,000 and the publication of her book. At the time she received it she had been publishing her poems in British and American literary magazines, including the *Dial*, for nearly ten years. Three years earlier, in 1921, Moore's friends H.D., Bryher, and Robert McAlmon published a collection of her poetry, called *Poems*, in Britain without her knowledge or consent. Her friends were acting in what they thought was Moore's best interest; they had been urging her to publish her first book for some time, and apparently mistook her refusals as coy self-effacement. Moore's correspondence from the time shows her genuine distress at the book's existence, but also her recognition of her friends' good intentions in creating it.[2]

---

2   For a detailed account of how *Observations* came to be, including Moore's

Observations was her chance to set the record of her own publication straight. As a collection of her work titled, selected, ordered, and edited entirely by her, published in the United States, it was the start of Moore's career as a major Modernist poet on her own terms. Because Moore ordered its contents more or less chronologically one can watch her poems develop from short, epigrammatic lyrics of the late teens to longer, complexly associative poems, built largely on wide-ranging quotations, of the mid-twenties. Reading *Observations* whole allows us to understand how Moore matured as an artist in the first decade of her published work, and shows us the poet that T. S. Eliot, Ezra Pound, Wallace Stevens, William Carlos Williams, and others recognized immediately as an innovative leader of the art.

The irony is particularly striking, then, that Eliot's conscientious and canny work on Moore's next book, *Selected Poems* (1935) resulted in the lasting erasure of *Observations* from her canon. After the second edition of *Observations* was published in 1925, Moore assumed the editorship of the *Dial*. She wrote voluminously for the *Dial* during the four years she worked as its editor, but none of that writing was poetry. It was not until 1929, when the journal closed due to a dispute between its owners, that Moore began writing poems again, and not until 1932 that she returned to publishing them. Her new poems were spectacular, long, intricately wrought meditations on history, ethics, commerce, and art that were simultaneously minutely attentive portraits of whatever interested Moore at the moment: a jerboa, Chinese porcelain, hothouse flowers. Eliot, who had corresponded with Moore since the early twenties about publishing a book of her poetry, suggested in 1934 that the time was right for Moore's second book, and offered to publish it with Faber & Faber where he was editor. He further suggested that, in the interest of presenting her to a British audience as an established, eminent poet, they publish a "selected" volume as they had recently and successfully done for Ezra Pound. Moore gratefully agreed and Eliot set to work on the table of contents for *Selected Poems*.

Eliot's explicit goal in editing and publishing this book was to entrench Moore's standing in the literary world. To this end he did two things, both effective. First, he wrote an introductory essay that not only asserted that Moore's contribution to literature was "permanent," but preemptively described as virtues those features of her work that had been criticized. Second, and more consequentially

---

reactions to *Poems* three years earlier, see Moore (ed. Schulze), *Becoming Marianne Moore*, 18–38.

for all of Moore's subsequent readers, he arranged the contents of *Selected Poems* so that her most recent poems, those written in the 1930s, appeared first, followed by a re-ordered selection of poems from *Observations*. This choice worked beautifully in the way Eliot meant it to, presenting Moore to a wide audience primarily as the writer of the elaborate, densely allusive, and freely associative poems she had written most recently. It was an admirable act of editorship in which each choice pertaining to individual poems contributed to the larger purpose of the book. Moore expressed her own satisfaction with it by enshrining *Selected Poems*, not *Observations*, as the first book listed in both her 1951 *Collected Poems* and her 1967 *Complete Poems*.

That choice has meant that most of Moore's readers have encountered a deliberately achronological ordering of her work, designed to privilege her aesthetic choices of the 1930s and obscure the process by which she reached them. Moore preferred it that way. In fact "preference" is not a strong enough word to describe what was really her insistence that books were opportunities to re-make her past work according to her present intentions. That insistence is visible in her books of the late thirties and forties, but became a declaration of sorts in 1951 when she edited *Collected Poems*. One writer titled his review of it "The Revised Poems of Marianne Moore" and called it "a report of her endless revisions" (Gregory, 154). Moore's decision to make *Selected Poems*, rather than *Observations*, the first listed book in the table of contents preserved the rearranged, partial picture in *Selected Poems* of her early years as a poet. She went further in revising the record of her work, however: the section within that edition called "Selected Poems" was itself only a selection from the 1935 book of the same name. *Selected Poems* (1935) has forty-nine poems; the "Selected Poems" section of *Collected Poems* has forty-five. The next section in the table of contents, "What Are Years," contains eleven of *What Are Years*'s original fifteen poems.

More significantly, Moore made deep cuts to some of her best-known poems: "The Steeple-Jack" went from twelve stanzas to seven and a half; "The Frigate Pelican" from twelve stanzas to five and a half. Other poems (such as "An Octopus," "The Jerboa," "The Buffalo," "Nine Nectarines," and "He 'Digesteth Harde Yron'") lost passages as well. In this way Moore used the landmark status a volume of collected poems has in a poet's career to make at least two implicit statements about her work. First, she demonstrated that the chronology of her poems' publications was of limited interest to her. Second, she established that each poem, irrespective of when it was written, could always be changed to reflect her present concerns. She made it plain, in other words, that the poet she had been, as well as her audience's expectations, were always secondary to the poet she had become.

Having definitively established that hierarchy in 1951, in 1967, at the age of eighty, Moore made it permanent in her *Complete Poems*. Rarely has a title been more misleading. *Complete Poems* (1967), like the updated 1981 edition that has been the standard Moore edition for more than three decades, contains just over half the poems Moore published during her lifetime. It is structured like *Collected Poems* (1951): a "Selected Poems" section comes first, followed by sections for each volume she published after it. Moore reprinted nearly all of the revised versions of her poems she created in 1951, and added a raft of new revisions as well. As a result, the situation since 1981 has been this: Moore's readers have had available to them approximately half of what she actually published. Her work has been presented in such a way that we read first poems she wrote in the thirties, then work back (without being told so) to poems she wrote in the teens and twenties, then leap forward to the forties and beyond. All the while, the poems we are reading are in many cases revised versions created twenty to thirty years after she first wrote and published the originals (again, we are not told that this is the case).

This state of affairs has only one virtue: it is what Moore wanted. In a prefatory "Note on the Text" in the 1981 edition of *Complete Poems* the editors, Clive Driver and Patricia Willis, state "the text conforms as closely as is now possible to the author's final intentions" (viii). They use the phrase "final intentions" because it signals their adherence both to Moore's wishes and to the dominant school of thought guiding Anglo-American editing since the 1950s. That school is called Greg/Bowers, after the widely influential work of W. W. Greg and Fredson Bowers.[3] The Greg/Bowers principle of final intentions is succinctly formulated in a classic essay on editorial theory by Thomas Tanselle. "An editor's judgment," he writes,

> is directed toward the recovery of what the author wrote, not toward an evaluation of the effectiveness of the author's revisions . . . [W]hen an editor has strong reason to attribute a revision to the author, he will accept that revision as "final" on the grounds that, coming second, it represents the author's considered and more mature judgment. (Tanselle, 169)

---

3 For a useful history of the Greg/Bowers method, and the challenges to it that have followed, see Moore (ed. Schulze), *Becoming Marianne Moore*, 1–6.

Determining an author's "final intentions" is a multi-faceted process, requiring an editor to seek out the last known instance of the text approved by the author herself, learning where possible the difference between changes made to texts by editors, typesetters, proof-readers, and the like, with and without the author's knowledge and approval, and combing the author's archive for indications about what further changes she would have made, given the chance. By Greg/Bowers standards the 1981 *Complete Poems* remains an exemplary work of editorship. Readers wishing to know what Moore's last recorded intentions for her work were may consult it with confidence, as Driver and Willis are scrupulous about representing, without cavil, Moore's latest known choices. However, as the quotations by Eliot, Hecht, and Kenner with which this essay began suggest, Moore's choices about her work have seldom pleased her readers. Many of those readers, who include a number of her century's best poets, did not hesitate to (as Tanselle says an editor should not) evaluate "the effectiveness" of her revisions at the time she made them. Those readers are now gone, and with them their advocacy for the poems she chose not to reprint, and their protest at poems she revised until they bore little relation to their former selves. This edition takes up their cause.

II. Editing the *New Collected Poems*

The premise on which I have selected and arranged this book's contents is quite different from that underlying the idea of an author's final intentions, and works directly counter to many of Moore's own choices. My presentation of Moore the poet will frequently entail overriding Moore the editor, and doing so requires some justification. The "final intentions" principle assumes, as Tanselle says, that the older an author is, the more "considered and . . . mature" his or her judgment will be. Such an assumption has on its side intuitive plausibility, and displays an appealingly courteous deference to the author: an editor who seeks out and records final intentions is also not presuming to second-guess the artist. As its proponents are the first to acknowledge, however, no procedure can actually evade the issue of "evaluating" an author's decisions. Deciding that "considered and mature" changes are desirable is itself an evaluative act. Moreover, there are any number of circumstances that might call into question the idea that a writer's final changes are the result of consideration and maturity. Breakdowns in health, bereavements, and seismic shifts of political or religious beliefs have all been the occasions of literary revisions. One could argue that the poet who revises after such a change, or after any change of time and circumstance, is not the same poet who wrote before it. Yeats cheerfully said as much in the dedicatory poem to his *Collected Poetry and Prose*:

> The friends that have it I do wrong
> Whenever I remake a song
> Should know what issue is at stake,
> It is myself that I remake.

According to Yeats's logic here, choices about which text to reprint in a given edition are really choices about which poet to present to a reading audience. As the number of extant versions of a poem increases, it multiplies the array of poets an editor may choose to present: the poet the editor likes best? The youngest poet, the oldest poet, the poet writing at a time of greatest personal or societal significance? The reader has a right to know what rationale an editor has followed in choosing texts to reproduce. The greater the number of possible texts that exist, the more complexly reasoned such a rationale may need to be. In Moore's case, the number and entanglements of the available texts makes it necessary to keep in play different, sometimes competing, principles of selection.

In brief, three aims guided my selections for this volume: to present the poems grouped by the individual books Moore published, starting with *Observations*; to print versions of poems that represent Moore's intentions for them near to the time she wrote them; and to get back into print many, but not all, of the poems Moore herself chose not to include in her own books. These principles inevitably come into conflict with one another. The textual history of Moore's poem "The Student," to choose only one example, shows why.

Moore first published "The Student" in the June 1932 issue of *Poetry* magazine. She placed it second in a trio of poems (between "The Steeple-Jack" and "The Hero") to which she gave the collective title "Part of a Novel, Part of a Poem, Part of a Play." Her publication of these poems was an event, the end of the seven-year hiatus in her poetry publishing while she edited the *Dial*. The poems themselves were quickly recognized as major work from an artist doing some of her strongest writing to date, and two of them, "The Steeple-Jack" and "The Hero," continue to be among the handful that define for many readers the beauty, intricacy, and ethical ambition of her poetry at its best. "The Student" is not included in that handful because of what Moore did to it subsequently. When Eliot edited *Selected Poems* in 1935 Moore chose to leave it out. There is no record of her thinking on the subject, merely the fact that while the first listing in *Selected Poems'* table of contents is the tri-partite title "Part of a Novel, Part of a Poem, Part of a Play," only "The Steeple-Jack" and "The Hero" are actually included in the book.

The poem's omission from *Selected Poems*, the book on which Moore's transatlantic reputation was largely founded, sealed its fate. Most readers don't know it exists, and scholars have ignored it. Moore expunged even its lingering trace as the ghostly "Part of a Poem" hinted at in the group title when she edited her 1951 *Collected Poems*. The table of contents for the "Selected Poems" section of that book simply begins with "The Steeple-Jack" and "The Hero." The poem's 1935 disappearance, however, was not the end of its story. In 1941 Moore published *What Are Years*, her first trade edition since *Selected Poems*. In it there appears a poem called "The Student." That poem shares many lines and phrases with its 1932 predecessor, though it is significantly shorter, has an entirely different formal scheme, and posits substantially different lessons to be drawn from its subject. When Moore's readers refer to "The Student" it is to this later composition, which has successfully effaced the earlier poem.

The 1941 "Student" raises the question of when a poem's alterations make it not simply another version of an earlier poem, but a new poem altogether. In calling this new poem by an old name, Moore added another level to the puzzle of her work's history. There is no indication in *Complete Poems* (again, the text of record since 1967) that "The Steeple-Jack" and "The Hero" were originally conceived as related to one another, let alone that they used to be part of a trio including "The Student." A reader who does somehow find out that they used to be a trio could be forgiven for attempting to reconstruct it by reading the 1941 "Student," which appears later in the *What Are Years* section. The resultant sequence, however, would bear a tenuous relation to the 1932 group, consisting as it would of a "Steeple-Jack" revised in 1935 and 1951 (though restored to its 1935 state in 1967), a "Student" almost wholly rewritten in 1941, and a "Hero" that remains close to what it was in 1932.

I have described this case at some length to dramatize the way a given poem can bring into conflict seemingly harmonious editorial principles. In this case, for example, restoring the original order of Moore's books (my first goal) suggests following Moore's own procedure, reprinting the 1941 "Student" in the *What Are Years* section of this edition. My second and third goals, however, argue for printing the original 1932 "Student," thereby presenting the poem as it was near to the time when it was written, and putting back into circulation a poem currently lost to readers. I made the latter choice, as I have done in numerous similar cases, because in my judgment Moore's primary contribution to twentieth-century poetry lies in the poems her contemporaries knew her by rather than in the later editorial choices she made about them.

Which is not to say those choices are not themselves fascinating. The mere fact of their existence is fascinating, whether or not one likes what resulted from them, because they show that a Moore poem was never definitively finished. For Moore a poem was always in the process of becoming, and any one printed incarnation of it was not its essence, but only the visible souvenir of a living process of composition. In this respect Moore's closest predecessor is Walt Whitman, both of them working until the end of their lives not simply on new poems, but on re-making the whole of their work. Moore's *Complete Poems* may be seen as her *Leaves of Grass*.

I have suggested that editing is largely a matter of choosing, if not actually inventing, the poet to represent. It is equally an act of imagining a reading audience and responding to its needs. The broader the imagined audience is the more complex the editor's work becomes, because the Moore specialist will want things from a Moore edition that a reader new to Moore may not want, and would likely find obtrusive if they were there. For example, a long-time reader of Moore's might enjoy being presented with three new versions of a poem she already knows well, while a reader new to Moore might well be put off by the unfamiliarity and confusion of three poems presented under one title.

Since both such readers need a new and reliable edition of Moore's work, both are included in my imagined audience. The format of the book itself requires, for the most part, choosing only one version of each poem to print. Since no single choice will be right for every reader, I have focused on making the reasons behind my choices, as well as the range of possibilities available, as clear as possible. To this end the apparatus at the back of the book has a more fine-grained portrait of the poems chosen and, to some extent, the poems not chosen. The "Editor's Notes" gives citations for the versions I have taken as copy-text, and explains, where relevant, how I chose between versions that had strong claims for use. The "Original Tables of Contents" section offers all the original tables of contents for collections of Moore's work published during her lifetime, starting with the unauthorized *Poems* (1921), and ending with *Complete Poems* (1967). These lists (excluding *Poems*) can guide a reader interested in Moore's always careful choices about ordering her poems in books, as well as a reader interested to know how her book-reading audience (including readers of *Poems*) first saw her. Since the table of contents of the present book often privileges the integrity of the poem over the integrity of the collection in which it first appeared, the original tables of contents are essential to keeping Moore's publication history visible.

This book is an edition of Moore's original poetry that was in print on a national and international scale. As such it does not reproduce draft material, or poems published in magazines associated with her alma mater Bryn Mawr (except where Moore herself reprinted them in books). It also omits Moore's translation of *The Fables of La Fontaine*, a substantial project she published in 1954. My table of contents presents an implicit argument that Moore was a major force in American Modernism, and that the best way to understand that force now is to encounter her work in the forms it took at the time it was written—not as she later revised it. Wherever presenting a poem in an early version conflicts with representing a book as it first appeared, I have most often chosen in favor of the poem.

This means that although the table of contents is mainly divided into sections that reflect Moore's discrete books, some of those sections are preceded with "from." That "from" does not mean I have not reprinted every poem in the book it precedes. Rather, it means that some poems appear in other sections, grouped with poems published contemporaneously. For example, the section called "*from* What Are Years" does not include eight poems she included in that book. These eight can still be found in this volume in other, earlier sections, in the versions Moore published before deciding to revise them and collect them in *What Are Years*. I have documented the particulars of each poem in the "Editor's Notes," and direct readers to the "Original Tables of Contents" section to see how Moore grouped them.

The example of the poem "Sun" will show why I decided this procedure is the least of editorial evils. Moore included a poem called "Sun" in three of her books: it is the penultimate poem in *The Arctic Ox* (1964), the last poem in *Tell Me, Tell Me* (1966), and again the last poem in the "Tell Me, Tell Me" section of *Complete Poems* (1967). The variants between each of these printings are minor. Since it would be confusing and redundant to include the poem in both the "Arctic Ox" and "Tell Me, Tell Me" sections of this book, the right choice would seem to be to reprint it in the "Arctic Ox" section, since it is earlier, and leave it at that. There is a problem, however.

Moore actually wrote the poem nearly fifty years before, publishing it (again, with minor variants) in the January 1916 issue of a magazine called *Contemporary Verse*. Remaining faithful to the poem in its earliest form, then, would suggest using that version as copy-text and collecting it in the "Appendix" of this book. However, there is (it may not be surprising to learn) another problem. Moore actually did publish the poem (with, as ever, minor variants) in *Observations*, but took care to obscure that fact by retitling it "Fear is Hope." Because one of my primary aims in this edition is restoring *Observations* to its rightful place as the beginning of Moore's career as a major American modernist, I chose to print it, under its *Observations* title, in the "Observations" section of this volume.[4]

My several references to "minor" variants suggest a further wrinkle in keeping the record of Moore's work straight. In addition to show-stopping, statement-making revisions, Moore made innumerable smaller changes to her poems nearly each time she reprinted them. The greater a reader's interest in Moore's work, the less likely he is to consider any change to the poems "minor." Because this is not a full variorum edition (such a work would run to multiple volumes) I have had to decide which variants are interesting enough to document in the "Editor's Notes."

Some such decisions are easier. For example, there are many extant versions of Moore's most famous poem, "Poetry," but four of these stand out as the most significant. "Poetry" started its long published life in the July 1919 issue of *Others* magazine. In this version it is a poem of five stanzas, each containing six lines that follow a regular pattern of syllable count and rhyme. Moore reprinted a slightly modified version of it in the first edition of *Observations*, in 1924, which is the poem I use as copy-text for the "Observations" section of this edition. Within months, however, she changed the poem radically for the second edition of *Observations* in 1925, turning it into a free-verse poem of merely thirteen lines, and later published a three-stanza version in a 1932 anthology. Most notorious of all, however, is the version she printed in her 1967 *Complete Poems*. For that occasion she cut all but the first three lines, and appended the five-stanza version as a note to it in the back of the book. The reader of this edition can find the latter three versions in the "Editor's Notes" (pp. 363–4), because

---

4   It is worth adding that while "Sun" shows that Moore was capable of publishing the same poem multiple times under different names, she was also capable of doing the opposite, as when she published two different, entirely unrelated poems under the same title, "The Past is the Present." Both poems appear in this edition with their chronologically appropriate cohorts.

Moore's decades of work on the poem have become emblematic of her practice as a whole. The poet who was never done revising became, in her old age, the poet determined to assert her continuing right to do as she pleased with her work.

Other decisions are less easy. For example, Moore frequently re-punctuated her poems. Changes in punctuation are visually less prominent than changes in wording, and often more subtle in their effects. They are easier to treat as (to use a distinction made in traditional editorial theory) "incidentals" rather than "substantives." However, the very fact that Moore so often made such changes suggests that they were not incidental to her. Few twentieth-century writers consider punctuation unimportant, and Moore was writing in the age when authors such as Virginia Woolf and Gertrude Stein were consciously bringing artistic scrutiny to bear on the mechanics of sentences, including most especially their punctuation. Fully honoring this context requires a meticulous record of changes in punctuation.

Some of this detailed variorum work has been done elsewhere, and I have referred interested readers to it wherever possible.[5] For this edition, however, I made a conventional choice in deciding to record only changes in wording and form, for the conventional reason that page space and the reader's patience are limited. With respect to the poems written before 1944 and revised later, that most often means including the poems' final, revised versions in the notes. For instance, in 1967, for *Complete Poems*, Moore took three syllabic poems from the 1920s, "Peter," "England," and "Picking and Choosing," and reprinted them as free verse. In each case I use the original syllabic version from *Observations* as copy-text for the main body of this edition, but reprint the free-verse variants in the notes. I hope in this way to set the record straight about Moore's formal choices in the 1920s, while allowing the reader to experience these exciting examples of Moore's embodiment of the same material in two different formal structures.

With respect to the poems written after 1944, which Moore most often published in periodicals, collected in books, and then left alone, I have usually noted any significant revisions Moore made between the periodical versions and the book versions. These changes are seldom as radical as the changes she made to her early poems, and are interesting in a different way. If Moore's late revisions of early poems show mostly what a different poet she became over decades, her more

---

5 See Moore (ed. Schulze), *Becoming Marianne Moore*, and (ed. White) *A-Quiver* and *Adversity*.

immediate revisions of new poems show how she thought about them as they came into being.

*

When I began editing Moore's poems I was frustrated by the fact that no one edition can do everything. As I finished editing that same fact became a comfort. However clearly an editor articulates principles, and however consistently she follows them, the complexities of actual works of art will vex and exceed them. I began by thinking that inconsistent decisions were unpardonable editorial faults. I ended thinking that careful record-keeping with respect to unavoidable inconsistencies is the greatest virtue. As I reflect on the endless challenges Moore's poems present, I have come to believe that the most dangerous pitfalls of editing are the questions the editor lacks the wit to ask. Editing is a discipline and the practice of scholarship; it is also an act of imagination in the face of wide possibility. In all respects curiosity vitalizes it more than any principle or theory; where curiosity lapses no system can reliably compensate, as Moore herself knew well. "Be infallible at your peril," she warns us, "for your system will fail" ("Tom Fool at Jamaica": 198).

The answer is not to abandon systems, but to avoid becoming a slave to them, a point about which Moore was equally clear: "Too stern an intellectual emphasis upon this quality or that, detracts from one's enjoyment" ("When I Buy Pictures": 51). In editions as in mathematical proofs, then, rigorous reason is required, but the ultimate test is beauty. In all cases where I was up to the task of asking the right questions I have worked to make my answers reasonable and beautiful. When reasons themselves were too profuse and contradictory to point me to simple answers I kept faith with one of Moore's most striking rhetorical questions. In the poem "Black Earth" (41–2), considering the elephant's superb skin, at once magnificently protective of the elephant's inner life and expressive of its worldly experience, Moore challenges the reader of poems and, I think, the maker of editions: "Will/depth be depth, thick skin be thick, to one who can see no/beautiful element of unreason under it?"

NOTES

OBSERVATIONS

Copy-text for all poems except "Poetry," "The Monkey Puzzler," and the "Index" is the second edition of *Observations* (New York: The Dial Press, 1925). I have used the second edition because the first, 1924, edition was rushed to press and contains numerous errors. In correcting the text for the second edition, Moore inserted the poem "The Monkey Puzzler," and substituted a much shorter version of "Poetry." In this volume I have included "The Monkey Puzzler," re-substituted the 1924 "Poetry," and used the slightly more extensive 1924 "Index." For full documentation of all variants for each poem until 1924, including facsimile reproductions of each poem's first publication and of O, see Moore (ed. Schulze), *Becoming Marianne Moore.*

To an Intra-Mural Rat

FIRST PUBLISHED: *Poetry* 6.2 (May 1915): 71.

COLLECTED: O.

Reticence and Volubility

FIRST PUBLISHED: As "The Wizard in Words." *Poetry* 6.2 (May 1915): 72.

COLLECTED: O.

To a Chameleon

FIRST PUBLISHED: As "You Are Like the Realistic Product of an Idealistic Search for Gold at the Foot of the Rainbow" in *The Egoist* 5.3 (May 1, 1916): 71.

COLLECTED: P under the original title. As "To a Chameleon" in O, OD, AO, ComP.

A Talisman

FIRST PUBLISHED: *The Lantern* 20 (Spring 1912): 61.
COLLECTED: *P* (as "Talisman"), *O*.

To a Prize Bird

FIRST PUBLISHED: As "To Bernard Shaw: A Prize Bird." *The Egoist* 8.2 (August 2, 1915): 126.
COLLECTED: *O*, *ComP*.

Injudicious Gardening

FIRST PUBLISHED: As "To Browning." *The Egoist* 8.2 (August 2, 1915): 126.
COLLECTED: *O*, *SP*, *ColP*, *ComP*.

Fear is Hope

FIRST PUBLISHED: As "Sun!" *Contemporary Verse* 1.1 (January 1916): 7.
COLLECTED: *O*. As "Sun" in *AO*, *TM*, *ComP*.

To a Strategist

FIRST PUBLISHED: As "To Disraeli on Conservatism." *The Lantern* 23 (Spring 1915): 60.
COLLECTED: *O*.

Is Your Town Nineveh?

FIRST PUBLISHED: *The Lantern* 24 (Spring 1916): 19.
COLLECTED: *P*, *O*, *SP* (as "Is Your Town Nineveh").

A Fool, a Foul Thing, a Distressful Lunatic

FIRST PUBLISHED: In a substantially different version, as "Masks" in *Contemporary Verse* 1.1 (January 1916): 6.

COLLECTED: O.

The variants in "Masks" are likely the work of an editor, not Moore.

To Military Progress

FIRST PUBLISHED: As "To the Soul of 'Progress'" in *The Egoist* 4.2 (April 1, 1915): 62.

COLLECTED: O, SP, ColP, ComP.

An Egyptian Pulled Glass Bottle in the Shape of a Fish

FIRST PUBLISHED: In O.

COLLECTED: O, SP (as "An Egyptian Pulled Glass Bottle"), ColP, ComP.

To a Steam Roller

FIRST PUBLISHED: *The Egoist* 10.2 (October 1, 1915): 104.

COLLECTED: P, O, SP, ColP, ComP.

Diligence is to Magic as Progress is to Flight

FIRST PUBLISHED: *The Egoist* 10.2 (October 1, 1915): 158.

COLLECTED: P, O.

To a Snail

FIRST PUBLISHED: In O.

COLLECTED: O, SP, ColP, ComP.

"The Bricks are Fallen Down, We Will Build with Hewn Stones. The Sycamores are Cut Down, We Will Change to Cedars."

FIRST PUBLISHED: In *O*.

COLLECTED: *O*.

George Moore

FIRST PUBLISHED: *Others* 1.6 (December 1915): 105–6.

COLLECTED: *O*.

"Nothing will Cure the Sick Lion but to Eat an Ape"

FIRST PUBLISHED: In *O*.

COLLECTED: *O*, *SP* (as "'Nothing Will Cure'"), *ColP*, *ComP*.

To the Peacock of France

FIRST PUBLISHED: As "French Peacock" in *Others: An Anthology of the New Verse (1917)*, ed. Alfred Kreymborg (New York: Knopf, 1917), 77.

COLLECTED: *O*, *SP*, *ColP*, *ComP*.

In this Age of Hard Trying, Nonchalance is Good and

FIRST PUBLISHED: *The Chimaera* 1.2 (July 1916): 52–5.

COLLECTED: *P*, *O*, *ComP*. As "In This Age of Hard Trying" in *SP*, *ColP*.

The 1925 *Observations* version has the phrase "They need not" rather than "They did not" at the end of the second line. Because all other versions, including the first periodical publication, have "They did not" I have used that phrase in the main text.

To Statecraft Embalmed

FIRST PUBLISHED: *Others* 1.6 (December 1915): 104.
COLLECTED: *O, SP, ColP, Comp*.

The Monkey Puzzler

FIRST PUBLISHED: *Dial* 78 (January 1925): 8.
COLLECTED: *O* (second edition), as "The Monkey Puzzle" in *SP, ColP, Comp*.

Poetry

FIRST PUBLISHED: *Others* 5.6 (July 1919): 5.
COLLECTED: *P, O, SP, ColP, Comp*.
Copy-text is *Observations* (New York: The Dial Press, 1924). Arguably Moore's most famous poem, it is also her most reprinted and most revised. In addition to the 1924 version printed in this volume there are three other notable versions, from 1925, 1932, and 1967.

a) from *O* (1925):

Poetry

I too, dislike it:
there are things that are important beyond all this fiddle.
The bat, upside down; the elephant pushing,
a tireless wolf under a tree,
the base-ball fan, the statistician—
"business documents and schoolbooks"—
these phenomena are pleasing,
but when they have been fashioned
into that which is unknowable,
we are not entertained.
It may be said of all of us
that we do not admire what we cannot understand;
enigmas are not poetry.

b) from *The New Poetry*, eds. Harriet Monroe and Alice Corbin Henderson (New York: Macmillan, 1932), 414:

Poetry

I too, dislike it; there are things
   that are important beyond all this fiddle. Reading it,
     however, with a perfect contempt for it,
       one discovers that there is in it, after all, a place for
        the genuine:
         hands that can grasp, eyes that can dilate, hair that
          can rise if it must,

the bat holding on upside down,
   an elephant pushing, a tireless wolf under a tree,
   the immovable critic twitching his skin
     like a horse that feels a fly, the base-ball fan,
       the statistician—nor is it
        valid to discriminate against business documents,
        school-books,

trade reports—these phenomena
   are important; but dragged into conscious oddity by
   half poets, the result is not poetry.
     This we know. In a liking for the raw material in all
      its rawness,
      and for that which is genuine, there is liking for
       poetry.

c) from *ComP*:

Poetry

I, too, dislike it.
  Reading it, however, with a perfect contempt for it,
     one discovers in
  it, after all, a place for the genuine.

The Past is the Present

There is another poem with this title in the Appendix to this volume. They are two different poems, despite sharing a title. The poem called "The Past is the Present" in this, the *Observations* section, was first published as "So far as the future is concerned, 'Shall not one say, with the Russian philosopher, "How is one to know what one doesn't know?"' So far as the present is concerned," (*Others* 1.6 [December 1915]: 106).

COLLECTED: *O*, *SP*, *ColP*, *ComP*.

Pedantic Literalist

FIRST PUBLISHED: *The Egoist* 6.3 (June 1, 1916): 95.
COLLECTED: *P*, *O*, *SP*, *ColP*, *ComP*.

"He Wrote The History Book"

FIRST PUBLISHED: As "'He Wrote the History Book, It Said'" in *The Egoist* 5.3 (May 1, 1916): 71.
COLLECTED: *O*, *SP*, *ColP*, *ComP*.

Critics and Connoisseurs

FIRST PUBLISHED: *Others* 3.1 (July 1916): 4–5.
COLLECTED: *O*, *SP*, *ColP*, *ComP*.

To be Liked by You Would be a Calamity

FIRST PUBLISHED: *The Chimaera* 1.2 (July 1916): 56.
COLLECTED: *O*.

Like a Bulrush

FIRST PUBLISHED: *Others: An Anthology of the New Verse (1917)*, ed. Alfred Kreymborg (New York: Knopf, 1917), 76.
COLLECTED: *O*, *SP*.

Sojourn in the Whale

FIRST PUBLISHED: *Others: An Anthology of the New Verse (1917)*, ed. Alfred Kreymborg (New York: Knopf, 1917), 78.
COLLECTED: *O, SP, ColP, ComP.*

My Apish Cousins

FIRST PUBLISHED: *Others: An Anthology of the New Verse (1917)*, ed. Alfred Kreymborg (New York: Knopf, 1917), 83–4.
COLLECTED: *P, O.* As "The Monkeys" in *SP, ColP, ComP.*

Roses Only

FIRST PUBLISHED: *Others: An Anthology of the New Verse (1917)*, ed. Alfred Kreymborg (New York: Knopf, 1917), 80–1.
COLLECTED: *P, O, SP.*

Reinforcements

FIRST PUBLISHED: *The Egoist* 6.5 (June–July 1918): 83.
COLLECTED: *P, O.*

The Fish

FIRST PUBLISHED: *The Egoist* 7.5 (August 1918): 95.
COLLECTED: *P, O, SP, ColP, ComP.*

Black Earth

FIRST PUBLISHED: *The Egoist* 4.5 (April 1918): 55–6.
COLLECTED: *P, O, SP.* As "Melanchthon" in *ColP.*

Radical

FIRST PUBLISHED: *Others* 5 (March 1919): 15.
COLLECTED: *P*, *O*.

In the Days of Prismatic Color

FIRST PUBLISHED: *The Lantern* 27 (Spring 1919): 35.
COLLECTED: *P*, *O*, *SP*, *ColP* (using the spelling "Colour"), *ComP*.

Peter

FIRST PUBLISHED: *O*.
COLLECTED: *O*, *SP*, *ColP*, *ComP*.
In *ComP* the poem appears in the following free-verse version:

Peter

   Strong and slippery,
built for the midnight grass-party
confronted by four cats, he sleeps his time away—
the detached first claw on the foreleg corresponding
to the thumb, retracted to its tip; the small tuft of fronds
or katydid-legs above each eye numbering all units
in each group; the shadbones regularly set about the mouth
to droop or rise in unison like porcupine-quills.
He lets himself be flattened out by gravity,
as seaweed is tamed and weakened by the sun,
compelled when extended, to lie stationary.
Sleep is the result of his delusion that one must
do as well as one can for oneself,
sleep—epitome of what is to him the end of life.
Demonstrate on him how the lady placed a forked stick
on the innocuous neck-sides of the dangerous southern snake.
One need not try to stir him up; his prune-shaped head
and alligator-eyes are not party to the joke.
Lifted and handled, he may be dangled like an eel
or set up on the forearm like a mouse;
his eyes bisected by pupils of a pin's width,
are flickeringly exhibited, then covered up.

May be? I should have said might have been;
when he has been got the better of in a dream—
as in a fight with nature or with cats, we all know it.
Profound sleep is not with him a fixed illusion.
Springing about with froglike accuracy, with jerky cries
when taken in hand, he is himself again;
to sit caged by the rungs of a domestic chair
would be unprofitable—human. What is the good of
        hypocrisy?
It is permissible to choose one's employment,
to abandon the nail, or roly-poly,
when it shows signs of being no longer a pleasure,
to score the nearby magazine with a double line of strokes.
He can talk but insolently says nothing. What of it?
When one is frank, one's very presence is a compliment.
It is clear that he can see the virtue of naturalness,
that he does not regard the published fact as a surrender.
As for the disposition invariably to affront,
an animal with claws should have an opportunity to use them.
The eel-like extension of trunk into tail is not an accident.
To leap, to lengthen out, divide the air, to purloin, to pursue.
To tell the hen: fly over the fence, go in the wrong way
in your perturbation—this is life;
to do less would be nothing but dishonesty.

Dock Rats

FIRST PUBLISHED: *Others for 1919: An Anthology of the New Verse*, ed. Alfred Kreymborg (New York: Nicholas Brown, 1920), 127–8.

COLLECTED: *P, O.*

Picking And Choosing

FIRST PUBLISHED: *Dial* 68 (April 1920): 421–2.

COLLECTED: *P, O, SP, ColP, Comp*.

In *Comp* the poem appears in the following free-verse version:

Picking and Choosing

Literature is a phase of life. If one is afraid of it,
the situation is irremediable; if one approaches it familiarly,
what one says of it is worthless.
The opaque allusion, the simulated flight upward,
accomplishes nothing. Why cloud the fact
that Shaw is self-conscious in the field of sentiment
but is otherwise rewarding; that James
is all that has been said of him. It is not Hardy the novelist
and Hardy the poet, but one man interpreting life as emotion.
The critic should know what he likes:
Gordon Craig with his "this is I" and "this is mine,"
with his three wise men, his "sad French greens," and his
            "Chinese cherry"
Gordon Craig so inclinational and unashamed—a critic.
And Burke is a psychologist, of acute raccoon-like curiosity.
Summa diligentia; to the humbug whose name is so
            amusing—
very young and very rushed—Caesar crossed the Alps
on the top of a *"diligence"*!
We are not daft about the meaning,
but this familiarity with wrong meanings puzzles one.
Humming-bug, the candles are not wired for electricity.
Small dog, going over the lawn nipping the linen and saying
that you have a badger—remember Xenophon;
only rudimentary behavior is necessary to put us on the scent.
"A right good salvo of barks," a few strong wrinkles
            puckering
the skin between the ears, is all we ask.

England

FIRST PUBLISHED: *Dial* 68 (April 1920): 422–3.

COLLECTED: *P, O, SP, ColP, ComP.*

In *ComP* the poem appears in the following free-verse version:

England

with its baby rivers and little towns, each with its abbey or
        its cathedral,
with voices—one voice perhaps, echoing through the
        transept—the
criterion of suitability and convenience: and Italy
with its equal shores—contriving an epicureanism
from which the grossness has been extracted,

and Greece with its goat and its gourds,
the nest of modified illusions: and France,
the "chrysalis of the nocturnal butterfly,"
in whose products mystery of construction
diverts one from what was originally one's object—
substance at the core: and the East with its snails,
        its emotional

shorthand and jade cockroaches, its rock crystal and
        its imperturbability,
all of museum quality: and America where there
is the little old ramshackle victoria in the south,
where cigars are smoked on the street in the north;
where there are no proofreaders, no silkworms,
        no digressions;

the wild man's land; grassless, linksless, languageless country
        in which letters are written
not in Spanish, not in Greek, not in Latin, not in shorthand,
but in plain American which cats and dogs can read!
The letter *a* in psalm and calm when
pronounced with the sound of *a* in candle, is very noticeable,
        but

why should continents of misapprehension
have to be accounted for by the fact?
Does it follow that because there are poisonous toadstools
which resemble mushrooms, both are dangerous?

Of mettlesomeness which may be mistaken for appetite,
of heat which may appear to be haste,
no conclusions may be drawn.

To have misapprehended the matter is to have confessed that
                    one has not looked far enough.
The sublimated wisdom of China, Egyptian discernment,
the cataclysmic torrent of emotion
compressed in the verbs of the Hebrew language,
the books of the man who is able to say,
"I envy nobody but him, and him only,
who catches more fish than
I do"—the flower and fruit of all that noted superiority—
if not stumbled upon in America,
must one imagine that it is not there?
It has never been confined to one locality.

When I Buy Pictures

FIRST PUBLISHED: *Dial* 71 (July 1921): 33.

COLLECTED: *P, O, SP, ColP, ComP*.

In addition to the 1925 version reprinted in this volume there are two
other notable versions, both from 1921.

a) from the *Dial*:

When I Buy Pictures

or what is closer to the truth,
when I look at that of which I may regard myself as the
                    imaginary possessor,
I fix upon what would give me pleasure in my average
                    moments:
the satire upon curiosity, in which no more is discernible than
                    the intensity of the mood;
or quite the opposite—the old thing, the mediaeval decorated
                    hat-box,
in which there are hounds with waists diminishing like the
                    waist of the hour-glass
and deer and birds and seated people;
it may be no more than a square of parquetry; the literal
                    biography perhaps—

in letters standing well apart upon a parchment-like expanse;
an artichoke in six varieties of blue; the snipe-legged
        hieroglyphic in three parts;
the silver fence protecting Adam's grave or Michael taking
        Adam by the wrist.
Too stern an intellectual emphasis upon this quality or that,
        detracts from one's enjoyment;
it must not wish to disarm anything; nor may the approved
        triumph easily be honoured—
that which is great because something else is small.
It comes to this: of whatever sort it is,
it must acknowledge the forces which have made it;
it must be "lit with piercing glances into the life of things;"
then I "take it in hand as a savage would take a looking-
        glass."

b) from *Poems* (Egoist Press, 1921): 17:

When I Buy Pictures

or what is closer to the truth, when I look at
    that of which I may regard myself as the
        imaginary possessor, I fix upon that which would
    give me pleasure in my average moments: the satire
            upon curiosity,
        in which no more is discernible than the intensity of
            the mood;

or quite the opposite—the old thing, the medi-
    aeval decorated hat-box, in which there
        are hounds with waists diminishing like the waist of
            the hour-glass
    and deer, both white and brown, and birds and seated
            people; it may be no more than a square
    of parquetry; the literal biography perhaps—in letters
            stand-

ing well apart upon a parchment-like expanse;
    or that which is better without words, which means
        just as much or just as little as it is understood to
        mean by the observer—the grave of Adam, prefigured
            by himself; a bed of beans
        or artichokes in six varieties of blue; the snipe-legged
            hiero-

glyphic in three parts; it may be anything. Too
    stern an intellectual emphasis, i-
        ronic or other—upon this quality or that, detracts
    from one's enjoyment; it must not wish to disarm anything;
        nor may the approved tri-
        umph easily be honoured—that which is great because
        something else is small.

    It comes to this: of whatever sort it is, it
        must make known the fact that it has been displayed
        to acknowledge the spiritual forces which have made it;
    and it must admit that it is the work of X, if X produced it;
        of Y, if made
    by Y. It must be a voluntary gift with the name written
        on it.

A Grave

FIRST PUBLISHED: As "A Graveyard" in *Dial* 71 (July 1921): 34.
COLLECTED: *O, SP, ColP, ComP.*

Those Various Scalpels

FIRST PUBLISHED: *Lantern* 25 (Spring 1917): 50–1.
COLLECTED: *P, O, SP, ColP, ComP.*

The Labors of Hercules

FIRST PUBLISHED: *Dial* 71 (December 1921): 638.
COLLECTED: *O, SP* (using the spelling "Labours"), *ColP* (using the spelling "Labours"), *ComP.*

New York

FIRST PUBLISHED: *Dial* 71 (December 1921): 637.
COLLECTED: *O, SP, ColP, ComP.*

People's Surroundings

FIRST PUBLISHED: *Dial* 72 (June 1922): 588–90.
COLLECTED: O, SP, ColP, ComP.

Snakes, Mongooses, Snake-Charmers, and the Like

FIRST PUBLISHED: *Broom* 1.3 (January 1922): 193.
COLLECTED: O, ComP. As "Snakes, Mongooses" in *SP* and *ColP*.

Bowls

FIRST PUBLISHED: *Secession* 5 (July 1923): 12.
COLLECTED: O, SP, ColP, ComP.

Novices

FIRST PUBLISHED: *Dial* 74 (February 1923): 183–4.
COLLECTED: O, SP, ColP, ComP.

Marriage

FIRST PUBLISHED: *Manikin Number Three* (New York: Monroe Wheeler, 1923).
COLLECTED: O, SP, ColP, ComP.

Silence

FIRST PUBLISHED: *Dial* 77 (October 1924): 290.
COLLECTED: O, SP, ColP, ComP.

An Octopus

FIRST PUBLISHED: *Dial* 77 (December 1924): 475–81.
COLLECTED: O, *SP*, *ColP*, *ComP*.
Both *ColP* and *ComP* omit thirty-two lines, from "Larkspur, blue pincushions, blue pease, and lupin;" through "by the collision of knowledge with knowledge."

Sea Unicorns and Land Unicorns

FIRST PUBLISHED: *Dial* 77 (November 1924): 411–13.
COLLECTED: O, *SP*, *ColP*, *ComP*.

Index

O. Copy-text is the 1924 version. The page numbers have been changed to refer to the present edition.

POEMS 1932–1936

This section includes the new poems Moore published in *SP*, and those she published in periodicals after *SP* but did not collect in *POV*. I have placed the poems in chronological order of their first periodical publication. Unless otherwise noted copy-text for all poems is *SP*, as the variants between the first printings and *SP* versions are minor and include copy-editing corrections. For full documentation of all variants for each poem until 1936, including facsimile reproductions of each poem's first publication, see Moore (ed. White) *A-Quiver*.

Part of a Novel, Part of a Poem, Part of a Play

Copy-text *Poetry* 40 (June 1932): 119–28. Moore first published "The Steeple-Jack," "The Hero," and "The Student" under this group title in *Poetry*. She preserved the group title in *SP*, listing it (instead of the poems' individual titles) in the table of contents. However, although she preserved the tripartite title in *SP*, she did not include "The Student." Instead, she included an extensively revised version of that poem, nine years later, in *WAY*. She left that version out of *ColP*, then re-inserted it in *ComP*.

The Steeple-Jack

COLLECTED: *SP*, *ColP*, *ComP*.

The *SP* version omits stanza six, and the *ColP* version omits stanzas five through nine. The *ComP* version restores all of the original stanzas, making the 1967 version of "The Steeple-Jack" the only example of a poem returned to its original length as a result of Moore's revisions.

From *CoIP*:

The Steeple-Jack

Dürer would have seen a reason for living
    in a town like this, with eight stranded whales
to look at; with the sweet sea air coming into your house
on a fine day, from water etched
    with waves as formal as the scales
on a fish.

One by one, in two's, in three's, the seagulls keep
    flying back and forth over the town clock,
or sailing around the lighthouse without moving their
    wings—
rising steadily with a slight
    quiver of the body—or flock
mewing where

a sea the purple of the peacock's neck is
    paled to greenish azure as Dürer changed
the pine green of the Tyrol to peacock blue and guinea
grey. You can see a twenty-five-
    pound lobster and fish-nets arranged
to dry. The

whirlwind fife-and-drum of the storm bends the salt
    marsh grass, disturbs stars in the sky and the
star on the steeple; it is a privilege to see so
much confusion.

            A steeple-jack in red, has let
    a rope down as a spider spins a thread;
he might be part of a novel, but on the sidewalk a
sign says C. J. Poole, Steeple-Jack,
    in black and white; and one in red
and white says

Danger. The church portico has four fluted
    columns, each a single piece of stone, made
modester by white-wash. This would be a fit haven for
waifs, children, animals, prisoners,
    and presidents who have repaid
sin-driven

senators by not thinking about them. One
    sees a school-house, a post-office in a
store, fish-houses, hen-houses, a three-masted schooner on
the stocks. The hero, the student,
    the steeple-jack, each in his way,
is at home.

It scarcely could be dangerous to be living
    in a town like this, of simple people
who have a steeple-jack placing danger-signs by the church
when he is gilding the solid-
    pointed star, which on a steeple
stands for hope.

The Student

COLLECTED: *WAY, ComP*, in the following version:

The Student

"In America," began
the lecturer, "everyone must have a
degree. The French do not think that
all can have it, they don't say everyone
    must go to college." We
do incline to feel
    that although it may be unnecessary

to know fifteen languages,
one degree is not too much. With us, a
school—like the singing tree of which
the leaves were mouths singing in concert—is
    both a tree of knowledge
and of liberty,—
    seen in the unanimity of college

mottoes, *lux et veritas,*
Christo et ecclesiae, sapiet
felici. It may be that we
have not knowledge, just opinions, that we
    are undergraduates,
not students; we know
    we have been told with smiles, by expatriates

of whom we had asked "When will
your experiment be finished?" "Science
is never finished." Secluded
from domestic strife, Jack Bookworm led a
    college life, says Goldsmith;
and here also as
    in France or Oxford, study is beset with

dangers,—with bookworms, mildews,
and complaisancies. But someone in New
England has known enough to say
the student is patience personified,
    is a variety
of hero, "patient
    of neglect and of reproach,"—who can "hold by

himself." You can't beat hens to
make them lay. Wolf's wool is the best of wool,
but it cannot be sheared because
the wolf will not comply. With knowledge as
    with the wolf's surliness,
the student studies
    voluntarily, refusing to be less

than individual. He
"gives his opinion and then rests on it;"
he renders service when there is
no reward, and is too reclusive for
    some things to seem to touch
him, not because he
    has no feeling but because he has so much.

The Hero

COLLECTED: *SP*, *ColP*, *ComP*.

No Swan So Fine

FIRST PUBLISHED: *Poetry* 41 (October 1932): 7.

COLLECTED: *SP, ColP, ComP.*

In its first publication "ambidextrous" takes the place of "gondoliering" in line four.

The Jerboa

FIRST PUBLISHED: *Hound & Horn* 6 (October–December 1932): 108–13.

COLLECTED: *SP, ColP, ComP.*

ColP and *ComP* omit the fourth stanza of the "Abundance" section. The surrounding lines from stanzas three and five are rewritten to conceal the omission:

> with the tail as a weight,
> undulated out by speed, straight.

> Looked at by daylight,
> the underside's white,
>   though the fur on the back
> is buff-brown

Camellia Sabina

FIRST PUBLISHED: *Active Anthology* ed. Ezra Pound (London: Faber & Faber, 1933): 189–91.

COLLECTED: *SP, ColP, ComP.*

In its first publication the penultimate line of each stanza has a caesura of four spaces after the first three syllables of the line (always corresponding to a word break). Cf. "Nine Nectarines and Other Porcelain," "The Pangolin," and "Spenser's Ireland."

The Plumet Basilisk

FIRST PUBLISHED: *Active Anthology* ed. Ezra Pound (London: Faber & Faber, 1933): 199–205.

COLLECTED: *SP, ColP, ComP.*

Moore allowed Pound to print "The Plumet Basilisk" (along with "The Steeple-Jack," "No Swan So Fine," "The Jerboa," and "Camellia Sabina") in his 1933 *Active Anthology*. The anthology appeared nearly simultaneously with the poem's publication in *Hound & Horn* 7 (October–December 1933): 29–34. In the *Hound & Horn* version, as in all subsequent versions, Moore omitted the last four stanzas of the first section, "In Costa Rica."

The Frigate Pelican

FIRST PUBLISHED: *Criterion* 13 (July 1934): 557–60.

COLLECTED: *SP, ColP, ComP.*

ColP and *ComP* omit six and a half stanzas, marking the omission in the middle of the poem with an ellipsis, and ending the poem with a four-line stanza:

The Frigate Pelican

Rapidly cruising or lying on the air there is a bird
    that realizes Rasselas's friend's project
    of wings uniting levity with strength. This
        hell-diver, frigate-bird, hurricane-
bird; unless swift is the proper word
    for him, the storm omen when
he flies close to the waves, should be seen
    fishing, although oftener
    he appears to prefer

to take, on the wing, from industrious crude-winged species
    the fish they have caught, and is seldom successless.
    A marvel of grace, no matter how fast his
        victim may fly or how often may
turn. The others with similar ease,
    slowly rising once more,
        move out to the top
        of the circle and stop

and blow back, allowing the wind to reverse their direction—
  Unlike the more stalwart swan that can ferry the
  woodcutter's two children home. Make hay; keep
    the shop; I have one sheep; were a less
limber animal's mottoes. This one
    finds sticks for the swan's-down-dress
  of his child to rest upon and would
    not know Gretel from Hänsel.
    As impassioned Handel—

meant for a lawyer and a masculine German domestic
  career—clandestinely studied the harpsichord
  and never was known to have fallen in love,
    the unconfiding frigate-bird hides
in the height and in the majestic
    display of his art. He glides
  a hundred feet or quivers about
    as charred paper behaves—full
    of feints; and an eagle

of vigilance. . . . *Festina lente.* Be gay
  civilly? How so? 'If I do well I am blessed
  whether any bless me or not, and if I do
    ill I am cursed.' We watch the moon rise
on the Susquehanna. In his way,
    this most romantic bird flies
  to a more mundane place, the mangrove
    swamp to sleep. He wastes the moon.
    But he and others, soon

rise from the bough and though flying, are able to foil
        the tired
  moment of danger that lays on heart and lungs the
  weight of the python that crushes to powder.

The Buffalo

FIRST PUBLISHED: *Poetry* 45 (November 1934): 61–4.

COLLECTED: *SP, ColP, ComP*.

ColP and *ComP* versions omit the last three lines of stanza two, and the first half of the first line of stanza three. The omission is marked by a line of six evenly-spaced dots:

> tail; what would that express?
> And John Steuart Curry's Ajax pulling
> grass—no ring
>   in his nose—two birds standing on the back?
>
> .   .   .   .   .   .
>
>   The modern
> ox does not look like the Augsburg ox's
> portrait. Yes,

Nine Nectarines and Other Porcelain

FIRST PUBLISHED: *Poetry* 45 (November 1934): 64–7.

COLLECTED: *SP, ColP* (as "Nine Nectarines"), *ComP* (as "Nine Nectarines").

In *Poetry* 45 the penultimate line of each stanza has a caesura of four spaces before the final syllables of the line (always corresponding with a word break). Cf. "Camellia Sabina," "The Pangolin" and "Spenser's Ireland." *ColP* and *ComP* versions omit three and a half stanzas. The omission is marked by a line of five evenly-spaced dots:

Nine Nectarines

> Arranged by two's as peaches are,
> at intervals that all may live—
>   eight and a single one, on twigs that
>   grew the year before—they look like
> a derivative;
>   although not uncommonly
> the opposite is seen—
> nine peaches on a nectarine.
>   Fuzzless through slender crescent leaves
>   of green or blue or
>   both, in the Chinese style, the four

pairs' half-moon leaf-mosaic turns
out to the sun the sprinkled blush
   of puce-American-Beauty pink
   applied to bees-wax grey by the
unenquiring brush
   of mercantile bookbinding.
Like the peach *Yu,* the red-
cheeked peach which cannot aid the dead,
      but eaten in time prevents death,
         the Italian
         peach-nut, Persian plum, Ispahan

      secluded wall-grown nectarine,
as wild spontaneous fruit was
      found in China first. But was it wild?
      Prudent de Candolle would not say.
One perceives no flaws
   in this emblematic group
of nine, with leaf window
unquilted by *curculio*
   which someone once depicted on
      this much-mended plate or
      in the also accurate

   unantlered moose or Iceland horse
or ass asleep against the old
   thick, low-leaning nectarine that is the
   colour of the shrub-tree's brownish
flower.

               .   .   .   .   .

   A Chinese 'understands
the spirit of the wilderness'
   and the nectarine-loving kylin
   of pony appearance—the long-
tailed or the tailless
   small cinnamon-brown, common
camel-haired unicorn
with antelope feet and no horn,
   here enamelled on porcelain.
      It was a Chinese
      who imagined this masterpiece.

Pigeons

FIRST PUBLISHED: *Poetry* 47 (November 1935): 61–5. Copy-text.
COLLECTED: Uncollected.

See in the Midst of Fair Leaves

FIRST PUBLISHED: *New Directions in Prose and Poetry*, ed. James
Laughlin (Norfolk, Conn.: New Directions, 1936), 56. Copy-text.
COLLECTED: *WAY.*

Walking-Sticks and Paperweights and Watermarks

FIRST PUBLISHED: *Poetry* 49 (November 1936): 59–64. Copy-text.
COLLECTED: *WAY* in the following version:

Walking-Sticks and Paper-Weights and Water Marks

Jointed against indecision,
the three legs of the triskelion
    meeting in the
middle between triangles, run
in unison,
    self-assisted. And yet, trudging
    on two legs that move contradictorily,
despite ghosts and witches, one
    does not fear to ask for beauty.

Stepped glass has been made in Ireland;
they still have blackthorn walking-sticks, and
    flax and linen
and paper-mills; and reprimand
you if you stand
    your stick on such and such a spot.
    You must keep to the path "on account of the
souls." And all can understand
    how centralizing loyalty

shapes matter as a die is hid
while used; and that such power, unavid
    since secure, can

mold an at first fluid solid
glass weight. Amid
   the wax the seal is safe. Also
   as the water mark's translucence clearly seen
can fascinate, the vivid-
    ly white flower attracts one lightly

brushing against sceptre-headed
weeds and daisies swayed by wind. [They said,
   "Do not scatter
your stick, on account of the dead."]
The pathway led
   into woods "where leafy trees meet
   overhead and noise of traffic is unknown"—
the mind exhilarated
   by life all round, so stirringly

alive. Fancy's rude root cudgel
with the bark left on, the woodbine smell-
   ing of the rain,
the very stones had life. Little
scars on churchbell-
   tongues, put there by the Devil's claws,
   and other forms of negativeness need but
be expressed and visible,
   to prove their unauthority.

Patience, with its superlatives,
firmness and loyalty and faith, gives
   intensive fruit.
As a device before it leaves
the wax, receives
   to give, and giving must itself
   receive, "difficulty is ordained to check
poltroons," and courage achieves
   despaired-of ends inversely,—

mute with power and strong with fear.
A bold outspoken gentleman, cheer-
   ful, plodding, to-
the-point, used to the atmosphere
of work, and there-
   fore author of the permanent,
   says modestly, "This is my taste, it might not

be another man's." Sincere
    unforced unconscious honesty,

sine cera, can be furthest
from self-defensiveness and nearest;
    as when a seal
without haste, slowly is impressed,
and forms a nest
    on which the raised device reversed,
    shows round. It must have been an able workman,
humorous and self-possessed,
        a liker of solidity,

who gave this greenish Waterford
glass weight with the summit curled down toward
    itself as the
    glass grew, the look of tempered sword-
steel; of three-ore-d
    fishscale-burnished antimony-
    lead-and-tin smoky water-drop type-metal
smoothness emery-armored
        against rust. Its subdued glossy

splendor leaps out at the eye as
the light does not shine even from glass
    air-twist canes, or
witchballs. This paperweight, in mass
a stone, surpass-
    ing it in tint, enlarges the
    fine chain-lines on the letter-flap weighted by
its hardened rain-drop surface.
        The paper-mold's similarly

at first unsolid blues, yellow-
whites and lavenders, when seen through, show
    leopards, eagles,
quills, acorns and anvils. "Stones grow,"
as volcano-
    sides and quartz mines prove. "Plants feel? Men
    think." "Airmail is quick." "Save rags, bones, metals."
            Hopes
are harvest when deeds follow
        words postmarked "Dig for victory."

Postmark behests are clearer than
the water marks beneath,—than ox, swan,
    crane, or dolphin,
than eastern, open, jewelled, Span-
ish, Umbrian
    crown,—as symbols of endurance.
    And making the envelope secure, the sealed
wax reveals a pelican
        studying affectionately

the nest's three-in-one upturned tri-
form face. "For those we love, live and die"
    the motto reads.
The pelican's community
of throats, the high-
    way's trivia or crow's-foot where
    three roads meet, the fugue, the awl-leafed juniper's
whorls of three, objectify
        welded divisiveness. Of the

juniper that in balladry
has been kept green, the fugue's three times three
    reiterat-
ed chain of interactingly
linked harmony,
    says "On the first day of Christmas
    my true love he sent unto me, part of a
bough of a juniper-tree,"
        repeated to infinity.

THE PANGOLIN AND OTHER VERSE (1936)

Copy-text for all poems is *The Pangolin and Other Verse* (London: The Brendin Publishing Co., 1936). In *POV* Moore grouped "Virginia Britannia," "Bird-Witted," "Half Deity," and "Smooth Gnarled Crape Myrtle" as a series, under the common title "The Old Dominion." For full documentation of all variants for each poem until 1936, including facsimile reproductions of each poem's first publication, and *POV* itself, see Moore (ed. White), *A-Quiver*.

Virginia Britannia

FIRST PUBLISHED: *Life and Letters Today* 13 (December 1935): 61–5.

COLLECTED: *POV, WAY, ColP, ComP.*

In addition to the *POV* version printed in this volume there are two significant variant versions of the poem's final stanza:

a) *Life and Letters Today*:

> they say. The live-oak's moss-draped
> undulating massiveness, the white
>   pine, the English hackberry—handsomest vis-
> itor of all, the
>   cedar's etched solidity,
>   the cypress, lose identity
> and are one tree, as
>   sunset flames increasingly
>   over the leaf-chis-
> selled blackening ridge of green.
> Expanding to
> earth size, igniting redundantly
> wind-widened clouds, it can
>   not move bothered-with-wages
>   new savages,
> but gives the child an intimation
>   of what glory is.

b) *WAY, ColP, Comp* (*ColP* and *Comp* compress the final seven lines into six):

> The live oak's darkening fila-
> gree of undulating boughs, the etched
>   solidity of a cypress indivis-
>   ible from the now
>   agèd English hackberry,
>   become with lost identity,
>   part of the ground, as
>   sunset flames increasingly
>   against the leaf-chis-
> selled blackening ridge of green;
> while clouds, expanding above
> the town's assertiveness, dwarf
> it, dwarf arrogance
>   that can misunderstand
>   importance; and
> are to the child an intimation of
>   what glory is.

Bird-Witted

FIRST PUBLISHED: *New Republic* 85 (January 22, 1936): 311.
COLLECTED: *POV, WAY, ColP, Comp.*

Half Deity

FIRST PUBLISHED: *Direction* 1 (January–March 1935): 74–5.
COLLECTED: *POV, WAY.*

Moore revised the poem extensively for *WAY*, removing all direct references to the myth of Eros and Psyche:

Half Deity

> half worm. We all, infant and adult, have
>   stopped to watch the butterfly, last of the
>   elves, and learned to spare the wingless worm
>   that hopefully ascends the tree. What zebra
>   could surpass the zebra-

striped swallow-tail of South America
on whose half-transparent wings, crescents engrave

the silken edge with dragon's blood, weightless?
    They that have wings must not have weights. The north's
    yellower swallow-tail with a pitch-
        fork-scalloped edge, has tails blunter at the tip.
    Flying with droverlike
        tenacity and weary from its trip,
one has lighted on the elm. Its yellowness

that almost counterfeits a leaf's, has just
    now been observed. A nymph approaches, dressed
    in Wedgwood blue, tries to touch it and
        must follow to *micromalus,* the midget
    crab-tree, to a pear-tree,
        and from that, to the flowering pomegranate.
Defeated but encouraged by each new gust

of wind, forced by the summer sun to pant,
    she stands on rug-soft grass; though some are not
    permitted to gaze informally
        on majesty in such a manner as she
    is gazing here. The blind
        all-seeing butterfly, afraid of the
slight finger, floats as though it were ignorant,

across the path, and choosing a flower's palm
    of air and stamens, settles; then pawing
    like a horse, turns round,—apostrophe-
        tipped brown antennae porcupining out as
    it arranges nervous
        wings. Aware that curiosity has
been pursuing it, it cannot now be calm.

The butterfly's tobacco-brown unglazed
    china eyes and furry countenance confront
    the nymph's large eyes—gray eyes that now are
        black, for she with controlled agitated glance
    explores the insect's face
        and all's a-quiver with significance.
It is Goya's scene of the tame magpie faced

by crouching cats. Butterflies do not need
    home advice. As though the admiring nymph

were patent-leather cricket singing
   loud or gnat-catching garden-toad, the swallow-
tail bewitched and haughty,
   springs away; flies where she cannot follow,
trampling the air as it trampled the flowers, feed-

ing where it pivots. Equine irascible
   unwormlike unteachable butterfly-
zebra! Sometimes one is grateful to
   a stranger for looking very nice; to the
friendly outspread hand. But
   it flies, drunken with triviality
or guided by visions of strength, off until,

diminishing like wreckage on the sea,
   rising and falling easily, it mounts
the swell and keeping its true course with
   what swift majesty, indifferent to
her, is gone. Deaf to ap-
   proval, magnet-nice as it fluttered through
airs now slack now fresh, it had strict ears when the

west wind spoke; for pleased by the butterfly's
   inconsequential ease, he held no net,
did not regard the butterfly-bush
   as a trap, hid no decoy in half-shut
palm since his is not a
   covetous hand. It was not Oberon, but
this quietest wind with piano replies,

the zephyr, whose detachment was enough
   to tempt the fiery tiger-horse to stand,
eyes staring skyward and chest arching
   bravely out—historic metamorphoser
and saintly animal
   in India, in Egypt, anywhere.
Their talk was as strange as my grandmother's muff.

Smooth Gnarled Crape Myrtle

FIRST PUBLISHED: As "Smooth Gnarled Crepe Myrtle!" in *New English Weekly* 8 (October 17, 1935): 13.
COLLECTED: *POV, WAY, ColP, ComP.*

The Pangolin

FIRST PUBLISHED: *POV.*
COLLECTED: *POV, WAY, ColP, ComP.*
In *POV* and *WAY* the eighth line of each stanza has a caesura of four spaces after the first four syllables of the line (always corresponding to a word break). Cf. "Camellia Sabina," "Nine Nectarines and Other Porcelain," and "Spenser's Ireland."

from WHAT ARE YEARS (1941)

Copy-text for all poems is *What Are Years* (New York: Macmillan, 1941). In addition to the poems included in this section, *WAY* contains revised versions of "Walking-Sticks and Paper-Weights and Water Marks," "The Student," "Half Deity," "Smooth Gnarled Crape Myrtle," "Bird-Witted," "Virginia Britannia," "See in the Midst of Fair Leaves," and "The Pangolin." See the "Original Tables of Contents" section of this volume for Moore's ordering. For full documentation of all variants for each poem until 1941, including facsimile reproductions of each poem's first publication and of *WAY*, see Moore (ed. White) *Adversity*.

What are Years?

FIRST PUBLISHED: *Kenyon Review* 2 (Summer 1940): 286.
COLLECTED: *WAY, ColP, ComP.*

Rigorists

FIRST PUBLISHED: *Life and Letters Today* 26 (September 1940): 243–4.
COLLECTED: *WAY, ColP, ComP.*
In *Life and Letters Today* the poem's final four lines are:

of the Esquimaux ; a stubborn race, gone

  but for it—for
it, imported by a missionary,
fervent man. Its firm face is augury.

Light is Speech

FIRST PUBLISHED: *Decision* 1 (March 1941): 26.
COLLECTED: *WAY*, *ColP*, *ComP*.

He "Digesteth Harde Yron"

FIRST PUBLISHED: *Partisan Review* 8 (July–August 1941): 312–14.
COLLECTED: *WAY*, *ColP*, *ComP*.

ColP and *ComP* omit half of stanza six, and all of stanzas seven and eight. The omission is marked with a line of six evenly-spaced dots:

> He 'Digesteth Harde Yron'
>
> Although the aepyornis
>   or roc that lived in Madagascar, and
> the moa are extinct,
> the camel-sparrow, linked
>   with them in size—the large sparrow
> Xenophon saw walking by a stream—was and is
> a symbol of justice.
>
>   This bird watches his chicks with
>   a maternal concentration—and he's
>   been mothering the eggs
>   at night six weeks—his legs
>   their only weapon of defence.
>   He is swifter than a horse; he has a foot hard
>   as a hoof; the leopard
>
>   is not more suspicious. How
>   could he, prized for plumes and eggs and young, used
>   even as a riding-
>   beast, respect men hiding
>   actor-like in ostrich-skins, with
>   the right hand making the neck move as if alive and
>   from a bag the left hand
>
>   strewing grain, that ostriches
>   might be decoyed and killed! Yes this is he
>   whose plume was anciently
>   the plume of justice; he

whose comic duckling head on its
great neck revolves with compass-needle nervousness
when he stands guard, in S-

   like foragings as he is
   preening the down on his leaden-skinned back.
The egg piously shown
as Leda's very own
   from which Castor and Pollux hatched,
was an ostrich-egg. And what could have been more fit
for the Chinese lawn it

   grazed on as a gift to an
   emperor who admired strange birds, than this
one who builds his mud-made
nest in dust yet will wade
   in lake or sea till only the head shows.

        .   .   .   .   .   .

   Six hundred ostrich-brains served
   at one banquet, the ostrich-plume-tipped tent
and desert spear, jewel-
gorgeous ugly egg-shell
   goblets, eight pairs of ostriches
in harness, dramatize a meaning always missed
by the externalist.

   The power of the visible
   is the invisible; as even where
no tree of freedom grows,
so-called brute courage knows.
   Heroism is exhausting, yet
it contradicts a greed that did not wisely spare
the harmless solitaire

   or great auk in its grandeur;
   unsolicitude having swallowed up
all giant birds but an
alert gargantuan
   little-winged, magnificently speedy running-bird. This one
remaining rebel
is the sparrow-camel.

Spenser's Ireland

FIRST PUBLISHED: *Furioso* 1 (Summer 1941): 22–5.

COLLECTED: *WAY, ColP, ComP*.

In *Furioso* 1 and *WAY* the sixth line of each stanza has a caesura of four spaces after the first three syllables of the line (always corresponding to a word break). Cf. "Camellia Sabina," "Nine Nectarines and Other Porcelain," and "The Pangolin."

Four Quartz Crystal Clocks

FIRST PUBLISHED: *Kenyon Review* 2 (Summer 1940): 284–5.

COLLECTED: *WAY, ColP, ComP*.

The Paper Nautilus

FIRST PUBLISHED: As "A Glass-Ribbed Nest" in *Kenyon Review* 2 (Summer 1940): 287–8; and *Life and Letters Today* 26 (September 1940): 244–5.

COLLECTED: *WAY, ColP, ComP*.

In both periodical publications the last two lines of stanza two and the first line of stanza three contain variants.

From the *Kenyon Review:*

> animal takes charge of
> it herself and scarcely
>
> leaves it till the eggs are hatched.

From *Life and Letters Today:*

> the tense mother, clutches
> it, scarcely leaving or
>
> eating till the eggs are hatched.

NEVERTHELESS (1944)

Copy-text for all poems is *Nevertheless* (New York: Macmillan, 1944).

Nevertheless

FIRST PUBLISHED: *Contemporary Poetry* 3 (Summer 1943): 5.
COLLECTED: *N, ColP, ComP*.

The Wood-Weasel

FIRST PUBLISHED: *Harvard Advocate* 128 (April 1942): 11.
COLLECTED: *N, ColP, ComP*.

Elephants

FIRST PUBLISHED: *New Republic* 109 (August 23, 1943): 250–1.
COLLECTED: *N, ColP, ComP*.

ColP and *ComP* omit stanzas fifteen and sixteen; stanza seventeen is re-written to conceal the omission.

From *ColP* and *ComP*:

> small word with the dot, meaning know,—the verb bùd.
>
> These knowers "arouse the feeling that they are
> allied to man" and can change roles with their trustees.
> Hardship makes the soldier; then teachableness
> makes him the philosopher—as Socrates,
>
> prudently testing the suspicious thing, knew

A Carriage from Sweden

FIRST PUBLISHED: *Nation* 158 (March 11, 1944): 311.
COLLECTED: N, *ColP*, *ComP*.

The Mind is an Enchanting Thing

FIRST PUBLISHED: *Nation* 157 (December 18, 1943): 735.
COLLECTED: N, *ColP*, *ComP*.

In Distrust of Merits

FIRST PUBLISHED: *Nation* 156 (May 1, 1943): 636.
COLLECTED: N, *ColP*, *ComP*.

POEMS 1944–1951

This section consists of poems first published between 1944 and 1951. Unless otherwise noted copy-text for all poems is *ColP*, as variants between first printings and *ColP* are minor and include copy-editing corrections. With the exception of "Pretiolae," "Quoting An Also Private Thought," and "We Call them Brave," Moore printed all of these poems in the "Hitherto Uncollected" section of *ColP*, and the "Collected Later" section of *ComP* (see the "Original Tables of Contents" section for Moore's 1951 and 1967 ordering). I have placed the poems in the order of their first periodical publication.

"Keeping Their World Large"

FIRST PUBLISHED: *Contemporary Poetry* 4 (Autumn 1944): 5–6.
COLLECTED: *ColP*, *ComP*.

His Shield

FIRST PUBLISHED: *Title* (November 1944): 4.
COLLECTED: *ColP*, *ComP*.

Propriety

FIRST PUBLISHED: *Nation* 159 (November 25, 1944): 656.
COLLECTED: *ColP*, *ComP*.

The version in *Nation* contains variants in its first eighteen lines:

> It's a chord
> like one word
>   Brahms had heard
>   from a bird
> warbling at the root of its throat.

It's the little downy woodpecker
    spiraling a tree
    up up up like mercury.

A bird song
is not long,
    a wayside
    of hayseed
tune; a reticence with rigor
from strength at the source. Propriety's
    Bach's *Solfegietto,*
    harmonica, and basso.

The fish-spines
of fir pines—

Voracities and Verities Sometimes are Interacting

FIRST PUBLISHED: *Spearhead: Ten Years' Experimental Writing in America,* ed. James Laughlin (New York: New Directions, 1947): 190.

COLLECTED: *ColP, ComP.*

A Face

FIRST PUBLISHED: *Horizon* 16 (October 1947): 58.

COLLECTED: *ColP, ComP.*

By Disposition of Angels

FIRST PUBLISHED: *Quarterly Review of Literature* 4 (1948): 121.

COLLECTED: *ColP, ComP.*

Efforts of Affection

FIRST PUBLISHED: *Nation* 167 (October 16, 1948): 430.

COLLECTED: *ColP, ComP.*

In the poem's first publication the final three lines are:

> Bless wholeness—
>
> Namely wholesomeness too tough for infraction.
> No saint? A godsend. Bless efforts of affection.

The Icosasphere

FIRST PUBLISHED: *Imagi* 5 (1950): 2.
COLLECTED: *ColP, ComP.*

Pretiolae

FIRST PUBLISHED: *Wake* 9 (1950): 4. Copy-text.
COLLECTED: Uncollected.

Armor's Undermining Modesty

FIRST PUBLISHED: As "Armour's Undermining Modesty" in *Nation* 170 (February 25, 1950): 181.
COLLECTED: *ColP* ("Armour's"), *ComP* ("Armor's").

Quoting An Also Private Thought

FIRST PUBLISHED: *University of Kansas City Review* 16 (Spring 1950): 163. Copy-text.
COLLECTED: Uncollected.

We Call Them the Brave

FIRST PUBLISHED: *Nation* 172 (May 5, 1951): 423. Copy-text.
COLLECTED: Uncollected.

LIKE A BULWARK (1956)

Unless otherwise noted copy-text for all poems is *Like a Bulwark* (New York: Viking, 1956).

Bulwarked against Fate

The earliest version of this poem, printed below, was called "At Rest in the Blast" (*Botteghe Oscure,* no. 2 [1948]: 287). Before collecting it in *LB* Moore revised and re-titled it "Bulwarked Against Fate" for publication in the *New York Times Book Review* (November 18, 1956): 2.

COLLECTED: *LB, ComP.*

From *Botteghe Oscure:*

At Rest in the Blast

Like a bulwark against fate,
    By the thrust of the blast
  Lead-saluted;
Saluted by lead?
As though flying
    Old Glory full mast.

Pent by power that holds it fast—
    A paradox . . . Hard-pressed,
  You take the blame
And are inviolate—
    Down-cast but not cast

Down. Some bind by promises,
    But not the tempest-tossed—
  Borne by the might
Of the storm to a height,
From destruction;
    At rest in the blast.

Apparition of Splendor

FIRST PUBLISHED: *Nation* 175 (October 25, 1952): 383.
COLLECTED: *LB, ComP.*

Then the Ermine:

FIRST PUBLISHED: *Poetry* 81 (October 1952): 55–6.
COLLECTED: *LB, ComP.*
The *Poetry* version is longer by one stanza and contains significant variants in the final line of stanza three through its stanza eight:

> non timeo
>
> *vel mutare*—I don't change or frighten;
>   though all it means is really,
> *am* I craven?
> Nothing's certain.
>
> Fail, and Lavater's physiography
>   has another admirer
> of skill that axiomatically
> flowers obscurely.
>
> Both paler and purpler than azure, note marine
>   uncompliance—bewarer
> of the weak analogy—between
> waves in motion.
>
> Change? Of course, if the palisandre settee can express
>   for us, "ebony violet"—
> Master Corbo in full dress
> and shepherdess
>
> at once—exhilarating hoarse crownote
>   and dignity with intimacy.
> Our foiled explosiveness is yet
> a kind of prophet,

Tom Fool at Jamaica

FIRST PUBLISHED: *New Yorker* 29 (June 13, 1953): 32.
COLLECTED: *LB, ComP*.

The Web One Weaves of Italy

FIRST PUBLISHED: *Times Literary Supplement* (September 17, 1954):
xlviii.
COLLECTED: *LB, ComP*.

The Staff of Aesculapius

FIRST PUBLISHED: *What's New* (Abbott Laboratories) 186
(December 1954): 9.
COLLECTED: *LB, ComP*.

The Sycamore

FIRST PUBLISHED: *Art News Annual* 24 (1955): 94.
COLLECTED: *LB, ComP*.
The *Art News* version contains variants throughout:

The Sycamore

Against a darker sky,
I saw an albino giraffe. Without
   leaves to modify,
      chamois-white as
         I've said, although partly pied near the base,
it towered where a chain of stepping-stones lay
   in a stream nearby—
   glamor to stir the envy

   of inkier anonimi—
Hampshire pig, the living lucky-stone,
   moth or butterfly.
      Well; I digress
      from animals to likenesses—

but not of flowers that do not wilt; they must die
and a nine-hair brush of she
camel-hairs aid memory.

Worthy of Imami,
the Persian—clinging to a stiffer stalk,
was a little dry
thing from the grass,
in the shape of a Maltese cross—
retiringly formal as if to say:
"And there was I,
like a field-mouse at Versailles."

Rosemary

FIRST PUBLISHED: *Vogue* 124 (December 1954): 101.
COLLECTED: *LB, ComP.*

Style

FIRST PUBLISHED: *Listener* 55 (April 12, 1956): 423.
COLLECTED: *LB, ComP.*

Logic and "The Magic Flute"

FIRST PUBLISHED: *Shenandoah* 7 (Summer 1956): 18–19.
COLLECTED: *LB, ComP.*

Blessed is the Man

FIRST PUBLISHED: *Ladies' Home Journal* 73 (August 1956): 101.
COLLECTED: *LB, ComP.*

from O TO BE A DRAGON (1959)

Copy-text for all poems is *O to be a Dragon* (New York: Viking, 1959). Although printed for the first time in book form in *OD*, "I May, I Might, I Must" and "A Jellyfish" were written and first published fifty years earlier. "I May, I Might, I Must" was originally titled "Progress" (*Tipyn O'Bob* 6 [June 1909]: 10). Under the title "A Jelly-Fish" a slightly longer version of "A Jellyfish" appeared in *The Lantern* 17 (Spring 1909): 110.

See the "Original Tables of Contents" section for Moore's ordering.

O to Be a Dragon

FIRST PUBLISHED: *Sequoia* 3 (Autumn 1957): 20, as "Oh, to Be a Dragon."
COLLECTED: *OD, ComP.*

I May, I Might, I Must

See note above.
COLLECTED: *OD, ComP.*

A Jellyfish

See note above.
COLLECTED: *OD, ComP.*

Values in Use

FIRST PUBLISHED: *Partisan Review* 23 (Fall 1956): 506.
COLLECTED: *OD, ComP*.

Hometown Piece for Messrs. Alston and Reese

FIRST PUBLISHED: *New York Herald Tribune* (October 3, 1956): 1.
COLLECTED: *OD, ComP*.
The *New York Herald Tribune* version omits stanzas sixteen through twenty-two.

Enough: Jamestown, 1607–1957

FIRST PUBLISHED: *Virginia Quarterly Review* 33 (Fall 1957): 500–2.
COLLECTED: *OD, ComP*.
Moore reworked two notable portions of this poem each time she reprinted it. In *Virginia Quarterly Review* the first five stanzas and the eighteenth stanza appear as follows:

> The Godspeed, The Discovery, and one more—
> till The Deliverance made four—
>
> found their too earthly paradise.
> The colonists with grateful cries
>
> clutched the soil; then worked upstream,
> inward to safety, it would seem;
>
> to pests and pestilence instead—
> the living outnumbered by the dead.
>
> Their ships have namesakes. All did not die,
> as jets to Jamestown verify.
>
> [. . .]
>
> mattered at first. . . . Pernicious—rhymes
> for maddened men in starving-times.

When Moore collected the poem in *ComP* she reduced the first five stanzas to three, and revised the (formerly) eighteenth stanza as follows:

> Some in the Godspeed, the Susan C.,
> others in the Discovery,
>
> found their too earthly paradise,
> a paradise in which hope dies,
>
> found pests and pestilence instead,
> the living outnumbered by the dead.
>
> [. . .]
>
> mattered at first. (Don't speak in rhyme
> of maddened men in starving-time.)

Melchior Vulpius

FIRST PUBLISHED: *Atlantic* 201 (January 1958): 59.

COLLECTED: *OD, ComP.*

In its first publication the first five lines of stanza two are:

> Ear chained, we have to trust
>   this mastery—"one which
> no one understands—which someone has
> acquired and is able to
>   direct." Mouse-skin-bellows'-breath

No better than "a withered daffodil"

FIRST PUBLISHED: *Art News* 58 (March 1959): 44.

COLLECTED: *OD, ComP.*

This poem was first published in a section called "Poets on Pictures." Moore's poem is set above an illustration, and an asterisk appears in the middle of line ten, with the accompanying caption:

> * Sir Isaac Oliver: *Portrait of Sir Philip Sidney,* ca 1580–86, miniature on ivory.
> Windsor Castle

In the Public Garden

FIRST PUBLISHED: As "A Festival" in *Boston Globe* (June 15, 1958).
COLLECTED: *OD, ComP.*
The *Boston Globe* version contains minor variants throughout, most notably in the first two lines:

> Here we have a festival,
> a holiday for all:

The Arctic Ox (or Goat)

FIRST PUBLISHED: As "The Arctic Ox" in *New Yorker* 34 (September 13, 1958): 40.
COLLECTED: *OD, ComP.*

Saint Nicholas,

FIRST PUBLISHED: *New Yorker* 34 (December 27, 1958): 28.
COLLECTED: *OD, ComP.*

For February 14th

FIRST PUBLISHED: *New York Herald Tribune* (February 13, 1959): 1.
COLLECTED: *OD, ComP.*

Combat Cultural

FIRST PUBLISHED: *New Yorker* 35 (June 6, 1959): 40.
COLLECTED: *OD, ComP*.

In its first published version the poem's first stanza is a series of rhetorical questions:

> Who does not like a laggard rook's high
> speed at sunset to outfly the dark?
> Or a mount well-schooled for a medal—
> front legs tucked under for the barrier?
> Or team of leapers turned aerial?

Leonardo da Vinci's

FIRST PUBLISHED: *New Yorker* 35 (July 18, 1959): 22.
COLLECTED: *OD, ComP*.

from THE ARCTIC OX (1964)

Unless otherwise noted copy-text for all poems is *The Arctic Ox.* (London: Faber, 1964). *AO* contains, in addition to those printed here, all poems in *OD* except for "Values in Use" and "Hometown Piece for Messrs. Alston and Reese." *AO* also contains "'Sun,'" a poem Moore first published in 1916. She later re-titled it "Fear is Hope" and collected it in *O*. It appears under the latter title in the *Observations* section of this volume. All poems are collected in the "Tell Me, Tell Me" section of *ComP*. See the "Original Tables of Contents" section of this volume for Moore's ordering.

Blue Bug

FIRST PUBLISHED: *New Yorker* 38 (May 26, 1962): 40.
COLLECTED: *AO, TM, ComP.*

To Victor Hugo of My Crow Pluto

FIRST PUBLISHED: *Harper's Bazaar* 94 (October 1961): 185.
COLLECTED: *AO, TM, ComP.*
Moore changed her mind about one "esperanto madinusa" phrase spelled, in *AO*, "beto e totto." In the poem's first publication she spelled it "bóto e tótto," while it appears in *ComP* as "botto e totto."

Baseball and Writing

FIRST PUBLISHED: *New Yorker* 37 (December 9, 1961): 48.
COLLECTED: *AO, TM, ComP.*

Moore re-worked lines eight and nine of stanza three several times. In the poem's first publication they are:

> "Mickey, leaping like a—" deer ("devil"
>   is not so complimentary),

In *TM*, *ComP*:

> "Mickey, leaping like the devil"—why
>   gild it, although deer sounds better—

To a Giraffe

FIRST PUBLISHED: *Poetry in Crystal* (New York: Steuben Glass, 1963): 44.

COLLECTED: *AO, TM, ComP.*

Arthur Mitchell

FIRST PUBLISHED: *City Center Music and Drama Souvenir Program,* January 1962.

COLLECTED: *AO, TM, ComP.*

Tell Me, Tell Me

FIRST PUBLISHED: *New Yorker* 36 (April 30, 1960): 44.

COLLECTED: *AO, TM, ComP.*

Because of several likely copy-editing mistakes in *AO*, copy-text is the *New Yorker* version.

Rescue with Yul Brynner

FIRST PUBLISHED: *New Yorker* 37 (May 20, 1961): 40.

COLLECTED: *AO, TM, ComP.*

Carnegie Hall: Rescued

FIRST PUBLISHED: As "Glory" in *New Yorker* 36 (August 13, 1960): 37.

COLLECTED: *AO, TM, ComP.*

Copy-text is the *New Yorker* version, as that is the version reprinted in both *TM* and *ComP*. Variants in the *AO* version occur in the first and second stanzas:

> It spreads, 'the campaign carried on
> by long distance telephone—
>   with Saint Diogenes
>   supreme commander
>   at the 59th minute
>   of the eleventh hour; stirred, sir,
>
> to rescue Mr. Carnegie's
> music hall which by degrees
>   became and still is
>   our music stronghold;

An Expedient—Leonardo da Vinci's—and a Query

FIRST PUBLISHED: *New Yorker* 40 (April 18, 1964): 52.

COLLECTED: *AO, TM, ComP.*

In the poem's first publication the final stanza has ten lines instead of nine. In that version the third line, later omitted, is:

> that leaves one resistless—

from TELL ME, TELL ME (1966)

Copy-text for all poems is *Tell Me, Tell Me* (New York: Viking, 1966). *TM* includes ten poems from *AO* that were not themselves reprinted from *OD*. These poems include "'Sun,'" a poem Moore first published in 1916. She later re-titled it "Fear is Hope" and collected it in *O*. It appears under the latter title in the *Observations* section of this volume. *Tell Me, Tell Me* also includes four prose pieces, "A Burning Desire to be Explicit," "Profit is a Dead Weight," "My Crow Pluto— a Fantasy," and "Subject, Predicate, Object." See the "Original Tables of Contents" section of this volume for Moore's ordering.

Granite and Steel

FIRST PUBLISHED: *New Yorker* 42 (July 9, 1966): 32.
COLLECTED: *TM, ComP.*
In *ComP* the second line of stanza four is omitted.

In Lieu of the Lyre

FIRST PUBLISHED: *Harvard Advocate* 100 (November 1965): 5.
COLLECTED: *TM, ComP.*

The mind, intractable thing

FIRST PUBLISHED: *New Yorker* 41 (November 27, 1965): 60.
COLLECTED: *TM, ComP.*

Dream

FIRST PUBLISHED: *New Yorker* 41 (October 16, 1965): 52.
COLLECTED: *TM, ComP.*

Old Amusement Park

FIRST PUBLISHED: *New Yorker* 40 (August 29, 1964): 34.
COLLECTED: *TM, ComP.*

W. S. Landor

FIRST PUBLISHED: *New Yorker* 40 (February 22, 1964): 26.
COLLECTED: *TM, ComP.*

Charity Overcoming Envy

FIRST PUBLISHED: *New Yorker* 39 (March 30, 1963): 44.
COLLECTED: *TM, ComP.*
In the poem's first publication lines eleven and twelve are as follows:

> daisies, pink harebells, little flattened-out
> sunflowers, thin arched coral stems, and—

Saint Valentine,

FIRST PUBLISHED: *New Yorker* 35 (February 13, 1960): 30.
COLLECTED: *TM, ComP.*

POEMS 1963–1970

This section consists of poems first published between 1963 and 1970. Unless otherwise noted copy-text for all poems is *Complete Poems* (New York: Macmillan/Viking, 1967).

Moore printed the first four of these poems in the "Hitherto Uncollected" section of her 1967 *Complete Poems* (see the "Original Tables of Contents" section of this volume for Moore's 1967 titling and ordering). The last four were included in the posthumous 1981 edition. I have placed the poems in the order of their first periodical publication.

I've been Thinking . . .

FIRST PUBLISHED: As "Occasionem Cognosce" in *New York Review of Books* 1 (October 31, 1963): 19.

COLLECTED: *ComP* (1981) as "Avec Ardeur."

To the *ComP* (1981) printing the editors Willis and Driver added Moore's dedication: "*Dear Ezra, who knows what cadence is.*"

Love in America?

FIRST PUBLISHED: *Saturday Evening Post* 239 (December 31, 1966): 78.

COLLECTED: *ComP*.

Tippoo's Tiger

FIRST PUBLISHED: *ComP*.

The Camperdown Elm

FIRST PUBLISHED: *New Yorker* 43 (September 23, 1967): 48.
COLLECTED: *ComP.*

Mercifully,

FIRST PUBLISHED: *New Yorker* 44 (July 20, 1968): 34.
COLLECTED: *ComP* (1981).

"Like a Wave at the Curl"

FIRST PUBLISHED: *New Yorker* 45 (November 29, 1969): 50. Copy-text.
COLLECTED: *ComP* (1981) as "Reminiscent of a Wave at the Curl."

Enough

FIRST PUBLISHED: *New Yorker* 45 (January 17, 1970): 28. Copy-text.
COLLECTED: As "Enough: 1969" in *ComP* (1981).

The Magician's Retreat

FIRST PUBLISHED: *New Yorker* 46 (February 21, 1970): 40. Copy-text.
COLLECTED: *ComP* (1981).

*

During this period Moore also published five occasional poems she chose not to collect in books. I have followed her lead by not introducing them into the main text of this edition, but present them here, in order of their first publication, in the interest of completeness.

The Master Tailor

by comparison with whose materials,
   Zephyrs seem coarse;
Whose seaming is all of a piece,
as Praxiteles would say
   Invisibly executed pockets
Buttons of ocean pearl—no two alike:
   Each, a study; varying like the
Silvery face of the moon.
   It is an event for any one who admires
perfection to own it
   Excited and thus disabled to use
pen or write words.

Copy-text *New York Herald Tribune* (November 27, 1963): 19.

Velvet Mat

Velvet mat
is my cat.
Beaver fur
makes my hat.
Our best pencils
write like that.

Copy-text *New York Post* (February 18, 1967): 31.

For Katherine Elizabeth McBride

Dear Katharine McBride
words have no way
of conveying to you what achievement should say,
since we have not replicas of your insight enriching our school—
of your kindled vision discerning individual promise.

What is a college?
a place where freedom is rooted in vitality,
where faith is the substance of things hoped for,
where things seen were not made with hands—
where the school's initiator being dead, yet speaketh,
where virtue trod a rough and thorny path,
finding itself and losing itself—
the student her own taskmaster,
tenacious of one hour's meaning sought
that could not be found elsewhere.

Students—foster-plants of scholarship—
at the beginning of the year,
bewildered by anxiety and opportunity
in the vibrant dried-leaf-tinctured autumn air,
pause and capitulate, compelled to ponder
intimations of divinity—
recurrent words of an unaccompanied hymn:

Ancient of Days, who sittest throned in glory.

O fosterer of promise, aware that danger is always imminent—
The free believe in Destiny, not Fate.
O fortunate Bryn Mawr with her creatively unarrogant
President
unique in her exceptional unpresidential constant:

a liking for people as they are.

Copy-text *Bryn Mawr Alumnae Bulletin* 48 (1966–67): front cover.

Assistance

If unselfish ingenious
Mona Van Duyn Thurston

could send me on a post-card,
despite inconvenience and
a dearth of wild animals—
a wild moose making its way through
a Maine lake in deep water—

could I not ignore disability
and fly to Washington University?

Copy-text *Tambourine* (Washington University, 1967–68): 1.

Santa Claus

Santa Claus,
How would it be
if you gave it to me
all at once for Christmas.
Three dark sapphires
all the same size, Love

    Marianne Moore

Copy-text *New York Times Magazine* (December 21, 1969): 5.
Retitled "A Christmas Poem" in *Philadelphia Evening Bulletin Focus* (December 22, 1969): 3.

APPENDIX: POEMS 1915–1918

This section is comprised of poems Moore published in magazines other than those affiliated with Bryn Mawr, and that do not appear in O. The one apparent chronological anomaly in this section is "Old Tiger." It appears here because Moore wrote the poem and sent it to Ezra Pound in 1918, although he published it, for the first and only time it appeared in print, in a 1932 anthology.

To a Man Working his Way through the Crowd

FIRST PUBLISHED: *Egoist* 4.2 (April 1, 1915): 62.

To the Soul of "Progress"

FIRST PUBLISHED: *The Egoist* 4.2 (April 1, 1915): 62.

That Harp You Play So Well

FIRST PUBLISHED: *Poetry* 6.2 (May 1915): 70.

Counseil to a Bacheler

FIRST PUBLISHED: *Poetry* 6.2 (May 1915): 71.

Appellate Jurisdiction

FIRST PUBLISHED: *Poetry* 6.2 (May 1915): 71.

To William Butler Yeats on Tagore

FIRST PUBLISHED: *Egoist* 5.2 (May 1, 1915): 77.

To a Friend in the Making

FIRST PUBLISHED: *Others* 1.6 (December 1915): 105.

Blake

FIRST PUBLISHED: *Others* 1.6 (December 1915): 105.

Diogenes

FIRST PUBLISHED: *Contemporary Verse* 1.1 (January 1916): 6.

Feed Me, Also, River God

FIRST PUBLISHED: *Egoist* 8.3 (August 1916): 118.

He Made This Screen

FIRST PUBLISHED: *Egoist* 8.3 (August 1916): 118–19.

Holes Bored in a Workbag by the Scissors

FIRST PUBLISHED: *Bruno's Weekly* 3 (October 7, 1916): 1137.

Apropos of Mice

FIRST PUBLISHED: *Bruno's Weekly* 3 (October 7, 1916): 1137.

The Just Man And

FIRST PUBLISHED: *Bruno's Weekly* 3 (December 30, 1916): 1233.

In "Designing a Cloak to Cloak his Designs," you Wrested from Oblivion, a Coat of Immortality for your own Use.

FIRST PUBLISHED: *Bruno's Weekly* 3 (December 30, 1916): 1233.

The Past is the Present

FIRST PUBLISHED: *Others: An Anthology of the New Verse (1917)*, ed. Alfred Kreymborg (New York: Knopf, 1917), 74–5.

You Say You Said

FIRST PUBLISHED: *The Little Review* 5.8 (December 1918): 21.

Old Tiger

FIRST PUBLISHED: *Profile: An Anthology Collected in MCMXXXI*, ed. Ezra Pound (Milan: John Scheiwiller, 1932), 61–4.

SOURCES FOR MOORE'S NOTES

A Note on the Notes

Copy-text *WAY*. Moore subsequently reproduced this passage at the beginning of her notes for *ColP* and *ComP*.

Observations

Copy-text is 1925, except for the note on "Poetry," which is taken from the 1924 edition.

Marriage

In *ComP* Moore precedes the notes to this poem with the sentence "Statements that took my fancy which I tried to arrange plausibly."

Poems 1932–1936

Copy-text is *SP*, except for "The Student," "Walking-Sticks and Paperweights and Watermarks," and "See in the Midst of Fair Leaves," all from *WAY*.

Note that although the *WAY* versions of the poems "Walking-Sticks and Paperweights and Watermarks" and "The Student" differ significantly from those presented in this volume, the notes refer to elements consistent between versions.

The Pangolin and Other Verse

Copy-text *POV*.

What Are Years

Copy-text *WAY*.

Nevertheless

Copy-text *N*.

Poems 1944–1951

Copy-text is *ColP*, except for the notes to "The Icosasphere," which are from *Imagi* 5 (1950): 2, and "Pretiolae," from *Wake* 9 (1950): 4.

Like a Bulwark

Copy-text *LB*.

O to Be a Dragon

Copy-text *OD*.

The Arctic Ox

Copy-text *AO*.

Tell Me, Tell Me

Copy-text *TM*.

Poems 1963–1970

Copy-text for "Love in America?" and "Tippoo's Tiger" is *ComP*. Copy-text for "Mercifully," "'Like a Wave at the Curl,'" and "The Magician's Retreat" is *ComP* (1981).

ORIGINAL TABLES OF CONTENTS

Poems

London: The Egoist Press, 1921.

Pedantic Literalist
To a Steam Roller
Diligence is to Magic as Progress is to Flight
Those Various Scalpels
Feed Me, Also, River God,
To William Butler Yeats on Tagore
He Made This Screen
Talisman
Black Earth
"He Wrote The History Book," It Said
You Are Like the Realistic Product of an Idealistic Search
    for Gold at the Foot of the Rainbow
Reinforcements
Roses Only
In this Age of Hard Trying Nonchalance is Good, And
The Fish
My Apish Cousins
When I Buy Pictures
Picking and Choosing
England
Dock Rats
Radical
Poetry
In the Days of Prismatic Color
Is Your Town Nineveh?

Observations

New York: The Dial Press, 1924.

To An Intra-Mural Rat
Reticence and Volubility
To a Chameleon
A Talisman
To a Prize Bird
Injudicious Gardening
Fear Is Hope
To a Strategist
In Your Town Nineveh?
A Fool, a Foul Thing, a Distressful Lunatic
To Military Progress
An Egyptian Pulled Glass Bottle in the Shape of a Fish
Diligence Is To Magic As Progress Is To Flight
To a Snail
"The Bricks Are Fallen Down, We Will Build With Hewn Stones.
  The Sycamores Are Cut Down, We Will Change To Cedars"
George Moore
"Nothing Will Cure the Sick Lion But To Eat An Ape"
To the Peacock of France
In This Age of Hard Trying Nonchalance Is Good And
To Statecraft Embalmed
Poetry
The Past Is the Present
Pedantic Literalist
"He Wrote the History Book"
Critics and Connoisseurs
To Be Liked By You Would Be a Calamity
Like a Bulrush
Sojourn In the Whale
My Apish Cousins
Roses Only
Reinforcements
The Fish
Black Earth
Radical
In the Days of Prismatic Color
Peter
Dock Rats
Picking and Choosing

Selected Poems

New York: Macmillan/London: Faber, 1935.

The Pangolin and Other Verse

London: The Brendin Publishing Company, 1936.

What Are Years

New York: Macmillan, 1941.

What Are Years?
Rigorists
Light Is Speech
He "Digesteth Harde Yron"
Walking-Sticks and Paper-Weights and Water Marks
The Student
Half Deity
Smooth Gnarled Crape Myrtle
Bird-Witted
Virginia Britannia
See in the Midst of Fair Leaves
Spencer's Ireland
Four Quartz Crystal Clocks
The Pangolin
The Paper Nautilus

Notes

Nevertheless

New York: Macmillan, 1944.

Nevertheless
The Wood-Weasel
Elephants
A Carriage From Sweden
The Mind is an Enchanting Thing
In Distrust of Merits

Collected Poems

New York: Macmillan, 1951.

SELECTED POEMS, 1935

The Steeple-Jack
The Hero
The Jerboa
Camellia Sabina
No Swan So Fine
The Plumet Basilisk
The Frigate Pelican
The Buffalo
Nine Nectarines
The Fish
In This Age of Hard Trying
To Statecraft Embalmed
Poetry
Pedantic Literalist
Critics and Connoisseurs
The Monkeys
Melanchthon
In the Days of Prismatic Color
Peter
Picking and Choosing
England
When I Buy Pictures
A Grave
Those Various Scalpels
The Labours of Hercules
New York
People's Surroundings
Snakes, Mongooses
Bowls
Novices
Marriage
An Octopus
Sea Unicorns and Land Unicorns
The Monkey Puzzle
Injudicious Gardening
To Military Progress
An Egyptian Pulled Glass Bottle in the Shape of a Fish
To a Steam Roller

Like a Bulwark

New York: Viking, 1956.

Bulwarked against Fate
Apparition of Splendor
Then the Ermine
Tom Fool at Jamaica
The Web One Weaves of Italy
The Staff of Aesculapius
The Sycamore
Rosemary
Style
Logic and "The Magic Flute"
Blessed is the Man

Notes to the Poems

O to Be a Dragon

New York: Viking, 1959.

O to Be a Dragon
I May, I Might, I Must
To a Chameleon
A Jellyfish
Values in Use
Hometown Piece for Messrs. Alston and Reese
Enough: Jamestown, 1607–1957
Melchior Vulpius
No better than "a withered daffodil"
In the Public Garden
The Arctic Ox (or Goat)
Saint Nicholas
For February 14th
Combat Cultural
Leonardo da Vinci's

Notes

The Arctic Ox

London: Faber, 1964.

Tell Me, Tell Me

New York: Viking, 1966.

Complete Poems

New York: Macmillan/Viking, 1967.

Author's Note

The Monkey Puzzle
Injudicious Gardening
To Military Progress
An Egyptian Pulled Glass Bottle in the Shape of a Fish
To a Steam Roller
To a Snail
"Nothing Will Cure the Sick Lion but to Eat an Ape"
To the Peacock of France
The Past Is the Present
"He Wrote the History Book"
Sojourn in the Whale
Silence

What Are Years (1941)

What Are Years?
Rigorists
Light Is Speech
He "Digesteth Harde Yron"
The Student
Smooth Gnarled Crape Myrtle
Bird-Witted
Virginia Britannia
Spenser's Ireland
Four Quartz Crystal Clocks
The Pangolin
The Paper Nautilus

Nevertheless (1944)

Nevertheless
The Wood-Weasel
Elephants
A Carriage from Sweden
The Mind Is an Enchanting Thing
In Distrust of Merits

Collected Later (1951)

A Face
By Disposition of Angels
The Icosasphere
His Shield
"Keeping Their World Large"

WORKS CITED

Ashbery, John. Ed. Eugene Richie. *Selected Prose*. Ann Arbor: University of Michigan Press, 2004

Bishop, Elizabeth. *The Collected Prose*. New York: Farrar, Straus and Giroux, 1984

Frost, Robert. *Collected Poems, Prose, & Plays*. New York: Library of America, 1995

Gregory, Elizabeth. *The Critical Response to Marianne Moore*. Westport: Praeger, 2003

Hecht, Anthony. "Writer's Rights and Readers' Rights." *Hudson Review* 21 (1968): 208–9

Kenner, Hugh. *A Homemade World*. Baltimore: Johns Hopkins University Press, 1989

Leavell, Linda. *Holding on Upside Down: The Life and Work of Marianne Moore*. New York: Farrar, Straus and Giroux, 2013

Moore, Marianne. *A Marianne Moore Reader*. New York: Viking Press, 1961

———. Ed. White, Heather Cass. *A-Quiver with Significance: Marianne Moore 1932–1936*. Victoria, BC: ELS Editions, 2008

———. Ed. White, Heather Cass. *Adversity and Grace: Marianne Moore 1936–1941*. Victoria, BC: ELS Editions, 2012

———. Ed. Schulze, Robin G.. *Becoming Marianne Moore: The Early Poems, 1907–1924*. Berkeley, Los Angeles, and London: University of California Press, 2002

———. Eds. Willis, Patricia C., and Clive Driver. *The Complete Poems of Marianne Moore*. New York: Macmillan/Viking, 1981

———. Ed. Willis, Patricia C. *The Complete Prose of Marianne Moore*. New York: Penguin, 1987

———. Ed. Schulman, Grace. *The Poems of Marianne Moore*. New York: Viking Penguin, 2003

———. Eds. Costello, Bonnie, Celeste Goodridge, and Cristanne Miller. *The Selected Letters of Marianne Moore.* New York: Knopf, 1997

Stevens, Wallace. *Collected Poetry and Prose.* New York: Library of America, 1997

Tanselle, Thomas. "The Editorial Problem of Final Authorial Intention." *Studies in Bibliography* 29 (1976): 167–211

Williams, William Carlos. Ed. Webster Schott. *Imaginations.* New York: New Directions, 1970

Yeats, W. B., and A. Wade. *The Collected Works in Verse and Prose of William Butler Yeats.* London, Chapman & Hall, 1908

INDEX OF TITLES AND FIRST LINES